To

RoBBie & ....

enjoy the ride
enjoy the read (F did)

Louie O'Brien

by

Louis O'Brien

Grosvenor House
Publishing Limited

This book is published by
Grosvenor House Publishing Ltd
28-30 High Street, Guildford, Surrey, GU1 3EL.
www.grosvenorhousepublishing.co.uk

A CIP record for this book
is available from the British Library

ISBN 978-1-908447-97-5

LOUIE THE LIP SAYS THANKS!

I started Hasta La Flip-Flops! nearly ten years ago and my ambitions were originally pretty humble. I wanted my daughter Maria Engenes, now living in Oslo, Norway with her husband Jon and two boys Alexander and Jonathan, to know a little about what my life in Majorca was like.

But, somewhere along the way, my book turned into what you're holding in your hands. Some of the credit for this should go to David, my brilliant ghost-writer who, after reading some of my original chapters, got it straight away and has dedicated a year of his life to helping me write HLFF!

I'd also like to thank the people who've sponsored this book and taken out ads to help me pay the cost of publishing. A special thank you to easyJet who, apart from supporting HLFF!, made it a pleasure to be stranded in Majorca back in 2010 when Icelandic volcano ash grounded planes across Europe.

Along the way, David and I have spoken to a number of people who shared reminiscences of their time in Majorca with us. I'd like to thank Tumi Bestard, Francois Serra, Claude of La Baraka in particular and Anna of Fomento del Turismo de Majorca who helped put us together with Tumi and Francois.

Apart from offering her support and help wherever she could, Debbie Cameron of Justagreatlife.com, my mentor and PA (joke, I wish!), suggested I look for organisations to sponsor HLFF! and advertise, which was a brilliant idea.

If you'd like to know more about how this book is helping children in Africa, get in touch with Debbie direct at debbie@justagreatlife.com.

Thanks to Anna Nicholas, who I met completely by accident in a Chinese restaurant in London's Chinatown when David and I overheard her talking about books and Majorca. Anna has been kind enough to write a puff for the front cover. And she's a real writer! Like Hugh Ash, author of The Majorca Assignment, who was kind enough to give David and me the benefit of his experience.

Last but not least, I'd like to thank my family – my sisters Patsy Sullivan and Julie Mitchell, Julie's husband Mitch, my nephews Ricky Royalty and Mike Mitchell, niece Tina and her husband Stuart Nicholas.

Oh, and a big thanks to everyone who believed in Hasta La Flip-Flops! from the start. It's a great ride!

Louie The Lip

Hasta la Flip-Flops!

A PUFF OF SMOKE

I leaned forward into the mic. 'Welcome to Alexandra's all you early birds,' I said before fading the music back up again.

A few minutes later, I brought it down. 'We're gonna have another fantastic night at the number one disco on party island. Lots of party people are on their way down to dance the night away with you.' Music back up and down. 'We're open to 5 AM. And, don't forget, we'll be holding our original wet t-shirt contests a bit later on, where you'll see top international beauties get all wild, wet and willing. The original and still the best. In the meantime, HEEEEERE'S Madonna.'

Holiday. Celebrate. Holiday. Celebrate.

Looking out into the gloom of the club, I watched as maybe ten punters shifted from foot to foot in a half-hearted attempt to dance.

I pushed my rainbow-coloured wig back from my forehead, wiped away a trickle of sweat. My Carnaby Street Union Jack shoes were killing me and I had hours to go yet. I finished my rum and coke and lit yet another cigarette.

'Louie, Louie!' Someone was shouting to me over the booming noise of Madonna. 'Lou...pardon, Tom, Tom Brown.'

I was Tom Brown when I was the MC at Alex's, that was the rule. Tom Brown was a British DJ who was well-known on the radio in Scandinavia, where most of our punters came from.

No-one had ever seen Tom Brown so I figured I could get away with saying I was him. It was an extra draw for the club and it worked.

I looked down into the face of Paco our doorman. He looked sick. I stepped down from my booth, lifted my wig away from my ear so I could hear and Paco shouted 'Curly's just called from home.'

'I thought he was here,' I bellowed back.

'No, he went home. He called to tell you to turn everything off. We're closing.'

'Closing early?'

'No, closing *closing*.'

'You're kidding.'

Paco shook his big head. I squinted at him. He looked heartbroken. Paco was a cop who moonlighted at the club to make extra money and a tough guy. He'd been with us through all the glory years of Alex's since the middle of the 1970s and loved the place like it was his own. Gently, he put the keys to the club in my hand, patted me on the shoulder and turned and walked away into the darkness. Stunned, although I knew in my heart of hearts this had been coming for a long time, I climbed the steps to my booth like a man walking to his execution.

Fading down Madonna, I cleared my throat and leant into the mic. 'Sorry about this, party people but, due to circumstances beyond our control,' deep breath, 'Alexandra's is closing early tonight. Thank you for coming.' I turned the music back up and watched as the punters filed out of the club. They didn't seem too disappointed, to be honest.

Paco had sent the bar staff home and gone with them. It was 1992 and I was on my own in the club I'd given nearly 20 years of my life to, sweating blood to help turn Alex's into 'Majorca's Number One Nightspot'. Now it was all over and although I was shocked it had finally happened, I wasn't really surprised.

I walked to the bar, turned all the lights on and the place flooded with harsh, white light. It looked as sad as I felt. I fixed myself another drink and wandered into the back office. Sitting down, I eased the Union Jacks off my feet, leant back, took off my wig and carefully hung it on its stand with all the others.

I changed out of my Tom Brown clothes, put on a t-shirt, shorts and flip-flops, walked through the club, out the door, locked the heavy iron gates and climbed the 28 steps to the street. It was midnight. I raised my head to the sky. 'Tom Brown,' I shouted, 'has left the building.'

It was a hot summer night but a cool breeze came up the street from the sea, bringing with it the faint whiff of sewage that I'd come to know and love. I walked up to the top of the street, turned and looked back. I'd left the club's two big neon signs on and they blazed out the name Alexandra's. It was the only sign of life in our little square. I thought about going back to switch off the signs. 'Sod it,' I said out loud and kept on walking.

The only bar open on Plaza Gomila was one I couldn't remember having been in before, which was weird. I sat down. Eventually the bored barman came out and took my order for a 103 brandy with a San Miguel chaser.

I sipped the brandy, lit a cigarette, looked up into the blue velvet sky and decided to get drunk. A group of Spanish transvestites clattered past me on their high heels, all knock knees and bony arses in shiny hotpants, laughing and cackling like ugly birds. Probably on their way to a party, I thought. I felt even more like the last man standing.

Across the Plaza the drug dealers sat on a concrete bench drinking from big bottles of beer, passing a joint round and waiting for customers. Apart from me, they were the only people in the square.

There were no tourists. Nada.

I thought back to how Paco had broken the news that Curly had left me to close the club alone. I could picture Curly standing outside the club, looking up and down the street, scowling and smoking one of his cheap cigars. He would have thought 'balls to this, I'm going home.'

And in a puff of cigar smoke he'd have been gone.

For Curly, calling last orders on the club would have been just business. He was like that. I signalled for another large brandy.

I leant back in the yellow plastic chair, put my feet up on another, looked up at the sky and followed the blinking lights of an airplane as it came into land. I'd always loved the sight of planes landing, imagining they were filled with punters who'd find their way to Alex's. Now it just made me sad.

Sitting there in the deserted square, I felt my mind drift back to when it had all been so, so different.

I couldn't help it. I smiled.

EXCUSE ME, DO YOU SPEAK ENGLISH?

'Two San Miguels, mate.' The waiter looked at me, sat there on my own. I held up two fingers. He nodded. Went off into the café for my egg and bacon and the beers.

I was starving.

My first morning in Majorca and I was sat on the front at El Arenal, up the coast from the capital city of Palma de Majorca. Never been abroad before and I loved it right away.

It was late Sunday morning. I'd arrived the night before and I was pissed off because I thought the action only happened on a Saturday night. Like it did back in London.

I woke up too late for the buffet style hotel breakfast so I'd headed down the seafront.

The sun was already high and there wasn't a cloud in the sky. Even wearing shades, the Med was dazzling. I'd never seen a sky or sea so blue in my life.

Paradise.

From where I was sitting I could see the beach, rammed with seriously fit birds working on their suntans. The strip of British bars, Bavarian bierkellers and discos buzzed with tourists knocking back the cheap booze and kick-starting the day.

Music blared. A different song blasting out of each place. 'Black is Black'. 'San Francisco' – be sure to wear some flowers in your hair. 'A Whiter Shade of Pale'.

It was 1967. The Summer of Love.

Lambretta and Vespa scooters screamed up and down the front, on the wrong side of the road or so I thought. Buses dumped their loads of pasty kids with suitcases, all trying to look cool and failing miserably. The newly tanned made a point of looking like they owned the place.

I looked down at my clobber. Carnaby Street's finest. Black string vest. Three-quarter length Union Jack strides and flip-flops. Not too shabby. I'd just about got the hang of keeping the flip-flops on my feet.

And I was buzzing. It couldn't have been more different from rainy, grey old Bethnal Green. I felt like I was in a movie.

My own movie.

I lifted up my head and sniffed the air. Suntan lotion, spicy Spanish food, cigarette smoke, fresh coffee and underneath it all the smell of the sea.

The waiter bought out breakfast and the beers. The bacon was a bit funny-looking but there was plenty of it. The egg yolks were very yellow. He put the beers down. Watched to see what I would do. I took a drink straight from one bottle. My first ever Spanish beer. Cold and tasty. I did the same with the other San Miguel, picked both up and clinked them together.

'Cheers, Bern!' I said. The waiter looked at me, shook his head. 'I'm having one for my mate Bernie the Fox from Bethnal Green who couldn't be with us today,' I said. The waiter shrugged, disappeared inside.

Just another nutty foreigner.

'And I tell you what, Bern, mate,' I said. 'It ain't Margate.'

When I'd decided I was going on holiday in June and it was going to be Majorca, the only one of my friends who could make the week I wanted to go was Bernie the Fox but he was dead set on Margate. I'd had a choice to make. Majorca or Margate. I booked my ticket for Majorca the next day.

'Excuse me, do you speak English?' I peered up from my fried egg. Two blonde birds, brown as nuts, wearing only bikinis and with straw baskets hanging off their shoulders stood looking down at me. They were right darlings.

'Sorry?'

She smiled. 'Do you speak…?' Then she giggled. 'Course you do.' She was Northern, from Manchester I reckoned. 'Just got here?'

I grinned, looked down at my bare arms, which were turning a nice shade of pink. 'Nah, been here weeks, love.'

The other one laughed. She had a great smile. 'Right.' Another Northerner. 'Fancy going to a party?'

'Now? With you two?' I couldn't believe my luck. From out of the blue, two birds.

'No, tomorrow. We'll be there. It's a beach party. You know what they are?'

'Um, a party on a beach.'

Bird number one laughed. 'Right, but it's a boat trip, then the beach party and a disco to finish.'

'Fan-bloody-tastic! Count me in. When? Where.'

The girls looked at each other. Girl number two fiddled around in her basket, took out a block of tickets and tore one off. 'This is your ticket...'

'You mean I have to pay?'

'Cheeky! Don't worry. You'll get your money's worth. It's 100 pesetas deposit – that's about six bob – and another 250 on the day. The price includes the boat trip, food, free champagne, sangria...'

'What's that?'

Girl number one giggled again. She really did have a great giggle. 'You'll love it!'

Number two continued. 'And you also get into La Babalu, this amazing disco.'

'It's brilliant,' her friend said.

I handed over a 100 peseta note, took my ticket and stowed it in the pocket of my Union Jack shorts. 'Tomorrow then,' I said.

'Ta,' girl number one said. 'Club Nautico on the harbour at eleven.' She pointed in the direction of the harbour. 'That's it there. See ya.'

'Bye,' said girl number two.

I watched as they started off down the front and stopped at a table of pale lads outside a bar. 'Oi!' I shouted.

The girls turned round and the geezers looked up. 'Don't sell to any more fellas,' I said. 'Only birds from now on.'

'Don't worry,' girl number two said. 'We told you we'd be there. And there'll be loads of girls to go round.'

* * * * * *

Next morning, I couldn't wait for it to be eleven. I checked my gear in the mirror three times before I went out. I'd been careful the day before and only got a bit of sun. Seen some right horrors. Looked like they'd been boiled.

It was another fantastic day. Hot, not a cloud in the sky. Med glittering. I could get used to this, I thought.

I didn't want to look too keen so I stopped and had a San Miguel before heading down to the Club Nautico. Now I was wise to the ticket sellers, I saw them all over the strip.

They looked to be doing great business touting gangs of lads and chicks who all handed over 100 peseta notes and got their tickets.

When I got to Club Nautico, fashionably late by ten minutes, I was amazed to see what looked like a good 100 punters lined up and ready to go, chatting and laughing. All fizzing with anticipation. Bursting for the off.

A Spanish guy took their ticket and the extra 250 pesetas, stamped their hand and let them on. When they were on the boat they looked around for a place to lay down their beach towel and staked out their territory.

I looked around for the two Northern birds who'd sold me the ticket but they were nowhere to be seen. Of course.

The Beach Boys' fantastic 'Good Vibrations' was pumping out from the boat so loud the sound system crackled. I was definitely picking them up.

I handed over my money, got my hand stamped, picked my way through the towels and squeezed in next to three birds in the front of the boat.

And then I saw them coming down the jetty. It was like they were walking in slow motion.

There were four of them, tanned a deep brown, wearing tight white t-shirts, swimming trunks and flip-flops. They looked like gladiators sharing a private joke. I watched them from behind my shades.

One of the lads was taller than the others, well over six foot and obviously the leader. As they got near to us, he said something and the others cracked up. Another lad, a little guy with hair so blonde it looked white, laughed so hard he nearly fell in the drink.

The four gladiators strutted past all of us lining up to get on the boat, making a big impression on the girls who clocked them with sideways looks. They hopped onto the boat like they'd been doing it all their lives. The tall guy started shouting orders while the others took a head count and checked the supplies.

The last two passengers were a couple of older men in smart mohair suits who looked like they should be getting on the 8.15 from Guildford to Waterloo.

Once the gladiators were satisfied everyone was on, we were off and chugging out of the harbour. We turned right and started to head down the coast.

We stopped at another beach resort called Can Pastilla and picked up a hundred more passengers. Now the boat was really filling up.

Music played nonstop. Beatles, Stones, Monkees, Hendrix, Animals, Beach Boys. Plenty of Motown.

As we sat in the sun, cooled by the spray from the sea, I introduced myself to the three girls, who turned out to be from Leeds. I told the girls I was a songwriter who knew all the stars, which was kind of true.

Even if I'm not sure the birds from Leeds believed it.

* * * * * *

One of my window cleaning jobs back in London had been doing the West End offices of a bloke called Tito Burns. Tito was one of the leading pop impresarios of the day and had famous pop acts like the Searchers, Zombies and Dusty Springield on his books.

I always loved music and fancied myself as a singer/songwriter like Cat Stevens. I used to make tapes of myself singing my own songs on a reel to reel tape recorder. One of them was called 'I Wish I Knew'. Once I registered whose windows I was cleaning it was too good an opportunity to miss.

Next time I cleaned Tito's windows, I breezed into the offices, handed the dolly bird receptionist my tape and asked her if she could give it to the right person. I think she fancied me because she agreed right away.

Two weeks later I got a call saying they'd loved my demo and would I come in for a meeting? Too right!

Next morning, I put on my best suit from Sam Arkus, the great tailor in Soho's Berwick Street that I and all my mates went to. I signed a five-year songwriters' contract, blew the receptionist a kiss, strolled out of the office feeling like the next big thing and hotfooted it back to Bethnal Green.

I told my family and friends about my big break and they were over the moon. Every lunchtime after I'd finished my window cleaning rounds – I started at seven in the morning - I hurtled back to the East End on my pushbike and recorded my songs, accompanying myself on a tambourine. I was driven to make it and writing came easily to me so I soon had two or three numbers I thought weren't too shabby. I popped them into Tito's office and waited for the success I knew was going to be mine to come knocking.

While I waited I realised I needed to change my surname. My given name was Kosky, on account of my Jewish dad but that didn't have the right ring to it. I settled on O'Brien. Louie O'Brien sounded like a proper pop star's name. Dusty Springfield's real name was O'Brien and my sisters told me it had a good ring to it. I changed my name for good by deed poll.

At first, it really felt like I was living the pop life, even though I was still cleaning windows to make ends meet – not Tito's, obviously. Tito's firm had a suite in one of the top London hotels where they held celebration parties every time a new record was launched. I was invited and introduced as the new kid on the block, with a great future ahead of him.

Which is what it felt like to me too. I was rubbing shoulders with the new pop royalty and pulling more classy birds than I ever had before.

But, even though the parties and promises continued, I felt like I wasn't getting anywhere. In six months I hadn't even had so much as an Interns b-side. So I knocked it on the head.

Another thing was my manager was gay, which I didn't realise until he propositioned me and I found out fast. When I told him to get lost, he gave up all interest in my career.

Still, I had a tumble with Dusty Springfield's secretary.

* * * * * *

Tall hotels gave way to a jumble of older looking buildings and what we were told was Palma cathedral. A bit down from the cathedral, just past a couple of windmills on a headland, we headed into land again.

We cruised in to the main harbour of Palma, steering carefully through huge, beautiful, shining yachts that must have cost thousands of pounds.

We moored next to the main drag that ran the length of the Bay of Palma. Hotels, cafés and restaurants lined the strip. The beautiful people strolled along, checking out menus and deciding what they were going to have for lunch. A cream coloured Roller glided past.

At our docking spot, another gang waited to climb on board. We pulled up alongside a boat called the Santa Maria that was half-full with beautiful, blonde, golden girls. From the ooby-dooby way they talked I knew they were Scandinavian girls.

I'd seen some Scandinavian girls before in London, where they often worked as au-pairs but never anything like this. These were goddesses.

As I eyeballed the boat, grateful for my dark glasses and trying to stop myself from drooling, a tourist bus pulled up. The door opened and out burst another party of gorgeous Vikings, all wearing t-shirts with a big Club 33 on them.

The Scandinavians piled onto the Santa Maria and our new arrivals found whatever space they could on the already crowded boat.

Two of the gladiators climbed onto the Santa Maria. The other two, the tall leader and the little blonde guy stayed on our boat.

When he was sure our boat was full and all eyes were on him, the leader of the gladiators raised his bottle of San Miguel high in the air, signalled to the Captain of the boat, behind the wheel with his own beer and smoking a fat cigar. Next, the leader threw back his head, shouted 'FORWAAAARRRRRDDD BABALU GOOWWWWW!' like John Wayne leading his troops into the Battle of the Little Bighorn and we were off.

Side by side with the Santa Maria, we cruised along a rocky coast studded with beaches packed with brightly coloured beach towels and sun umbrellas. Even from where we were out at sea, I could see it was wall to wall bodies.

I watched two of the gladiators work the crowd of about 200 overexcited teenage punters and two middle-aged sensibly dressed blokes, selling them on the delights of the beach party.

Whenever one of the guys spotted a girl he liked, he spent extra time chatting her up, getting her name and schmoozing her. I started to envy how it was easy for them. I wanted some of the action.

After we'd been at sea for a bit, the gladiators started handing out dripping bottles of ice-cold Spanish champagne. It didn't take long for us party people, as the gladiators called us, to begin shaking our bottles and start spraying each other, egged on by the gladiators. The smartly dressed older men, who turned out to be Germans got drenched but laughed it off.

I offered to lick the champagne off the girl next to me, a saucy little thing in a bright yellow bikini, but she wasn't having any of it.

We chugged nearer to land and started to head towards what we'd been told was a deserted beach you could only get to by boat. This was actually four small beaches, two on either side of a rocky headland covered with trees. When we got closer the captains of both boats steered for the centre of the rocks. From there you could either go to the two beaches to the left or to the right. For a while we sailed carefully through crystal clear water over rocks that looked only inches below the surface, loads of funny-looking fish darting away into the shadows we passed.

We came to a halt off the rocks. One of the gladiators, a dark, seriously tanned, good-looking bloke, dived like a blade into the water. When he was in and bobbing up and down both captains threw him a rope and he swam ashore, climbed out and looped the ropes round a metal post bashed into the rocks.

Once the boats were safely tied up, the boy helped the captains lower the gangplanks onto the rocks and, beaming from ear to ear, bowed and accepted the cheers from the boats. He'd immediately become the girls' hero. And he knew it. It must have been his party piece.

We started to file off. When I passed the boat's cabin I saw the captain, cigar clamped in his mouth, counting out wads of cash. It looked like a small fortune. But the big grin on his sweaty, unshaven face turned to a scowl when he saw that some kids, desperate to make the beach, were diving off the boat. He hadn't turned off the propellers and they could easily have been cut in half. He started shouting something in Spanish and the little blonde gladiator screamed 'no diving off the boat! The propeller's still turning.'

And we were all on the beach. 300 seriously excited kids and two slightly confused men in suits waiting for the party to really get started.

Once I'd laid out my towel, I went for a little stroll. It was boiling hot now. I walked towards a wooden bar at the back of the beach. Two of the gladiators brought out two plastic dustbins from the bar.

I sauntered over and watched as they danced round the dustbins, pouring red wine out of what looked like brown pottery barrels, tipped in lemonade, chucked in oranges and lemons cut into wedges, dropped in ice-cubes and emptied a bag of sugar into each bin. When they'd done this, they each uncorked a bottle of brandy. One lowered his head and stood with his hands in front of him like he was praying while his mate tipped his bottle of brandy into one of the bins. Then it was his turn to pour brandy into his bin while the other lad blessed the mixture.

Each dipped a plastic cup into his barrel and drained it in one. They nodded to each other and smacked their lips. One of them, the little lad who'd chatted up the Leeds girl on the boat saw me watching and said, 'sangria, mate. Bloody marvellous.' I nodded, chuffed that he'd spoken to me and wandered back down the beach to join the rest.

The big guy was standing in front of the crowd with another gladiator. He put his fingers between his teeth, let out an incredibly loud whistle. The other two gladiators jogged down from the beach bar and joined him.

'OK, everyone, listen,' the big guy shouted. 'Right, party people, gather round. Welcome to the Babalu Beach

Party. Let me introduce you to the lads. Little Jimmy! Jimmy, take a bow.' Little Jimmy, with the white-blonde hair, stepped forwards and bowed deeply. 'Next up is Buddy. If you're lucky Buddy might give us a tune later and you'll see how he got his name. Let's hear it for Buddyyy!' Buddy held up an imaginary microphone and struck a crooner's pose. 'And now, part dolphin, part human, the boy David!' The muscular guy who'd tied up the boats stepped forwards and flexed his biceps like a comedy Charles Atlas. The girls whistled and cheered. 'Looks like you've pulled, David,' the big guy said. 'Leave some for the rest of us.' The girls laughed and the blokes booed. 'And, ladeez and gentleman, I'm Peter. Your master of ceremonies for the best party of your life. I kid you not.' Peter did a little tap dance while the other lads bowed before him and we clapped. 'Right,' Peter said. 'Let's get this party started.' We all whistled, whooped and cheered and the lads on the stage grinned at each other.

'OK,' Peter continued. 'Let's find out what nationalities we've got today? Anybody here from Sweden?' The gorgeous Scandinavian girls and ridiculously tall Viking boys threw back their heads and whooped. 'Not bad, pretty loud. Right, England.' Us English shouted and whistled loud and long and the sound echoed round the beach.' Peter grinned and then, incredibly fast, he said 'Scotland, Ireland, Wales?' While the English laughed and booed, the rest tried to drown them out. When the cheering, whistling, laughter and booing calmed down, Peter said 'oh, I forgot, any krau... Germans here? No...'

The two sensibly dressed men, who seemed to have somehow got used to the idea that they were at a beach party full of revved-up teenagers by accident called out 'ja, ja' and waved.

Two girls, one with terrible sunburn, also shouted 'ja'.

'Fantastico,' Peter said. 'You four will be defending the honour of der Fazzerland. OK, there'll be free water-skiing later, if the instructor turns up and, as soon as we sober up the chef – or is he recovering from food poisoning? - we'll be serving barbeque. But first, let the games commence!'

We cheered and followed Peter into the shallows. The other lads stayed on the edge of the sea. When we were in up to our waists, Peter said 'everyone form a big circle – boy girl, boy, girl.' We arranged ourselves like he said and waited to see what would happen. The circle was huge and went from one side of the beach to the other. 'Right, excellent. Come in close. Closer. Closer...' He paused. 'And now, everyone kiss the person on their right.' Girls squealed as the boys planted a kiss on them. I was standing next to a Scandinavian and gave her a smacker on the lips. She blushed but smiled and didn't hit me! What a great way of breaking the ice.

Next, the gladiators began a slow hand clap and Peter started singing 'woh, the Okey Cokey'. We all put our left foot in and our right foot out – what the Germans were doing looked suspiciously like a goosestep - as the clapping got faster and we ended up falling about and laughing.

'OK, next game,' Peter said. He lowered his voice. 'Could all the girls come in as close to me as you can.

OK, that's perfect. Now the boys. Don't be shy. Great.' When we were all as close as we could get, waiting curiously to find out what was going to happen next, he whispered, 'right...' and then, shouting as loud as he could, he roared 'the first guy to bring a bikini top back the to the beach...' Whatever he said next was drowned out by giggling, squealing, shouting and laughing. The sea looked like a load of sharks were thrashing around. Strangely enough, though, the girls didn't put up much resistance. I was working on the bra of a Scandinavian girl who was helping me when I heard a cry of triumph and a guy went running ashore waving a bikini top round his head like a trophy and looking for his prize, which was a two bottles of champagne he shared with the girl and her mates.

After that, we had an underwater kissing contest. I saw a fat bird heading in my direction, ducked under water and swam out of range.

There was an international tug of war: Great Britain versus the rest of the world. This was just slightly rigged. Little Jimmy and Buddy tied the Brit end of the rope to a tree. Germany, in the shape of the older blokes – now tipsy and well and truly entering into the spirit of things – and the two girls launched a good-natured official protest but they were shouted down.

Lunch was next, barbeque chicken with salad and slices of watermelon. It tasted great after all that larking around. The gladiators handed out cups of sangria, which was delicious and pretty potent, as I discovered by my third glass. When I'd finished eating, I started to help the boys dole out the sangria and I could see some of the girls thought I was part of the crew. I liked that.

After lunch, there was water-skiing which proved to be a lot harder than it looked, judging by the way people kept taking a tumble. David, our very own Charles Atlas, made it look dead easy.

I didn't bother with the water-skiing. I swam, chatted up one of the birds from Leeds, who promised me a smooch at the disco, smeared myself with suntan lotion and dozed off to the sounds of happy, pissed people getting to know each other rather better.

The beach bar was doing a roaring trade and other boats had started to arrive, packed with people who watched us frolicking on the beach.

After a couple of hours of mellowing out, Peter called us to the front where there was more sangria and champagne. A couple of the gladiators bought out guitars and they played pretty well, doing Beatles and Bob Dylan numbers. Buddy sang a Buddy Greco song and he did sound exactly like his idol.

Peter prowled round the crowd, towering over the girls who giggled but were a bit nervous. Finally he dragged one of the shy German girls up on stage for a filthy version of 'Satisfaction' while rubbing himself gleefully against her. The more she blushed the worse he got.

And then it was time to go. As the boat slowly pulled away I looked back at the deserted beach and the bar staff clearing up the mess and felt a little sad. It had been one of the best days of my life and I didn't want it to end.

It wasn't just me. Something special *had* happened today, everyone on the boats knew it and it seemed like the gladiators and even Captain Deigo knew it too.

* * * * * *

La Babalu was a mostly open air disco and the outside area was full of palm trees and plants. Coloured lights twinkled between the trees. Music thumped. It looked the business.

When I stepped through the arch into La Babalu, the air felt electric. I worked my way round to the bar which looked down onto the outside dance floor, smiling as I squeezed in among the sexy tanned bodies. I took my time.

The air was thick with the great smell of sun tan lotion, perfume, cigarette smoke and pure lust. Everyone was on the pull, determined to have a bit of a holiday fling.

There was also the whiff of exhaust fumes from the go-cart track next door. As well as entry to La Babalu, the boat party ticket included ten free laps.

On my left as I went in was a bar with tables in front. I made it to the bar and ordered a San Miguel. When the barman slid it in front of me I drank deep, lit a cigarette and leant against the bar to watch the dance-floor.

I was tired from the beach party but determined to pull. I'd caught the sun but just enough. I knew I looked sharp.

I'd checked myself in the mirror enough times before I went out. Flared white Levis, loafers with no socks and a denim shirt with loads of zips on it I'd had specially made down Carnaby Street. Plenty of Old Spice.

The dance floor was a beautiful sight. Hundreds of tanned, blonde girls showed off their moves, pretending to ignore the blokes who tried to muscle in. I saw the Northern birds who'd sold me on the beach party in the arms of two Spanish lads who looked like the cats who'd got the cream.

Living their fantasy. I couldn't exactly blame them for not wanting to go on a boat trip.

I scanned the crowd for the Leeds girl but couldn't see her anywhere. Still, I was spoilt for choice.

While I stood and watched in a sort of trance, 'I Was Made To Love Her' by Stevie Wonder became 'The Letter' by The Boxtops became 'Sweet Soul Music' by Arthur Conley became 'Bernadette' by The Four Tops. And then I needed a slash.

On my way to the khazi I saw an empty table near the end of the bar. A sign on it said 'Reserved for Beach Boys'. I wondered who they were.

After checking my look in the mirror again, paying particularly close attention to my skin-tight white Levis, I headed back to the dance floor. Time to get serious about pulling.

The empty table had filled up. With the gladiators. Or The Beach Boys, as they were obviously called. As

I walked past the table I heard 'Oi!'. I looked round, pointed to my chest, mouthed 'me?' and felt daft.

Peter, the big bloke from the beach party shouted 'yeah, you. Fancy a bevvy?' I grinned, nodded. He scooted over and I sat down next to him.

All four Beach Boys were there, wearing brilliant white shirts that showed off their tans and teeth. There were a couple of ice-buckets on the table with champagne bottles in them. Peter put a glass in front of me and Little Jimmy poured me a drink. I raised my glass to them 'cheers and ta!'

'It's salud here, man,' Peter said, as all four lads hoisted their glasses.

'Salud!' I said. We chinked glasses and downed the champagne.

Peter held up the bottle for a refill, saw that it was empty, somehow got the attention of a waiter and waved the bottle at him. The waiter nodded and seconds later there was another full bottle in a fresh ice-bucket. Peter splashed the champagne around and we drank again.

'Great spot you've got here, mate,' I said, looking out over the dance floor.

'Isn't it?' Peter said, grinning. 'We can spot the talent and the talent can spot us.' He took a drink. 'Enjoy the beach party?'

'Brilliant!' I said. 'Best day of my life.'

He nodded. 'It's like that every time, man. Although today I did think was something else. Dos mucho! Pulled yet?'

'Not yet, I was just about to get down to it when you shouted me over.'

'You will, son, you will. Especially if you're with us. You're in with the in crowd now.' He didn't say this as a boast. It was more a matter of fact. And I could see why. While we chatted, a steady stream of lovely birds came up to the table to talk to the Beach Boys. Almost to pay their respects, if you like. Some stayed. Others, the less lovely, were frozen out.

Peter asked me where I was from. I told him Bethnal Green and he said he was from Tilbury, Essex. Buddy was White City in West London, David a nice Jewish boy from Golders Green, North London. Little Jimmy, who Peter called 'the baby', was from somewhere in the Midlands.

We talked and joked. I started to relax. And I was made up he'd asked me over, even if I still couldn't understand why.

'You've got it made in the shade, Peter,' I said. 'Champagne instead of beer, hot and cold running birds, waking up to the sun every morning, great job. Better than cleaning bleeding windows. Here's to you, mate!'

I raised my glass and it was filled with champagne yet again.

'Tell me about it, Louie,' he said. 'It's a dirty job but someone's got to do it.' He paused, then I thought I heard him say 'why don't you sell tickets with us?' I swallowed the smoke from my cigarette and exploded in a terrible coughing fit. Peter nearly pissed himself laughing and slapped my back as hard as he could with his huge hands. When he did I realised I was more sunburnt than I thought.

'Thanks, Peter,' I croaked, catching a hand that was hurtling towards my sore back yet again. 'I'm all right now.' I turned to him. 'What did you say?'

He looked at me, eyes half-closed. 'I said, why don't you chuck your job in, come back and work for us selling tickets? I'm serious, man.'

'Me?' I was flattered and a bit confused. 'Why?'

'I clocked you helping out with the sangria at the party today. You seem like a good guy and, tell you the truth, we're always looking for the right sort to become a PR.'

'PR?'

'Public Relations. Ticket tout to you and me, pal. And, listen, there's nothing to it. As long as you've got the gift of the gab and I think you have. The money's terrific. I get a commission on every ticket I sell, plus a bit more for pushing La Babalu and there's all kinds of wrinkles on the side you'll find out about. You'll be quids in, man.'

'But, I haven't got anywhere to live. I don't know Spanish. I...'

'We'll sort you out an apartment with a couple of PR geezers we know. No sweat. You don't need to speak Spanish. And, you can't tell me you're happy with your glittering career as a bleedin' window cleaner, Louie. You're hungry for something a bit better. We all are.'

'True.'

'So, there's nothing stopping you really is there? You've got sod all to lose.' He put his big arm round my shoulder, 'and everything to gain. This is it, boy. The good life. Think about it. You don't need to give us your answer right away.'

I looked out over the sea of blonde heads on the dance floor, felt the girl next to me press her warm bare thigh against mine, drained my glass of champagne. 'I don't need time to think, Pete,' I said. 'I'm in.'

I'd found my paradise.

LOUIE BABY'S HERE!

Two weeks after I'd left, I was back in Majorca, this time to stay for the rest of the summer.

I'd thrown in my job. The geezer I worked for had said I could have it back at the end of the summer if I wanted. My old man had given me his blessing and a few quid.

Stepping out of the airport doors into the fierce mid-day heat and blindingly bright sunlight already felt familiar but I was also bubbling with excitement about starting my new life.

Most of all, I felt really alive.

I hopped in a cab. 'El Arenal, por favor,' I said, feeling like I belonged. The cab dropped me in a little square just back from the front and I lugged my suitcase to the Beach Boys' favourite restaurant, where they'd told me to look for them. A three course menu del dia at this place, including bread and wine, was 25 pesetas. I opened the door, feeling a twinge in my guts. What if it had all been a wind-up and they weren't there?

The restaurant was crowded with Spanish workmen and foreign ticket touts and so noisy it was like being smacked round the ear. I loved it. I clocked Peter's head at the back. He towered above the dark-haired Spanish and I could hear his voice over theirs. I bumped my way through the narrow gaps between tables, careful not to send anyone's wine flying.

Little Jimmy was sitting opposite Peter, his back to me but I could tell it was him by the blonde hair. Just before I got to the table, Peter looked up. A grin split his tanned face. 'Louie, Louie, baby. You're here!' He stood up, threw his arms open wide, nearly knocking a stuffed bull's head off the wall, and gave me a bone-crushing hug. Grabbing his knife, he tapped an empty wine glass. 'Look everybody,' he shouted, 'Louie's here! Louie's here! The man has arrived.' I blushed but I needn't have worried. No-one took a blind bit of notice. They were all used to Peter. I parked my suitcase, sat down.

Slapping me on the back, Little Jimmy laughed and said 'next beach party's Friday. Wanna buy a ticket?'

Peter sloshed wine into our glasses and we raised them high. 'Here's to the beach parties,' he bellowed. We downed our wines in one and Peter called out for the waiter to bring another bottle. He was blanked.

As soon as we started gassing, it was like I'd never been away. It also felt like nothing had happened to me back in London while months of amazing adventures had passed for Peter and Little Jimmy in a matter of weeks.

Peter got the bill, paid it. As we passed the kitchen he shouted 'keep practicing, chef. You'll get it right one day.' Someone, presumably the offended chef, flung a rasping curse back at him, no doubt something filthy involving Peter's mother and a farm animal. Peter laughed, shrugged it off like he did everything else.

We walked to the boys' car, sticking to the shade. Peter grabbed a dusty lemon off a tree and, providing his own commentary, took a run up and bowled the lemon as you would a cricket ball. He looked like a natural. Dazzling, to be honest.

'You've done that before,' I shouted, laughing.

Bowing an apology to the little old Spanish lady he'd just nearly hit with the lemon, Peter trotted back to us. 'Fast bowler, Essex and England school boys,' he said. 'And you should see my googlies.' Little Jimmy groaned.

'It's true,' Peter said. 'Starting bowler 1964.'

We climbed into the boys' rented SEAT 600 car and rolled all the windows down as fast as we could. Little Jimmy drove, Peter sat in the front passenger seat and I was folded into the back with my case. 'Where's my drum then?' I said.

* * * * * *

'Why's it called a drum?' Little Jimmy said as Peter walloped the big wooden front door of my new home with a meaty fist.

'Drum and bass, place.' I said, pulling my shirt away from my sweaty back. 'How much did you say the damage was?'

'750 pertaters a week.'

'Is that a lot?'

'Nah,' Peter said over his shoulder. '100 pesetas a day. You'll make that in a morning, no sweat. But the bloke wants a month in advance. That's how it works.' He was about to thump the door again when it was yanked open by a sleepy-looking and pissed off Spanish geezer with a huge naked hairy belly, popped out belly button and sticking up hair. 'Hola, amigo,' Peter said, shaking his hand vigorously and stepping passed him fast at the same time. 'La habitación para mi amigo Louie, si?' I shook the man's hand and lugged the suitcase through the door, impressed at Peter's Spanish.

The owner unlocked the door to my room. I stepped inside while Peter did the deal with him. When he'd agreed a price, after much muttering and protesting from the owner, Peter asked me for 3000 pesetas. I peeled the alarmingly large number of notes off my shrinking roll and handed them over. The room was a furnace. And it looked like a cell in the prison where I'd had reason to visit Bernie The Fox not so long ago. There was a single bed, a small washbowl perched on a metal tripod and three nails banged in the wall to hang clothes on. No wardrobe. The only light came from a bare bulb hanging from the ceiling. There was nothing on the walls apart from nasty-looking stains. It was horrible.

The deal done, Peter poked his head round the door, handed me two keys – one for the front door and the other a Yale for the room. 'I know it ain't great, Louie

Baby,' Peter said, laughing. 'But there's nothing else going. It's the height of the season, man. Listen, the shower's in the courtyard and you share it with the other five people who live here. Maybe there's a fit bird or two. Never know. And we'll be keeping our eyes peeled for another place.'

'Is 3000 pesetas a month all right for this shithola?' I said.

'Sell one ticket a day, man, and you've paid your rent. And, like I said, we'll all keep an eye out for another place, don't worry.'

'Yeah, places come up all the time,' Little Jimmy said. 'See you at the club tonight.'

'We'll get you sorted with your beach party tickets tonight,' Peter added. 'Tomorrow's your big day, man. Your dayboo as a ticket seller.'

And they were gone, sucking all the air out of the room and leaving me sat on the bed wondering what I'd got myself into. I looked up at the only window in the room, which was tiny and up near the ceiling. It had three bars across it. Just like a prison.

* * * * * *

I woke up soaked with sweat, no idea where I was, heart thumping. Light from my high window tried to fight its way in through the thick dust in the air. I unpacked my suitcase, hanging my clobber as carefully as I could on the three bent nails, found my wash bag and towel and went for a shower. I took my passport and money with me, just in case. The fat Spanish landlord looked well shifty.

When I opened the door to the bathroom, this disgusting looking brownish red insect thing shot down the plug hole. I showered as fast as I could. The water was tepid and a bit rust-coloured. I went back to my room, dressed and left. By the time I hit the street I was sweating again.

One good thing was that the Arenal front and Club Nautico were only ten minutes walk away from my new, hopefully temporary, gaff.

By now, the sun was starting to go down. The last people were leaving the beach and their footprints behind, heading back to their apartments and hotels to have a bite to eat, shower, get togged up and go out. An old Spanish couple took their evening stroll, shadows long and narrow. Along the strip, neon lights came on in ice-cream colours. The sea was dark, the empty sky royal blue. The colour reminded me of something but I couldn't think what.

I strolled past the bars and discos, now filling up. A light breeze from the sea blew the smells of frying food, cigarettes, coffee and perfume in my direction. I breathed deeply, grinned to myself. I was really here. It was getting on now so I caught a bus to La Babalu in Can Pastilla, a short ride away along the front.

* * * * * *

The line of punters waiting to get into La Babalu was already long. Blonde girls with freshly washed hair, glowing from where the sun had kissed them, stood in groups, giggling, smoking their duty-free and pretending they hadn't noticed the boys eyeing them up.

I walked to the front of the queue like Peter had told me to, trying not to swagger too much. I could feel the girls' eyes on me, heard a couple of muttered 'oo's 'e, then?' from the gangs of lads in the queue. I felt bloody great!

When I got to the front, I said 'I'm with the Beach Boys' to the doorman, a big Spanish guy who Peter had told me was a moonlighting cop. His bored 'seen it all, take no shit' expression didn't change as he waved me through.

'I'm in with the in crowd,' I sang as I squeezed past all the gorgeous tanned lovelies at the bar on my way to the Beach Boys special table.

Peter, Little Jimmy and Buddy were sitting like tipsy kings surveying a table covered with San Miguel bottles. There was no sign of David. 'What, no champers tonight, boys?' I said, taking a seat.

'Only on beach party nights, Louie,' Buddy said. He shook my hand. 'Welcome aboard.'

'No David?' I said.

'Nah, he's gone soft on some sort. Staying in.'

'Pip Pip!' Peter bellowed, jumping unsteadily to his feet

and slapping a hand to his forehead in a naval salute. We saluted him back, laughing. 'Time for a Beach Boy knee wobble, lads.'

The others stood up. 'What's a Beach Boy knee wobble?' I said. It sounded suspiciously like knee-trembler. I knew what that was all right.

'First one to stop wobbling his knees gets the next round in,' Little Jimmy said.

'But I thought you got free drinks.'

'We do but that's not the point,' Peter said. 'We're welcoming you as one of us. It's a celebration. A ritual, dear boy. Right, ready? Form an orderly circle.' We did. 'Let the knee wobble commence.'

The knee wobbling began and the boys got serious. They kept their eyes locked onto each other's and wobbled their knees as fast and hard as they could. Of course, I was the first to crack and give up, partly because I was laughing so hard.

'Drinks are on Louie Baby amigos,' Peter said, rubbing his hands. He waved to the waiter and sat down as the guy came over. 'Bottle of your finest shampoo,' he said.

'Only beer tonight,' the waiter said.

Peter jerked a finger in my direction. 'He's paying.' I shrugged, nodded, and prayed the fizz wouldn't cost an

arm and a leg. 'Right, Buddy, reveal the ancient sacred mysteries of punting tickets to young Louie Baby here.'

Buddy explained that tickets for the beach parties were punted out at 350 pesetas. 100 of these was my commission. On the nights when there wasn't a beach party, I could push discount cards promoting La Babalu. 'Put your name on each card you give out, Louie,' Buddy said, 'and you get 20 pesetas commission on every one.'

The champagne arrived with four glasses and the waiter stood over me while I paid for it. He'd probably had plenty of people order a bottle and try to duck out of paying. I handed over the cash. Peter splashed champagne into the glasses and we all stood while he made a toast. 'Here's to Louie Baby. Good luck, man!' We chinked our glasses together, downed the champagne and sat down.

I looked around at my new pals, feeling like a million bucks.

'Give Louie the tools of his trade, Buddy boy,' Peter said. Buddy handed over a huge bundle of tickets and cards. I looked at them and my first thought was I'll never get rid of this lot. 'Tomorrow morning, you start by checking out the sales geezers on the front at El Arenal,' Peter said. 'See how they do it. You'll soon be able to blast out tickets by yourself. Oh, yeah, give him the folder with the pictures of the beach party and La Babalu too. ' Buddy handed this over. Peter grabbed both my cheeks, wobbled them and, in a granny voice, said 'lovely boy like you. Ooh, 'asn't he got a lovely smile.'

I grinned even wider. 'Best get an early night, Louie Baby,' Peter said. 'You'll need to be on top form tomorrow morning. Good luck.'

'Knock 'em dead, Louie,' Buddy said.

'Yeah, good luck,' Little Jimmy said.

'Here,' I said, sipping my champagne. 'There are these fat horrible looking brown insect things in the shower, move like greased lightning. What are they?'

The boys looked at each other. Little Jimmy burst out laughing. Between snorts of laughter, Peter said 'those, Louie Baby, are what's known as cockroaches.' I looked at him, none the wiser. He stood up, started clicking his thumb and index fingers together, singing 'La cucuracha, la cucuracha.' He sat down again. 'That's them, man. Cockroaches. They're everywhere so you better get used to your little brown flatmates.'

'Can you get rid of cuca...cockroaches?'

'You can get this spray stuff that'll kill 'em, leave 'em gasping, but they just come back bigger and stronger eventually. Learn to live with them, old son. Everyone else does.'

'Right.' I nodded, stood up, finished my glass of champagne, said good night to the lads and started to work my way through the sweet-smelling girls packed at the bar. Coming from the Beach Boys table I got plenty of looks.

I caught a bus back to Arenal and started walking back to my place. It felt like I was floating on air. The front was jumping. The hot summer air was bursting with music. Gangs of laughing, singing boys and girls wandered in and out of the bars and discos. Everyone seemed to be having the time of their lives.

I know I was.

I stopped into a bar not far from my prison cell and had a last beer, not letting go of the bundle of tickets and the folder for a second. I'm part of all this, I thought. I couldn't believe how much my life had changed in two weeks.

I was made up. And, sitting there, I laughed to myself. I now had a nickname, my first ever. I was Louie Baby.

* * * * * *

Next morning, I was up and about early. My room was already like an oven. If I'm going to stay here, I thought, I have to get a fan.

I showered, keeping an eye out for any more of those cockroach things, got dressed, stashed my passport under the stained mattress and locked my door. I made it as far as the front door to the hostel before I had to go back and check my room was really locked. The door felt like you could blow on it and it would open.

It was still early, only about eight but it was already hot. The strip was just waking up and the only people on the beach were families with kids and one bloke who'd presumably flaked out the night before and was lying in a heap on the sand.

I had two large café solos – black coffee – with plenty of sugar. I was too fired up to eat breakfast. Eating could wait. Peter had told me there was an official stand on the front that the salesmen worked out of. I sat down on a wall near the booth and waited for it to open.

When the salesmen turned up around nine, six boys and girls, I introduced myself and told them I'd been hired by Peter. They were a friendly bunch, mainly Londoners like me.

For the first hour, as it got hotter and hotter, I watched the salesmen do their thing. They were pretty slick – friendly and smiling, not too pushy – and also head over heels in love with life in Majorca.

When I felt I was ready, I strolled a decent distance away from the booth and started to look out for possible punters. By that time there were PRs all over the strip. Must have been at least 40 of them.

I spotted a likely looking couple of girls. 'Um, hello,' I said, flipping open my plastic folder, 'would you like…' They just looked at me. I took a deep breath. 'There's a fantastic…' They looked at each other. One said something and I realised they were foreign. I blushed and walked away quickly.

Now I understood why the ticket sellers' first question was always 'excuse me, do you speak English?'

I saw three lads with very white faces, arms and legs who'd obviously arrived the night before. I plastered a big grin on my face, opened my folder, 'excuse me, lads, do you speak English?'

'Bugger off!' the biggest lad said in a Northern accent. 'Course we do. Now sling your 'ook.'

'You what,' I said, a bit confused.

'You heard him,' a smaller lad with a face only a mother could love said. 'We know what your game is. Our courier told us not to buy tickets off the streets. It's a racket. Beach parties don't exist. Now bugger off.'

There was nothing I could say. Their couriers had obviously nobbled them because they'd be losing out if their punters spent money on one of our trips so they slagged us off big time. As I turned and walked away, I heard one of the Northern boys say 'Cockney bastard. Think we was born yesterday, does he?' One of the others said something and they all laughed.

Great, I thought. I'm off to a brilliant start. Two Krauts and three Northern Neanderthals. All around me PRs were making sales. I started to panic. Two pale birds strolled towards me. 'Excuse me, girls,' I said, opening my folder, which was getting pretty sweaty by now. 'Do you speak English?'

They looked at each other and laughed. Here we go again, I thought. 'Course we do, darling' one girl said. They were Londoners! Thank God for that.

'Great,' I said, trying not to sound too relieved. 'Are you here on Tuesday?' They nodded. 'Want to go to the party of a lifetime?'

'Go on, mate, tell us all about it', the first girl said. I could have kissed them. I did my spiel, they lapped it up and bought a ticket each. I was off the mark.

By mid-day I'd sold 17 tickets, which meant 1700 pesetas. I'd been at it nonstop and felt pretty good. I was walking down the front thinking about lunch and a cold beer when I heard a car roar up next to me. I looked round. It was the Beach Boys in their rusty, battered SEAT 600, Little Jimmy driving. Peter leant out the window. 'Louie Baby! How's it going?' he said.

'Sold 17,' I said.

'Well done, man! I knew you could do it.'

'What do I do now? Flog the rest of these?' I waved the tickets I had left.

'Nah. The party's sold out. Give us the tickets you haven't shifted.' I handed them over. Peter dropped them on the floor, rummaged around in his bag and handed me another bundle. 'Start selling for Friday's party.'

'No problem. See ya later?'

'Babalu tonight, my boy,' Peter said. 'Be there or be triangular.'

Little Jimmy gunned the car and, with screeching tires, the Beach Boys shot off down the road.

* * * * * *

Once more, it took me a minute to work out where I was when I woke up the next morning. I wasn't in my prison cell this time, though. I was on someone's balcony and the sun was coming up over the sea.

I stepped through the French doors and into the apartment. A red-haired girl with a sunburned back was lying face down on a sofa in nothing but her bra and panties. She was cute. I tiptoed past her and stepped on a full ashtray. 'Shit,' I said.

The girl rolled over, opened one eye. 'Hello,' she said, her voice croaky.

'Um, where am I?' I said. 'How did I get here?'

'Dunno, mate,' she said. 'All I know is last night you was leaning over the balcony waving a bunch of tickets at the people on the street shouting "beach party, beach party, anyone wanna come to a beach party".'

I laughed. It made my head hurt. 'What's your name?'

'I told you last night. It's Maureen.'

'Pleased to meet you. I'm Lou…'

'I know. Louie Baby. You told me about a hundred times last night. Louie Baby. Friend to the stars.'

46

'Sorry?' Then I realised I must have told her about my time as a singer-songwriter. I winced. 'Did we...?'

'Course not. Cheek! After you finished shouting at people you flaked out and that was that.'

'Sorry.' Maureen shrugged. 'Listen,' I said. 'Wanna go to a beach party?'

A FOX AMONG SWEDISH CHICKS

'All right?' I said, holding the telephone receiver away from my ear. After a day in the sun it was so hot I thought the receiver was going to melt down my neck.

'Who's that?'

'It's me, Louie!'

'Louie! How you doin', mate? I couldn't hear you through all that fizzing and popping. Sounds like you're phoning from a champagne factory.'

I looked around me. The Arenal strip was just warming up for another full-on night of the Mediterranean good life. It was Sunday, the best day for us ticket-sellers because this was when punters arrived to begin their week or two in the sun. I'd had a great day. After three months blasting tickets, I was a star salesman, shifting between 30 and 40 tickets on a good morning, which this Sunday's had been. This was 3,000 or 4,000 pesetas so I'd made my month's rent and more. I fingered the roll of greasy banknotes in my pocket, grinned.

The sun hung in the darkening sky, fat, heavy and tired-looking, ready to slide down behind the mountains. The moon waited to take its place. It was still hair-dryer hot. 'Not quite, Bern,' I said. 'So, how do you fancy coming out for my birthday?'

'When is it?' Bernie the Fox said.

'12th September.'

'Course it is.' Bernie coughed. 'Why not? Sure.' He made it sound like he was just hopping on a train up to Southend but I knew why. Bern was too cool to show any excitement even though I could almost see him grinning from ear to ear.

'I'm having a big do next Saturday, the 10th. Listen, Bern. There's this travel agent in Covent Garden, run by the dad of a geezer named Robin who sells tickets with us out here. You got a pen?'

'Hang on, I'll just get one. 'Ere, what's the time in sunny Spain?'

'Nine. Course, it's eight where you are. What are you doing?

'Not much. Watching telly. Probably pop out down The Marquis of Cornwallis for last orders a bit later. Let me get that pen.'

I heard the clunk as he put his receiver down and then I couldn't hear any more apart from the mutter of the telly in the background. There was not much point watching telly in Spain. It was utter crap, apart from when there was European Cup football. But I sometimes got so desperate I watched Bonanza dubbed into booming Spanish

I looked up at the stars. They seemed very close, much nearer than back home. Maybe it was how clear the air was and how, apart from all the neon on the strip, the rest of the island was just a huddled dark shape. I watched a set of tail-lights glide into land and thought, here comes another bunch of punters.

Another clunk as the phone was picked up. 'Right,' I said. 'Got that pen?'

'Si, si.'

I gave him the address. 'Robin's dad will do you a good deal. Tell him you know the Beach Boys.'

'What?'

'Sorry, not yer actual Beach Boys. It's what some of the lads out here call themselves. He'll know. You'll come, yeah?'

'Sounds like a great idea, Louie. Why not? Sea, sun, sangria. Few tarts. Lovely. I'll schlep down to this bloke's place tomorrow. What's the weather like...?'

'What do you think?

'Stupid question I suppose. Here, want me to bring anything? Special birthday present, like?'

I didn't have to think. 'Tea, Marmite, good bit of bacon, bagels, Cheddar chee...'

And the phone went dead before I had a chance to put any more money in it. Those phones ate money. I hung up, rubbed my sore ear, and stepped away from the phone box, lighting a cigarette.

I knew Bern would say yes. I was sure he'd been itching to find out what the score was out in Majorca.

When I was back in London before I came out for the whole summer I didn't even bother trying to persuade Bern to come with me, even though he was my best mate. He had the cushiest job of anyone I knew back home.

* * * * * *

Bern the Fox was a charmer in a neighbourhood that loved anyone who was a great pulling partner. He wasn't called the Fox for nothing.

Of course, Bernie took great care over his appearance. He was half-Italian, looked a bit like Dean Martin with his sharp suits and crocodile shoes. He played on this by having a permanent suntan, courtesy of a gigantic sun bed in the front room of his high-rise council flat in Old Street, East London. He'd positioned the sun bed so he could watch telly at the same time as working on his tan. Actually, there wasn't much space left in the room once Bern had installed his tanning machine and the telly.

Bern drove an early 60s four-door Caddy that looked like it had dropped out of the sky onto the grimy East

End street, still pockmarked by bomb damage from German bombs.

Of all my mates, Bernie had the most glamorous job. By day he worked for his brother-in-law Maxie, a big wheel in the fashion industry and absolutely loaded. Bern put on fashion shows at Max's warehouse and was his minder so he obviously knew how to handle himself.

I guess Maxie needed a minder because, like lots of businesses in the East End, he made regular payments to certain heavy people to keep his business trouble-free. The underworld was always there beneath the surface of everything, sometimes very close.

He was also a serious high roller and rumoured to drop up to £50,000 at the roulette tables some nights. Don't forget, this was the mid-60s so that was a lot of money. A few times Maxie even went to Vegas all expenses paid to gamble.

One time Bernie and his three brothers – he also had four sisters – had got into a situation with another little firm and he'd roped me into going down to the boozer where they all were going to sort it out with cut-down snooker cues and socks filled with billiard balls. Luckily for me, though, they'd had a meet the night before and managed to sort things out without a scrap.

I'd seen the sawn off shotgun Bern carried in the boot of his big yank car but he always played down his gangster connections, even with me.

I knew he'd been put away for six months for passing forged banknotes back in 1962 when he was 21. He asked me to come up and see him on visiting day and bring him some cash for fags and toothpaste. When I slipped him a twenty, I said 'don't worry, mate. It's not one of yours.'

It was the time of the Kray Twins and all the other gangsters who knocked around with them. Bern was on nodding terms with the Krays because he knew Tony Lambrianou, another face and one of their firm.

I only met the Krays face to face once, when I went along with Bern to the Regency Club, the place they owned on Amhurst Road, Stoke Newington. Bern introduced me to them but I just stood there like a rabbit caught in the headlights and shook their hands. I'm sure the Twins found that hilarious.

I could understand what Bern got out of being around gangsters. Like plenty of people, he was fascinated by the air of danger around them. You simply had no idea what they were going to do next and they had this 'who gives a shit?' attitude which was very exciting. Of course, they also had the best birds – not that you dared even look at a girl who was going out with a villain – and were very free with the cash. It wasn't theirs, was it?

Some of the guys were also very funny. Mind you, we split our sides at everything they said. Just in case.

For me, though, villains always made me pretty nervous though I was careful not to show it. I was never a scrapper, unless I had no choice, so the air of menace around gangssters and the ever present potential for them to rip someone's head off if the poor sod looked at them the wrong way wasn't really my cup of tea.

I saw myself as an entertainer, always ready to leap onto a pub stage and belt out a song – as was Bern – and I could feel that this was my way out.

* * * * * *

When we'd talked in the pub, I could tell Bern was a little envious of what was going to be my new life and, at the very least, wanted to see it to convince himself it wasn't all it was cracked up to be and put his mind at rest.

And, of all my mates, he was the only one who could take time off at such short notice. Apart from that, though, Bern was my best mate and he'd come just because of that.

* * * * * *

I turned to stroll in the direction of La Babalu, where I was meeting the Beach Boys. I thought about how I'd automatically assumed Bern would know who I was talking about when I called Peter, Jimmy and Buddy by that name and smiled to myself.

I stopped at the green traffic lights, waited till they were red and stepped out into the road. A Vespa horn squealed and someone shouted my name. I jumped back just in time. The driver of the Vespa did a Hitler salute and his passenger shook her bright blonde hair. 'You vanker, Villi!' I shouted, even though I knew he couldn't hear me.

Willi was one of the faces on the strip. A German, he was a fantastic ticket seller. All of us PRs who'd made the grade and stuck it out for the summer, which would stumble to an end at the beginning of October, watched each other like hawks and were ferociously competitive.

Willi was so good he didn't just sell to the Germans but to the Brits as well. The Germans and the Brits really didn't mix, apart from in the big discos. Not that there was any real needle between us.

One of the Beach Boys favourite tricks when were out on the the piss was to pop into one of the bierkellers where they had that terrible oompah-oompah music and ask the German DJ if they had 'Twist and Shoot' by Gerry and the Panzers on the Goosestep label. The DJs would just laugh and tell us to bugger off.

So, for Willi to punt tickets to Brits was a big coup and he knew it.

By now I'd rented my own Vespa and gone mobile, although I didn't drive it at night. I'd woken up back in my prison cell bedroom a couple of times with no memory of having got there and I really didn't want to get on the wrong side of the cops.

Even though they turned a blind eye to most things, they could still decide to make an example of you and then you'd had it. Sometimes the coppers would come up to the stand we worked out of on the front and check our permits, even though they knew we were legal. If they caught us selling on the beach - which we weren't supposed to do - they came down on us like a ton of bricks.

One time, the cops were checking us out to see whether we had permits or not and there was a salesman there by the name of Johnny who didn't have a shirt on. He was a little, skinny guy. A big monster of a Guardia Civil gave him an almighty slap across the chest in front of all of us. He just had to stand there and take it.

Most of the Spanish didn't like us much and I could understand why. Some of the ticket sellers, like Willi, were outrageous and worse than the punters when they got drunk.

I'd realised that the discos tolerated us, not much more, and then only because they needed the business we bought them. The bars on the strip hated us.

Fat Paco, my landlord never did anything more than grunt and scratch his arse when I handed over my Duke of Kent. I'd become obsessed with trying to get a smile out of him. So far I'd had no luck.

Now, as I walked towards La Babalu, singing The Loving Spoonful's 'Summer In the City' to myself, I thought about what *my* summer had given me.

* * * * * *

For a start, no matter what state I was in when I woke up, where I was or who I was with, every day was a new adventure.

And some nights you didn't even want to sleep in case you missed out on something.

If I was selling tickets that day, I'd have a kind of tight feeling in my stomach. Even though I always sold plenty, I'd start the day nervous. But this was a buzz too.

I'd soon found out that if you didn't sell tickets, no-one was going to help. There was no-one to borrow money from. You were on your own.

But, I knew what I had to do and all of us ticket sellers were the same. There were usually about fifty of us on the strip and we were dead keen. We were all people who wanted more out of life, which is what Majorca was all about and we weren't going back to Blighty until the end of the summer. No chance.

Even though competition for punters was incredibly fierce, most of us played fair, maybe because it was about the status that came from proving you were a great ticket seller as much as the loot.

But, there was one time when Peter Bloss discovered that a couple of the ticket sellers who promoted discount entry tickets to La Babalu for a 20 peseta commission had come up with a pretty tasty scam.

To get your 20 peseta commission you had to prove you'd handed the punter who came into the club the discount entry ticket. You did this by writing your name on the ticket.

These two guys would wait a little way down the road from La Babalu and, as the punters streamed past on their way to the club, they'd ask to see their tickets. The story they gave punters was that they just wanted to check to make sure the tickets were genuine. They'd then switch the tickets for ones with their own names on them.

It was a neat racket but, when Peter rumbled the two guys, they were out on their ear pronto.

Life was an even bigger adventure when I was around the Beach Boys. It seemed like they made every second of the day magical. Larger than life.

The Beach Boys really were the stars of the strip, especially La Babalu. One night a bunch of international footballers, Dennis Law, Noel Cantwell, Georgie Best and Bobby Moore, captain of the England football team that won the 66 World Cup came into the club and were given a heroes welcome.

Peter went straight over to Bobby Moore's table and shook his hand. 'Nice one for winning the world cup, Bobby,' he said. 'Mind if I dance with your wife?'

All Bobby could do was look at his wife, Tina, who said 'sure, why not?' and, within seconds, she was dancing with Peter to the Jamaican house band.

Tina's reaction wasn't unusual. The first thing most people thought when they came into the orbit of Peter, the Beach Boys undisputed leader, was 'who is this guy? I want to know more about him.' There was just something about Peter that made people want to be around him.

Tall and good-looking, the loudest and funniest person I'd ever met in my life and one of those people who was a natural leader.

In Peter's world, he was the star.

Funnily enough, Peter was a terrible salesman. He admitted it himself. He'd start chatting to punters, get completely into what he was saying and forget he was meant to be selling tickets.

Peter and the rest of us ticket sellers worked for Harry Cohen AKA Harry the Horse, a hugely fat Jewish Londoner in his late 30s who loved to gamble, especially on jai alai, the national game of the Basque country. This incredibly fast and tough game is a bit like the French pelota, played with a ball and these scoop-like sticks. At that time there was a jai alai court in Palma where the Horse used to go. He also had a card school with his cronies, Jewish residents on the island. It was Harry who'd organised my work permit. Harry had an interest in La Babalu and leased La Corbetta and Santa Maria, the two boats we used for the Beach Parties, from a Cuban-Spanish guy called Julian who detested Harry the Horse. Julian stuck with Harry, though, because he was filling his boats.

Harry's wife was called Beauty. Really.

Although Julian earned good wedge out of the Beach Parties, he was also a real entrepreneur with fingers in loads of pies. Julian had a contract with the US Navy 6th Fleet to supply them with fresh fruit and veg. When they came into Palma he turned his boats into floating market stalls and steamed very slowly and carefully out to the aircraft carriers. It was rumoured that Julian also owned a brothel in Palma.

Buddy, the real ladies man of the Beach Boys was laid-back and easygoing. As I'd discovered, he sang just like Buddy Greco and used this to charm the pants off as many women as he could.

Ultra-fashionable, Little Jimmy was the baby of the group and all the girls thought he was cute. But like all small blokes, Jimmy felt he always had to prove himself. He hated 'Southern softies', as he called them. This, and the chip on his shoulder, sometimes made Jimmy pretty fiery when he'd had a few.

Even though I wasn't officially a Beach Boy – I didn't work the beach parties, just sold tickets – I knocked around with them so much it had started to feel a bit like I was. Like them, I was a big, extrovert character. In my case, I was the clown, the joker.

And, with the fourth original Beach Boy, David, back in Golders Green and working for his dad, the Beach Boys were down to three. Which didn't feel right.

I really didn't understand why David would have chosen miserable Britain and working for his dad over the incredible life he had as a Beach Boy and one of the princes of the strip.

For a start, you could have a different girl every night. No bother. All the Scandie birds were on the pill and as game for a bit of a tumble as us blokes were. If they did arrive with a boyfriend – some boring, straight, pasty-faced Herbert – they would often back-heel him and go for a Beach Boy or one of the Spanish guys.

Now the terror of getting some girl pregnant was out the way, the only thing to worry about was catching something. Many of the lads wound up with crabs, scabies or, if they were really unlucky, something worse.

Earlier in the summer, this guy called Barry from South London was out visiting one of the salesman and he got his leg over for the first time. He made the mistake of boasting about it in front of all of us. We knew the score so it wasn't like getting laid was a big deal.

We were sitting in front of one of the bars having a beer when Barry started on again about his amazing bunk-up. 'You've probably got half a gross,' Peter said. 'You know, a dose. All the girls have got something – VD, crabs or whatever.' Peter shuddered, shook his head.

Barry went white under his sunburn. 'Nah, she was a clean bird. I know it.'

Peter looked at us and we knew enough to jump in and back him up. We all nodded. 'It's true,' Little Jimmy said.

'We've all had a dose in our time.' Thinking fast, he said 'there's only thing what will cure it. Right, Pete?'

'That's right,' Peter said. 'I'll get you this special powder which you rub on your meat and two veg and under your armpits every morning and evening and that'll get rid of it. Works a treat, doesn't it lads?'

Once again, we all nodded.

Next day, Peter appeared with a pack of bright yellow powder. 'Right, Barry,' he said. 'Like I said, you rub this on your wedding tackle and under your arms every morning and night and it does the business.'

Barry was over the moon. He had a girlfriend back home in London who he was dead keen on. They were engaged and all that. She would have killed him if he'd come home with VD or God knows what. He couldn't thank Peter enough and disappeared off to the khazi to rub the stuff on his old chap.

When he'd gone, Buddy said 'what did you give him, Pete?'

'Saffron,' he said. 'Stains like a bastard. It's what they use to make the paella rice that colour. He'll go home with a bright yellow cock and balls and armpits and he'll have to explain that to Tracey, or whatever her name is. That'll teach him to shoot his mouth off.'

We all collapsed with laughter but I couldn't help feeling sorry for Barry. How would he explain that away?

The stuff that *really* did the trick was called Aceite Inglés, this oil you rubbed on yourself that stung like hell. I always thought that calling a VD treatment Aceite Inglés showed what the Spanish really thought of us. None of them ever got a half a gross, did they? Course not.

* * * * * *

I was beginning to feel accepted by the Beach Boys. I'd done a couple of things that made them look at me in a bit of a different light.

First of all, I'd saved a vital penalty as replacement goalie in a needle match between the La Babalu salesmen and the guys who worked for Sergeant Pepper's. This was a great little club in Gomila, in the middle of Palma, where about 2,000 kids partied in around a square kilometre of clubs and bars every night of the summer. Peter Bloss had introduced us to it and we'd go every now and again. Sergeant Pepper's was owned by a guy called Mike Jeffery, manager of Jimi Hendrix and the Animals.

We won 1-0 and I was a hero for a while after that.

The next thing was the Beach Boys discovering I could sing.

One night, we were all out at a birthday party for one of the ticket sellers at an open air BBQ place called Moli Can Perra in Arenal. It was one of those places with rows of big long wooden tables where you sit side by side. We were all well and truly bevvied up. I jumped on the table and started belting out 'It's Not Unusual' by Tom Jones.

I got a huge round of applause and quite a few surprised looks. When I followed up with 'Green, Green Grass of Home' and 'What's New Pussycat?', complete with over the top hip swivelling, the place went wild.

It erupted when Peter yanked my strides down. He couldn't stand anyone else being the star of the show for too long.

After that, once they knew I was an entertainer, the Beach Boys sometimes invited me along on beach party trips to help provide the entertainment.

On one of these, the real entertainment was provided by Captain Diego. Diego was the captain of La Corbetta, one of the boats Peter and the Beach Boys used for beach parties.

Most of the time Diego would swig his San Miguel, chew on a stinking cigar, occasionally wipe the sweat off his unshaven, grey face onto a filthy t-shirt and growl if anyone came too close. He was a foul-tempered guy and sometimes volatile.

This time, Captain Diego and Peter got into an argument over divvying up the tips for the trip. All the money was kept in a metal box and, when Diego got tired of Peter getting in his face with his foghorn voice, he threw the box over the side and into the Med. Stunned, Peter watched it sink. Then, being Peter, he shrugged, grinned and shook Captain Diego's hand.

Just another adventure.

* * * * * *

'Jesus, Louie,' Bernie the Fox said, 'thank Christ I'm not staying here. You can barely swing a cat.'

I'd just collected Bernie at the airport and bought him back to my gaff to show him it before we set off for his hotel. It was Saturday the 10th, the day of my birthday party. We were all going to La Babalu to make a night of it.

I was playing it cool but I was really chuffed Bern had come out and excited about showing him my new life.

'It's not that bad,' I said, thinking yes it was. I'd given up trying to find anywhere else, especially as I was never in the shitehola. But, at least I had a fan now and my new clobber lined up neat and tidy on a clothes rail I'd found beside a skip.

And my room was relatively cucaracha free for now. I'd got hold of some vicious insect spray that did for most of the huge cockroaches and I religiously sprayed along the door and under the bed every day. Even though the stuff was like poison gas – it made me cough and choke if I breathed it in – the odd cucaracha still got through. I'd find them upside down on the floor looking like some disgusting crunchy date, open the door and kick them spinning down the grimy hall.

Someone told me that cockroaches would survive a nuclear war. I could well believe it.

But, it was September now and I'd only need the room for about a month more. I kept myself from thinking about the end of the season and made sure I packed as much into every day as possible.

Bernie stepped forward, pulled a pair of brown leather trousers off the clothes rail and turned to me with a raised eyebrow. 'You actually wear these?' he said. Bernie was wearing the height of London fashion: Chelsea boots, mohair suit, shirt, tie, five-point hankie in his breast pocket and a heavy, bark finish gold bracelet. He'd splashed on so much Old Spice that, in my prison cell, it was making my eyes water as much as the cockroach poison.

I was secretly pleased to see Bern was sweating and finding it hard to keep his usual chutzpah.

'Course I do,' I said, mock-offended. I knew what he was like. 'Handmade those are. Quite the ticket, my son. Girls love 'em.'

Over the summer months, my style had relaxed and slowly become more San Tropez than Brick Lane. During the day, it was impossible to wear anything more than shorts and t-shirts and, because it was still hot at night, we all wore light cotton stuff, jeans and, every now and then, the leather trousers.

Mind you, I wasn't going to admit to Bernie I hardly ever wore the leather strides because they made me sweat so much I kind of slithered around inside them. It was like having a Turkish Bath in your pants.

My leather stuff – I also had a fantastic knee-length leather coat – was made for me by a tailor in nearby Coll den Rabassa who Peter had turned me onto. It was well-made and dirt cheap.

'Right, I said, 'let's get you checked in. You can have a shit, shower and shave and we'll head out, meet the Beach Boys, have a few sherberts and all that.'

I picked up Bern's case. 'What you got in here, Bern?' I said. 'Rocks?'

He grinned. 'Got to have the right schmutter when you go abroad, Louie,' he said. I didn't want to tell him that he already looked like a sharp-dressed shark out of water. He'd find that out for himself.

I swung the case out the door and followed it down the narrow stairs and into the street, Bernie strolling behind me.

I hailed a cab, told the driver the name of the hotel where Bernie was staying and we watched as the driver hauled the case into the boot of his cab. I'd soon learned that Majorcan cab-drivers were happy to let you do all the lugging and I took pleasure in making them work for their fare. They were usually miserable, foul-tempered sods. 'I'll come and meet you later, Bern,' I said. 'Couple of hours.'

He looked startled. 'I thought you was coming with me,' he said.

'What for? You'll want to freshen up, maybe have some shuteye. It'll be a long night.'

'I don't need a kip, mate. You're talking to Bernie the Fox here. It's just, I don't know where he's going to take me. What if he goes the long way round? Wouldn't put it past him, would you?'

'I wouldn't but your hotel's five minutes drive away.' I looked at Bern's face, knew that he was a bit rattled. I'd forgotten it was his first time abroad. I shrugged. 'All right, no sweat.'

Up in Bern's room, which had a great view of the bay of Palma, we caught up on what had been happening back home as he unpacked what looked like an entire boutique's worth of clobber. He watched as I pulled bits off the huge chunk of Cheddar cheese he'd bought me, made a disgusted face as I stuck my finger in the Marmite and licked it.

I asked after the gang back home. There was a group of us who'd grown up together in Bethnal Green and another bunch from Chelsea who I'd got friendly with and we all knocked around together.

'You know,' Bern said. 'The usual. Going up West, pulling birds, having a laugh. It's been a hot summer – course, not like this – so we all went down to Brighton a couple of times. The usual, like I say. What do you do?'

'It's great,' I said. 'Work's hard but I've got a knack for it so I do all right. Party every night. Plenty of birds – Brits and Scandies...'

'Scandies?'

'Scandinavians. You know, like the au pair sorts we met back in the Smoke but just a lot more of them and they're right up for a holiday fling. And, wait for it,' Bern raised an eyebrow, 'they're all on the pill. You'll pull tonight, no sweat. So, yeah, sun, sea, sangria, sex. Like they say. And I've got a proper great bunch of mates. They've showed me the ropes and they really look out for me. And we have a real laugh.'

'Sounds great,' he said.

'It is. I tell you, Bern, I've landed smack on my feet here.'

'You look good, Louie. Blinding Charlie Chan on your boat.' Bern was a connoisseur of tans. 'What are you going to do when the season finishes?'

'I don't want to think about that. Come on, have your shower and we'll go out.'

While Bernie showered, singing away, I sat on the balcony smoking one of his duty free Dunhill International cigarettes and watched a yellow ferry move slowly across the bay and out to sea. Seeing Bernie in my new life really made me aware of how much things had changed for me.

Bern appeared on the balcony, towel round his waist, showing off the gold chain round his neck and his weird, plastic looking tan. 'By the way,' he said. 'I forgot to tell you earlier but your dad, nan and sisters wish you happy birthday.'

* * * * * *

I didn't large it too much as we walked past the queue of excited kids waiting to get into La Babalu. I looked at Bern, who was staring at the massed ranks of gorgeous, tanned blonde girls chattering to each other and playing with their hair. 'Christ, Louie,' Bernie said. 'You can smell the fanny in the air.'

I looked at him, laughed and winked. He looked well sharp in a dark mohair suit, brilliant white shirt, tie and the highly-polished Chelsea Boots. These were obviously new and he was limping a bit.

The bouncer beamed at me as he waved us in, 'hola, Senor Louie,' he said. 'Feliz cumpleaños.'

'Gracias, Pedro,' I said. I couldn't do the lisp without feeling like a berk but I'd picked up a little Spanish.

'What did he say?' Bern said as we walked towards the VIP table where I could see the Beach Boys were already sat holding court.

'Happy Birthday.'

And, just as I said that, Eddie, the singer of La Babalu's Jamaican house band who were bashing out a Ska version of Chris Farlowe's 'Out of Time' bought the band to a stumbling halt.

'The birthday dude has arrived,' Eddie said. 'My man Louie. Come up here, my brother.' He waved me towards the low stage where the band was.

'Off you go, Louie,' Bern said, smiling.

Stunned, I made my way through the perfumed crowd who were looking at me like I was famous and climbed onto the stage. Eddie grinned at me, showing a row of big white teeth, and slapped me on the back. He turned to the crowd. 'It's my good friend Louie baby's birthday today,' he said.

Actually, my birthday was in two day's time but I wasn't going to argue with him. 'So, come on, everybody, what do we sing?'

Backed by the band, Eddie led the crowd in a Ska version of 'Happy Birthday To You' that got faster and faster until it ended in a thundering drum roll. When the song ended, I thanked Eddie, who gave me a big sweaty hug, bowed deeply and made my way back through the crowd, getting a few smackers on the cheek from the lovely Scandie girls.

I felt bloody fantastic.

When I got back to Bern, I could see he was gobsmacked in spite of himself. He slapped me on the back and followed me to the table where Peter, Little Jimmy and Buddy sat.'

'Did you put them up to this?' I said to Peter.

'Why, didn't you like it?' Peter said.

'It was horrible,' I said. 'Never been so embarrassed in my life.'

'You should get out more,' Peter said.

'No, it was blinding,' I said, wiping a pretend tear from my eye. 'Thanks lads.'

'Our pleasure,' Little Jimmy said. Buddy looked away from the girl he was busy snake-charming with his eyes and cocked an imaginary pistol at me before fixing her with his bright blue peepers again before she could come to her senses.

Peter stood up, put his arm round Bernie. 'And you must be the famous Bernie the Fox,' he said. 'Louie baby's told us you're a diamond geezer.' I knew Peter well enough to know he was hamming up the Cockney but Bernie didn't catch it. Peter didn't mean anything by it anyway. 'Shampoo?'

'Too right,' Bernie said, sitting down.

Peter stood up, took a bottle of champagne out of the bucket on the table and held it up to the moonlight. There was about a quarter of it left. Before I knew what was happening, he poured this over my head and planted a big kiss on my forehead. 'Look at that. Lovely French champagne all the way from France. Well, near France. Spain. Happy Birthday, Louie baby,' he said. 'Many happy returns, man.' He waved the bottle over his head, bellowed 'over here,' in the general direction of the nearest waiter. Satisfied that the waiter had heard him and was on his way over with fresh supplies, Peter sat down, looked at Bernie and said 'he's all right, Louie, isn't he? Well, he's a bit of vankaire but you know what I mean?'

Bernie laughed, lit up a cigarette with his gold-plated Ronson gas lighter, placed this and his fags on the table where everyone could see them, blew smoke out of the side of his mouth and said, 'you're not wrong, Pete.' He looked round at the golden lovelies spilling out of their summer dresses, waved at a girl who he caught looking over at our table and said, 'looks like you fellows have got it made in the shade. Made in the bleedin' shade.'

'True,' Peter said. 'It's paradise. If you can stand it. Someone famous said that. Who was it? I know. Me.' He chuckled to himself.

I looked at sharp-dressed Bernie, still with the smell of London on him, trying to relax and look laidback in his chair and at the Beach Boys, all deeply tanned and sprawled in their seats like lazy princes.

Made in the shade indeed, I thought.

1968 AND THE BEACH
BOYS INVADE EUROPE

As anyone who's ever worked a summer season like I just had will tell you, all you want to do when you get the chance is to sleep. Sleep and sleep some more.

That's the way it was for me. I was absolutely drained. And it wasn't just the work I'd been doing. The nonstop partying, the birds and whatever we used to help us be the life and soul of the endless parties also took it out of me.

To be honest, there also wasn't a lot to get out of bed for back in Bethnal Green. The only one of my mates who had a clue as to what my life had been like for the past few months was Bernie the Fox and he was busy hustling schmutter for his brother in law, cruising the narrow streets of East London in his beast of a Yank motor, chasing birds and lying on his sunbed.

The rest of the blokes had made a point of not being impressed when I tried to tell them what I'd been up to, about my new life. The first conversation I had back in the Marquis of Cornwallis pub went something like this. 'All right, Louie? What you having? Listen, there's a party over Chelsea later, fancy it? You wearing them leather strides for a bet?'

My tan, which I worked so hard to get, was long gone. Underneath my clothes, my body was yellowy-brown. Bernie The Fox was browner than I was and he always made some excuse so I couldn't use his sunbed.

That was that. It was like I'd never been away which, to say the least, was pretty depressing. As was the weather. The dirty grey skies over London, the endless drizzle that seemed to get inside your clothes and the biting wind all got to me. Being a window cleaner, I couldn't believe it'd never bothered me before.

But, of course, I'd never known anything different back then, had I?

So, now I was back cleaning windows up West and saving to get the cash I needed to be able to afford a decent apartment when I went back to the Rock, as we all called Majorca. That was months away but I was already dreaming of being back in what I now saw as my real life.

* * * * * *

She was coming towards me out of the clear blue Mediterranean water, arms open wide, water running down between her large, tanned, naked breasts, a big smile on her face when…

'Louie! LOUIE!' Dad's voice blasted that dream out of the water.

'Yeah?' I called back, the effort of raising my voice making me cough. I'd had a horrible cold ever since I'd been back and the fags didn't help.

'Some bloke called Peter's on the phone for you.'

'Peter 'oo?'

'Hang on.' A pause then Dad called up the stairs. 'He says his name's Peter Bloss. He's the Peter you've been raving about, I suppose. Christ, he's got a loud voice.'

I leapt out of bed and was down our stairs in a flash. Dad looked at me and raised an eyebrow as he handed over the phone before sitting back down in his chair by the gas fire to study the racing form. 'Blossy, old mate,' I said. 'Where are ya?'

'Never mind where I am, Louie Baby,' Blossy boomed. I held the phone away from my ear. I'd forgotten just how loud Peter was. 'I'm in sunny Essex freezing me nuts off, as it goes. But, listen. Buddy's only gone and bought a camper van and we're off on a European tour before we go back to the Rock. Yours truly, Buddy, Little Jimmy and, if you can swing it, you.'

'Sounds fantastic,' I said. 'Count me in.' I was over the moon just to be asked.

Peter chuckled. 'Hang on, Buddy's asking us all to chip in £600 towards the trip, for the van, gas and food. You got that?'

'Course. No sweat.' I didn't. I had the money I was saving from my window cleaning round but it was a long way short of what Buddy wanted. But I already knew I was going with them, whatever happened. I looked at

Dad pretending to read the racing form and thought fast. 'Give me a day, can you, Pete?' I said.

'Sure,' Peter said. He put on a German accent. 'If sings go to plan, ve vill be invading Europe Monday week at precisely 20 hundred hours. Be there or...'

'Be oblong, I know. What's your number, mate?' He reeled it off and I put the phone down. I was in my y-fronts and shivering but grinning from ear to ear.

'Hadn't you better put some clothes on?' Dad said without looking up.

'Right.' I paused. The air got thick and the ticking from the star clock above the gas fire became louder. I went to stand with my back to the fire. 'Dad?' I said.

'Yes son.'

'Um, that was a mate from Majorca. Peter.'

'He's got a bloody loud voice, ain't he?'

'I know. Sorry. He's invited me to go on a trip to Europe with the rest of the Beach Boys, you know, who I told you about.'

'And, are you going?' There was something in Dad's voice I couldn't quite pin down but he wasn't pissed off.

'My share's six hundred and I've got about a hundred quid saved.'

'So, what are you going to do, son?'

'I was wondering…'

'If I could give you the rest?' Dad's voice was still quiet and mild.

'It'll be a loan. I'll pay you back.' I didn't have to say anything else. Dad knew how desperate I was to get away from Bethnal Green.

'Let me think about it. It's a lot of money.'

'I know, dad.'

'Got any plans for today, son?'

'Meet the lads. Pub tonight. Maybe a party. Same old Saturday routine, I guess.' I sighed. 'But perhaps I should stay in tonight, save money.'

'Good idea,' Dad said. He licked his pencil and put a cross next to the name of a horse he fancied.

* * * * * *

I spent the day up West, mooching around, drinking endless cups of watery coffee and smoking. In my mind, I wasn't stepping round the puddles on Oxford Street or jumping back from the kerb when a bus splashed past. I was already swanning down a boulevard in Paris or Vienna or somewhere amazing like that.

A sandwich board man trudged past, his board hanging at a funny angle off his shoulders. He looked like I felt.

We locked eyes for a second and that decided me. Whatever it took, I was getting the hell out of Dodge.

But how?

* * * * * *

When I got back Dad wasn't around. I sat by the fire, scheming about how I could get my hands on the money I needed to make my great escape.

No matter how I looked at it, I always came up short. No-one I knew had that kind of dosh, not even Bernie. Maybe, I thought, he could help me do a job. A fiddle of some sort. I began to warm to the idea.

I was still sitting there, staring into space – visions of sauntering through Rome with an Italian bird hanging off my arm fading – when I heard the door open and close. Dad! My heart soared before I managed to get a grip on myself. What I was asking for was a lot of money for Dad too and it wasn't like he was loaded. I knew I couldn't ask him again.

When he came through the front door, Dad was whistling, which was unusual. It took a lot for him to do that. He also bought the strong smell of fish and chips with him. We only ever had fish and chips on Friday and my Nan made these and it was a Saturday. What was going on?

I said nothing, waited for him to come into the front room. When he did, he was beaming and carrying a tray with two plates of fish and chips, bread and butter, tomato sauce and two bottles of Worthington E beer. He put the tray down on the coffee table with exaggerated care and flopped down into the chair opposite mine on the other side of the fire.

'What's the special occasion, dad?' I said. 'Not that I'm complaining.'

'A result at the dogs, my boy,' he said. 'Very good result indeed.' Dad was a betting man but careful enough to always make sure he won more than he lost. And, as all gamblers know, you never tell people when you lose in any case.

I knew enough not to ask how much. Dad never bragged about his winnings. 'Nice one, Dad,' I said, 'ta very much'. I reached for a plate of fish and chips – one of the few things I'd really missed when I was out on the Rock. I picked up my plate and my eyes nearly popped out of my head when I saw what was below it. I looked at Dad. He was struggling to keep a grin from splitting his face in half.

'There you go, son,' he said.

Hands trembling, I put the plate down on the floor and picked up the banknotes Dad had fanned out on the tray. 'I...'

Dad saved me from losing it. 'It's a loan, Louie,' he said smoothly. 'And, like I said, I had a real result today.'

'Bloody 'ell, Dad,' I said, counting the crisp notes. 'There must be a monkey here.'

'I figured you'd need it. I want it back. Now, eat your fish and chips before they get cold. Nice piece of skate you've got there. Your favourite, right? And you won't be getting much of that where you're going. It'll be all goulash and spaghetti and all that foreign muck.'

And we settled back into our chairs on either side of the fire like bookends.

* * * * * *

'Is Peter there?'

'Can I say who's calling?' The woman, who I guessed was Blossy's mum, was very well spoken.

I made my voice sound a little posher even though I had no idea why I felt the need to do that. 'Louis O'Brien, Mrs Bloss,' I said. 'I'm a friend of Peter's from Majorca, from the summer.'

Her voice softened. 'Hello, Louie,' she said. 'He talks about you a lot.'

'Does he?' I said. That felt good.

'I'll just get him for you. Nice to speak to you.'

The phone went quiet and I heard Peter's voice echoing in the hallway. He was singing our patented version of 'Twist and Shout' by Gerry and The Panzers on the Goosestep label:

'Vell, shake it up, baby now, Tvist and shoot!'

I held the phone away from my ear in anticipation. 'All right, Louie Baby. You in?'

'I am.'

'You are?' He sounded a little surprised but soon recovered himself. 'Got the dosh? All of it?'

'Yep. I had a bit left and my old man lent me the rest. 500 sovs.'

'Nice one, old son. Nice one Louie Baby's old man. A prince among men.'

'He is,' I said. 'He says he won it on the dogs but I ain't so sure. It's a lot of money. I think he just wants me to have an adventure, wishes it was him who was going.'

'Ours not to reason why,' Peter said. 'Don't knock it, buddy.'

'I ain't. You've got the cash yourself then?' I said.

'Of course. Just don't ask me how.'

'What's the drill then? When's the off?'

Peter told me where and when we were all going to meet. I put the phone down, buzzing and headed up the stairs to my bedroom whistling 'Three Coins In The Fountain'.

* * * * * *

'Ain't it great to be leaving that shithole behind?' Buddy said as we watched the docks of Harwich fade away into the drizzle.

'Too right,' Little Jimmy said. Out of the sun, he'd taken to dying his hair blonde and it looked a bit weird with his white face.

When we were doing the off and Peter first saw Little Jimmy, he said 'blimey, Jim, you look like one of them Village of the Damned kids.'

We chinked our bottles of pale ale together. 'Next stop Norway,' Buddy said.

'Why exactly are we going to Norway?' I said. 'I thought the whole idea was to escape to the bleedin' sun.'

'Birds,' was all Buddy said. We'd all got a list of names and addresses of girls dotted all over Scandinavia we'd met in the summer. I'd put money on none of them ever expecting us to turn up on their doorstep. I was looking forward to the reaction.

Whatever happened, the camper van was a blinder, a Bedford Dormobile caravanette. There were four bunk beds, two on either side of the van so no-one had to crash out on the floor. The van even came with a two-ring stove, a fridge, cupboards with plenty of space for the food we'd got from the cash and carry before we left and a candy-striped pop-up roof.

I didn't have a full driving licence so I was made chef. I couldn't cook but the Beach Boys didn't know that. Yet.

Peter had decided that we should say we were a pop group and we certainly looked the part. He'd come up with the name 'Baby's Four', after his nickname for yours truly – Louie Baby - and this was written in black stick-on letters across the front of the van along with our names.

'Who cares where we're going, Peter said. 'So long as it's somewhere. Anywhere.' He drained his bottle of beer, dropped it over the side, rubbed his hands and said 'inside, lads? See if there's any talent at the bar?'

We followed him in.

* * * * * *

The only thing wrong with Scandinavia was the cold, especially when we didn't have warm Scandie chicks to bunk up with, which was more often than we liked. Most of the time we got the 'wow, lovely to see you, sorry, I have boyfriend now' routine. Tired of all the knockbacks in Norway, Sweden Denmark, we left after a few days, heading for Germany.

We met Abdul The Fat Turk at the Oktoberfest in Munich, the huge beer festival, while we were stuffing our faces with bratwurst and washing the sausage down with stein after stein of delicious beer.

The bratwurst made a much needed change from what I'd been cooking. This was mainly tinned Fray Bentos steak and kidney pies from a stash we'd invested in, accompanied by instant mash. We'd also bought a few cases of beans but hadn't read the label properly when we bought them. They were curried.

So, as we got to know each other better in the van, we also came to recognise the individual stench of each other's awful farts.

Actually, we didn't meet Abdul, he found us.

After a serious day's drinking and eating we staggered back to our van to find Abdul waiting. The first thing he said was 'is this your van?' He sounded like a villain from the movies. He had fat hands, one finger swollen round a huge gold knuckleduster ring.

'Oo's asking?'

'My name is Abdul. I am Turkish. I have been waiting for you.' If he'd added effendi, I wouldn't have been surprised. 'And, you, are you Baby's Four? What is Baby's Four? Are you pop group?'

'Kind of,' Peter said. 'Except we don't make music.' We looked at him.

Little Jimmy said 'you what?'

'It's a new concept,' Peter said. 'Now, Abdul, perhaps you'd be so good as to tell us what you want or sling your hook.'

'What is sling hook?'

'Never mind. What do you want?'

'I have friends in Istanbul with disco. They want to make it big success. You are English with the long hair and the cloth-es, you will help make disco big success. Yes? My friends pay you very well.'

We looked at each other. 'What do you reckon, playmates?' Peter said.

'Why not?' Buddy said. 'It's not like we've got anything to go back to. And it's hot in Turkey, ain't it?

'Is it hot in Turkey, Abdul?' Peter said.

'Very hot,' the Fat Turk said, nodding his head so vigorously his jowls wobbled. 'Oh yes.'

'I'm in,' I said.

'Me too,' added Little Jimmy.

Peter turned to Abdul. 'Looks like we're all up for it. But, first, we need to know what your mates are paying.'

'Wait here,' Abdul said. 'I make phone call.' He disappeared off in search of a phone box, leaving us looking at each other.

'Am I the only one that finds this all a little bit weird?' I said.

'A fat Turkish bloke at a German beer festival inviting us to Istanbul?' Peter said. 'Course not. But what have we got to lose? It's not like they're going to sell us into white slavery, are they?'

'Dunno. Are they?'

'Nah.' But he didn't sound too convinced.

'I ain't going back to the UK yet,' Buddy said. 'We've only been gone a couple of weeks.'

'Me neither,' Jimmy said. 'And what's white slavery when it's at home, Pete?'

'It'll be blonde slavery in your case, Jim,' Peter said.

'Don't get me wrong, lads,' I said. 'I'm up for it. I just think we should be careful.'

'Course,' Peter said. 'Aren't we always?' Little Jimmy snorted. 'Look, here he comes.'

Abdul was rubbing his hands and beaming as he waddled up to us. 'My friends,' he said. 'It is all agreed. You will make disco big success and my friends give you place to live and pay you big money. OK?'

We looked at each other. 'OK,' Peter said.

'Wonderful,' Abdul said. 'I give you address.' He handed Peter a grubby piece of paper which Peter stuffed into his jeans pocket. Abdul looked alarmed. 'You keep safe, yes? Is very long way to Istanbul. My friends expect you in one week.'

'No sweat,' Peter said. 'We'll be there.'

'Very good.' Abdul solemnly shook hands with each of us, turned and disappeared into the crowd of people. I half expected him to disappear in a puff of smoke.

When Abdul had gone, we turned and looked at each other. 'Istanbul here we come!' Little Jimmy shouted and we did the Beach Boys knee wobble, laughing and slapping each other on the back.

After a couple of minutes of ecstatic knee wobbling, Peter said 'anyone know where Istanbul actually is?'

* * * * * *

To get to Istanbul we drove through Austria, Yugoslavia and Bulgaria.

I didn't get to walk through the streets of Vienna but, while we were in Austria, we took a cable car to the top of a mountain and ran down, hand in hand, singing the 'the hills are alive with the sound of music' with Peter as Julie Andrews.

At that time, Yugoslavia and Bulgaria were communist. Little Jimmy's comment said it all: 'It's the spit of buggerin' Bradford and the birds all look like blokes.'

The best bit about the grindingly boring journey was the bond between us that was growing all the time, despite the poisonous farts we all brewed. We really did feel like a band of brothers.

* * * * * *

We found a camping site called the Mocamp on the outskirts of Istanbul run by a friendly young Turk. When we told him our story and gave him the name of the disco he warned us to be careful as the people running it were notorious local mafia and not to be trusted. He told us we could stay at the camp site as long as we wanted but that we shouldn't stick around.

'No way,' Peter said. 'We've come too far to turn back now.' The guy at Mocamp wrote down directions to the disco, which seemed to be famous and we headed into town.

Istanbul wasn't what we expected, even if we didn't know what to expect. It was on a big river called The Bosphorus, or the Phosphorus, as Little Jimmy called it, with the Black Sea on one side and something called The Sea of Marmara on the other. There were plenty of weird-looking mosques but also lots of ugly modern buildings springing up.

It wasn't warm.

We headed off to find the disco, flying the Union Jack as we'd done all the way across Europe. Big mistake.

In the middle of Istanbul a traffic cop – shiny boots, gun, big belly, deeply pissed off – took offense at the Union Jack, waved us down and told us to remove it as the only people allowed to fly a flag were embassy staff.

A large crowd including various touts selling fags and combs and a couple of shoeshine boys gathered to watch the cop take us hairy hippies down a peg or two. The air filled with the blare of car horns as traffic backed up. We obliged the cop and removed the flag, drove on a hundred metres, stopped and put it back on.

As we drove deeper into Istanbul, I began to realise just how foreign the place was. We inched our way through bazaars selling all sorts of strange clothes, sweets and mysterious food. Little boys were constantly thrusting their hands through the open van windows, asking for money, we guessed.

The Turkish blokes all dressed like they were in a 1920s gangster movie. They wore big floppy caps, double-breasted pinstripe jackets and had huge moustaches. Their shoes all had the back flattened like slippers. In among them was the odd hippy-looking westerner, which we didn't expect to see.

We saw some lovely birds, or Turkish Delights, as Peter predictably called them, including the first Muslim women I'd ever seen, covered from head to foot in black apart from a little slit for their eyes, which was strangely sexy.

The smell of the place was incredible. Petrol fumes, frying food, sewage and what smelt like several different kinds of animal shit.

As we got closer to where we'd been told the disco was, in the Sultan Ahmet part of the city, we saw a huge mosque that looked blue. The area around the mosque was pretty scruffy-looking but we noticed that there were more hippies wearing baggy, pajama-type trousers, shoulder bags, Afghan coats and little vests with bits of mirror on them. Most of these had long hair but some of them had shaved heads with a tuft left in the back.

'Where now?' Buddy, who was driving said to Peter, the navigator, as we came to a halt in a crowded street.

'Haven't a soddin' clue,' Peter said. 'I'll ask that geezer.' He pointed to a spaced out looking character wearing huge pajama trousers, a flowing striped shirt and one of the little mirror vests. 'Oi mate,' Peter bellowed. The guy turned round as if he'd been shot. He pointed his finger at his own chest. 'Yeah, you,' Peter said. The bloke came over to the van.

'Hey, guys,' he said. 'What's happening?' An American. 'Looking to score?'

Peter turned to us, his eyes lit up and he grinned. 'Not right now, mate,' he said, turning back. 'We're trying to find this place.' He pointed to the name of the disco on his piece of paper and the Yank hippy jabbed at each letter one by one. His fingernails were a bright red-orange. I looked at Peter. He shrugged.

'Just round the corner, dudes. Five minutes away.'

'Thanks,' Peter said.

The guy stepped back a little, took in the Union Jack and read the peeling letters that spelt out 'Baby's Four'. 'What are you guys, like a Bridish pop group or something?'

'Yeah, we're like a pop group only different,' Peter said.

'Cooool,' the guy said, very slowly. 'OK, guys, gotta boogie. Listen, you need to check out The Pudding Shop. It's way cool. You'll love it.'

'Pudding Shop?' Peter said.

'Yeah. Everyone knows where it is. Just ask anyone. It's seriously hip.' He paused. 'Yeah. OK, later.' He turned and melted into the crowd.

'Puddings?' Little Jimmy said. 'What the fook do we want with puddings?'

'Maybe it's a code,' Peter said. 'For hash or something. We'll find out.'

* * * * * *

We recognised the club by the two mohair suited heavies chatting outside it. It took us a bit of time to explain that we were the guys who'd been sent by Abdul – their English was a bit limited and our Turkish was non-existent – but we finally made ourselves understood and they led us inside.

It wasn't difficult to figure out who was the boss of the club. He was the guy in the back room smoking a huge cigar, a ring on every finger, whispering sweet nothings into the ear of a stunning green-eyed blonde curled on his lap. Shooing the blonde off, he stood up, straightened his trousers, shook hands with all of us and kissed us on both cheeks. He clicked his fingers, ordering the blonde to get us beers and she wiggled off into the gloom of the club.

'Abdul is one crazy man, no?' the boss said. He had a strong American accent.

'He is,' Peter said. We'd only known Abdul for about half an hour at the most but it wasn't hard to agree that he was crazy. 'So,' he continued, 'what's the deal?'

'It's very simple, boys,' the boss said. 'By day, you promote the club to the students in the colleges here in Istanbul and to the hippy Americans, English, Germans, Dutch, tourists – of which there are many. And, at night, you go crazy on dance floor. You do all the dances you know from London. You know, the Twist, the Mashed Potato, the Watusi.' He waved his hand. 'All this crazy stuff.'

The blonde appeared with a tray full of bottles of beers. I would have liked to see her do the Twist but I had the feeling looking at her for more than 60 seconds in front of the boss would be a bad idea.

The boss told us we'd be paid well, although none of had a clue about Turkish money so we had no idea whether the figure he named was high or low. We'd also have as much free beer as we could drink every night and we were to start that evening.

'So, where are we staying?' Peter said. 'Abdul say there'd be accommodation included.'

'Of course,' the boss said smoothly. 'I have beautiful hotel for you to stay in.'

The deal done, we shook hands once again, drank our beers and trooped out into the street.

Outside, Peter nodded to the mohair suited muscle and we wandered off. 'Fancy checking out that Pudding Shop?' he said.

'I'm not hungry,' Buddy said. 'Let's go look at the birds.'

Peter had a glint in his eye. 'Nah, let's find this place. It sounds cool.' Buddy shrugged and gave in, like we always did to Peter.

* * * * * *

What we didn't know was that Istanbul at that time was a magnet for all kinds of hippies and weird travellers heading to India, Nepal and beyond. It was where the Hippy Trail, or the Road to Katmandu, really started. There was something called the Magic Bus which took hippies from London to Istanbul and into India.

And the place all these hippies gathered to buy and sell hash or shit as they called it, tell stories about their adventures and hook up was The Pudding Shop.

After we'd asked a few people, we finally found the place. It was full of hippies dressed like our friend with the orange fingernails. The women were deeply tanned and mainly wore flowing flowery dresses or jeans. The air was thick with the smell of hash.

Peter's eyes lit up as we stepped through the door and into the haze of smoke. I didn't know about the rest of the lads but it all made me a bit nervous. I'd never really been around hippies and I certainly wasn't a dope smoker. We made our way to the back of the café, found a table and sat down. Within minutes Peter had bought a half inch thick piece of browny-green Turkish hash from a hippy and had borrowed what he needed to make a joint. We watched as, with nimble fingers, he rolled a long spliff, as he called it, lit up, inhaled and leant back in his chair.

After a few puffs, he passed the joint to Little Jimmy who inhaled and exploded into a spluttering mess. Jimmy handed it to Buddy, who did the same, much to Peter's delight. When it was my turn, I dragged the smoke in slowly and took it down into my lungs before letting it out gently.

This was actually the first time I'd ever smoked dope but I wasn't going to own up to that. To be honest, it didn't do a lot for me but, after a few minutes, I began to understand why the café did such a roaring trade in delicious, sweet puddings.

We sat for a bit. Somebody pulled out a guitar and plucked away until another person joined in with a harmonica. Peter chatted to the people around us, who were all very friendly and incredibly stoned, it seemed, while the rest of us drank Turkish coffee, ate pudding and stared into space.

When it was time to leave, Peter said 'you know we could always keep going don't you, lads? Make it all the way to Katmandu.'

'What about Majorca?' Little Jimmy said.

Peter said nothing. He smiled and unsteadily led the way back through the crowd to the van.

* * * * * *

It wasn't difficult for us to fill the club. After all, it was what we'd been doing all summer in Majorca.

The boss of the club obviously had good connections because we got our photo in the paper as a famous English band – I can only assume that because it was in Turkish.

We were photographed outside our van. From left to right: me holding some sort of bowl and a ladle, Buddy crooning into a big long stick, Peter wearing tartan shorts and waving his hands in the air, Jimmy leaning on the van holding a walking stick.

As Peter said, like a pop group only different.

My own musical career nearly took off in Istanbul, as did Buddy's. For some reason we were larking about in the Istanbul Hilton when we blundered into the resident hotel band rehearsing. Peter pushed me to the front and said to the leader 'ere, you should do original songs. Louie Baby here's a songwriter and a singer. Straight from London. You should give him a listen. Go on, Louie Baby.'

The band leader smiled and said 'why not?' so I taught them my song 'I Wish I Knew' and we ran through it a couple of times. They actually invited me to stay and sing with them, which was great but I didn't want to leave the boys and miss out on Majorca.

Buddy got to sing a Buddy Greco song at the Istanbul Playboy Club, which had nothing to do with Hugh Hefner's place and went down a storm, or at least pretty well. Two people clapped. They'd only let him sing if he had a tuxedo and he had to borrow one from one of the bouncers at the disco. It hung down almost to his knees. He too was invited to stay but like me he put the Beach Boys and Majorca before anything else.

Apart from musical adventures, we soon settled into a pleasant routine of hustling all day and, at night, showing the young Turks all the latest London dances – and some we'd made up, like the Beach Boys knee wobble – drinking as much free beer as we could neck and stuffing our faces with kebabs before driving the van back to the campsite.

We didn't actually stay in the hotel the boss had kindly arranged for us, even though it was free. There were plenty of cockroaches but we were used to that after Majorca. What freaked us out were the stand up toilets. We'd never seen them before and they struck us as the most primitive thing we'd ever encountered in our lives.

We headed straight back to the Mocamp.

The only problem with the Mocamp was the cold. Instanbul was definitely not hot, like Abdul said it was.

* * * * * *

When we weren't working, there was plenty for us to get up to.

In a rare display of cultural curiosity we decided one afternoon to pay a visit to the famous Blue Mosque, which towered over the dodgy bit the club was in. When we got there we saw that all the worshippers had carefully placed their shoes in compartments outside before they went in. There must have been a couple of hundred pairs of shoes. We switched all the shoes round, hid, and waited for the people to come out after prayers. Watching all these Turks get more and more pissed off as they tried to find their shoes and figure out what had happened was hilarious. Thank God, or Allah, they never heard us cracking up with laughter.

One afternoon in the Pudding Shop a dodgy looking hippy geezer asked us if we wanted to make a few bob smuggling hash to Copenhagen. The guy's idea was that we'd conceal the stuff about our person, as they say, in specially built body suits. Although it would have been a very good earner, the whole scheme sounded pretty nuts and he didn't exactly inspire confidence so we turned him down.

We were up for pretty much anything but drug smuggling wasn't on the agenda.

* * * * * *

'Bleedin' Abdul,' this became our standard curse as we woke up to yet another freezing morning on the campsite. Not only was Istanbul definitely not hot, as Christmas got closer, it became positively freezing.

It was Little Jimmy – white face, red nose, yellow hair – who said it first one bitterly cold morning. 'Shall we bugger off, boys?' he said, rubbing his hands together.

We looked at each other. 'I agree,' I said. 'Let's do the off before we freeze to death.'

Buddy and Peter agreed. We were a bit nervous about telling the club boss – Little Jimmy was convinced he'd have his goons take us hostage – but he was perfectly all right. For a mafia boss, he was rather laidback. Mind you, we didn't owe him money, none of us had been sniffing around his blondes and we'd had no chance to try out any scams.

'I will be sad to see you go,' the boss man said, 'but you have done excellent job. Abdul was right. You are good boys, Baby's Four.' He paid us in large bundles of Turkish lira and told us we could come back and work for him any time we liked. With that, he kissed us all on both cheeks and the latest blonde gave us a tiny wave.

The only problem, we discovered when we got talking to a pair of hippy girls in the Pudding Shop, was that Turkish lira weren't accepted outside Turkey. 'We could always buy a load of hash,' Peter said, skinning up another joint.

'Don't think so,' Buddy said. 'We'd get nicked at the first border. Four long-haired hippy herberts like us.'

The Petticoat Lane barrow boy in me came to the rescue. 'Why don't we go down one of those bazaars,' I said, 'buy some Afghan coats and big furry hats. They're all the rage in London.'

We found a bazaar, did a deal with a geezer who looked the spit of Abdul and bought twenty coats and fifty fur hats.

* * * * * *

It felt great to be back on the road again, especially as we were heading home and then on to Majorca. As we climbed away from yet another small, dusty town, Little Jimmy said 'I've just realised. We was only in Istanbul for three weeks.' He looked at us.

'Felt like months,' Peter said. 'Well weird. Look out, lads, here comes the border with Greece.' We were going back a different way to how we'd got to Turkey, through Greece, Italy, France and then across the channel.

The Greek border cops took one look at us and our van and got ready to tear it apart. Using sign language, one of them made it clear that we had to take our suitcases down from the roof of the van. 'Baggs not me,' Buddy said quickly and, according to the rules of the Baggsy game we'd played religiously all across Europe which we treated as if they were set in stone, he didn't have to help take down the luggage.

'I can't believe you even Baggsy'd that one,' Peter said, scowling at Buddy who watched as we dragged all our suitcases, including his, out of the van.

'Baggsy's Baggsy, man' Buddy said. 'And I'd have abided by the rules if you'd Baggsy'd it first.' Peter hated Baggsy. He was so slow he was nearly always last to blurt it out.

Luckily we had nothing to hide, even Peter, and they didn't think to take the Afghan coats and hats apart – not that we had anything hidden in them, it would have just scuppered us if they'd torn them to pieces.

We breathed a huge sigh of relief as soon as we were safely on the other side of the border. If Turkish nicks were full of characters like the night club boss's strong arm boys, it wouldn't have been any fun.

As we waved goodbye to the border, Peter was deep in thought. After a while, he said, 'you know what, I bags no more soddin' Baggsy.'

'Yeah, but...' Buddy said. Little Jimmy and I just looked at Peter open-mouthed.

But, as what has been Baggsed cannnot be Unbaggsed, we could never play the game again and had to take our turn washing up, driving or whatever like normal human beings.

* * * * * *

'Christ, that tastes awful! And it takes forever. There's got to be a better way,' Little Jimmy said.

'Shut up and keep sucking,' Peter said. Little Jimmy bent down again and sucked as hard as he could on the rubber tube that fed into the petrol tank of the parked car we'd found in a quiet side street in this little town in Northern France. This time it worked and fuel started to rush into the jerry can Peter was holding.

Buddy and I were keeping a lookout while Little Jimmy and Peter did the business. It was their turn. We'd been siphoning petrol out of cars all the way across Italy and now France. The owner of the Mocamp had shown us how to do it. I guess it was a vital skill in Turkey.

The last of our English money that we could change into francs was running out and we were saving it for essentials like food and plonk. We'd even decided fags were a luxury we couldn't afford.

'I have a cunning plan,' Peter said, as he shook the last few drops from the tube into his can while Little Jimmy replaced the cap and we crept back to the van. 'Why don't we just go straight to the source?'

'You what?' Little Jimmy said.

'We'll liberate fuel from petrol stations in future, my friends. And I will show you how.'

'Why couldn't you have come up with that stroke of genius before I had to get a gobful of petrol?' Little Jimmy said.

'Sorry, Jimmy,' Peter said. 'Who knows when inspiration will strike? Did Newton know the apple was going to hit him on the head? Did Einstein wake up and say "I think I'll come up with the theory of relatives today"? Don't think so.'

We climbed into the van and eased slowly off down the street. 'It's the theory of relativity,' Buddy said.

'Whatever,' Peter said. 'You know what I mean.'

* * * * * *

The next time the old red needle was well into empty and we were close to running out of gas, we had no choice but to try Peter's scam.

Little Jimmy and I went into the petrol station with our creased, stained road map and asked for directions for Paris, which was about 100 kilometres away. I felt a bit bad for the poor old dear who was trying to give us directions while we pretended not to understand and played dumb as our partners in crime filled the van up with gas before turning the dial back to zero.

After about ten minutes of giving the old dear the run around we figured Peter and Buddy must have done the deed and we thanked her before nipping off smartish.

It was midnight and we were on the outskirts of Paris, congratulating ourselves on being criminal masterminds when we hit the road block. The police ordered us out of the van at gunpoint, checked a few details by radio and confirmed that we were the desperadoes they were looking for.

We were absolutely bricking it. Those French cops looked terrifying, about as bad as the Guardia Civil back in Spain. And the problem was the old bird at the petrol station – suddenly I didn't feel so sorry for her – had called the cops and told them she'd been robbed without explaining that it was only a tankful of petrol.

So the cops thought we were hippy bank robbers or something. There was no chance of us explaining our way out of this one. After all, in one sense we were caught bang to rights and we couldn't pay for the petrol we'd stolen.

The cops took us to a nearby town and locked us up in two cells. We didn't feel like criminal masterminds now. It was an adventure too far. We had no idea how we were going to get out of this one.

* * * * * *

But, next morning, Buddy managed to persuade the chief of police to let us call the British Embassy. By now, the chief of police had figured out that we weren't criminal geniuses, which wasn't difficult, and wanted shot of us. The only problem was paying back the petrol station people, who still wanted blood.

Peter spoke to someone at the British Embassy and, for once, he must have made sense because the police agreed to let us go as long as we paid for the petrol.

The Embassy official, who'd taken a shine to us, suggested he hold our passports for security and gave us 24 hours to raise the money.

We hurtled down to one of the big shopping boulevards in Paris, dragged the Afghan coats and hats out of the van and, with Peter Bloss modelling the latest in hippy gear for the winter, we put on our own fashion show.

Two hours later we'd sold the lot. Desperation had made us blinding salesmen. We had just enough money to pay for the petrol and for the ferry back to Blighty.

And I was back in Bethnal Green by the next morning.

IBIZA CRACK-UP

After our adventures on the European Tour, I knuckled down to my window cleaning round and saving money to get a decent apartment on the Rock for the summer of 1968. No way was I going to spend another season in an overpriced airless shithole of a shoebox.

Back in Bethnal Green, I got used to the way in which my life of adventure and escape meant nothing to the fellows I knocked about with. They just didn't have itchy feet like I did and I couldn't understand why. As long as they had a few bob left over after their weeks spent working as fly-pitchers in Oxford Street selling Mickey Mouse perfumes, or as office cleaners or whatever to spend on fags, a few beers, clobber and maybe taking a bird to the pictures they seemed perfectly happy.

I started to feel like they refused to show any interest in what I'd been up to because it made them think about what they were or weren't doing with their lives. It put a bit of distance between us which made me look forward to getting back to the Rock and my Beach Boy pals even more.

Don't get me wrong, I still had plenty of fun. My best times were spent with Bernie The Fox, who I'd first met in the pub at the age of 16.

The only person who'd loved the stories of our rampage across Europe was my old man. I paid him back most of his loan of £500 with a bit out of my pay packet every week but he didn't seem to be in any tearing hurry to get his money back. It was like I'd told the Beach Boys, he wanted me to live in a way he hadn't had a chance to.

Dad worked as a Hoffman Presser in East End garment factories. He'd always been a hard worker so he was forever in demand.

After my mum died giving birth to my sister in hospital, who also died, Dad had to work seven days a week, as well as evenings, to pay the bills, clothe and feed us. When Dad wasn't around, our grandma Julie helped look after us, making sure we had a hot meal every night.

On Fridays, after we'd been to the public baths, this was always Jewish chicken soup, the best comfort food in the world. Dad's family was Jewish, although he wasn't strictly religious and never tried to impose the faith on us. When I was 13 I was supposed to be Barmitzvah'd but that didn't happen because Dad didn't have the money so I suppose you could say I never technically became a man. Dad gambled, worked on Saturdays – although he didn't have a lot of choice there – and loved a bacon bagel! But, for nan and our Jewish neighbours, who helped us out any way they could, Dad kept up appearances.

I always felt a bit guilty about what my two sisters and I put Dad through when we were kids. Dad was as strict as he could be when he was around but that wasn't often.

So we were always in trouble. One of our tricks was to go down to nearby Spitalfields Market and pinch fruit and veg for us and our neighbours. We managed to convince ourselves this wasn't nicking because we, and them, needed food. The stall owners didn't quite see things the same way though.

* * * * * *

It was March 1968 when I got back to the Rock. In the Med, spring had truly sprung. I took a cab the short distance from the airport to Can Pastilla and blew away the stink of the cabbie's pine air freshener by opening the window to let in the warm, soft island air. I could feel my shoulders coming down from either side of my ears as my soul warmed up.

I paid off the cabbie and sat on a concrete bench with my feet on my suitcase, had a smoke and looked out to the shimmering sea. Soon it would start all over again and I couldn't wait.

'Louie, Louie, baby!' As usual, I heard Peter before I saw him. I turned round. He was striding across the sleepy square, Buddy and Little Jimmy, his hair now a less frightening shade of blonde, hurrying to keep up with him. All three already had a nice looking tan on the go.

I leapt up. Peter threw his arms round me, gave me a ridiculously wet kiss on each cheek while I grinned from ear to ear. Buddy and Little Jimmy shook hands and patted me on the arm. Without a word we linked arms and launched into an insane Irish jig, hooting with laughter. When we'd finished and collapsed onto the bench, Little Jimmy said 'good to see you, Louie. We've got loads to tell you.'

'Where's David?' I said.

I saw the look Peter shot Jimmy before he said 'let's get Louie Baby checked into the hotel first shall we? And then we can tell all.' Peter stood up, grabbed my suitcase and staggered off with it, shouting over his shoulder, 'what have you got in 'ere, Louie, the soddin' family jewels?' Bored with the impossibly heavy suitcase routine, Peter settled for walking along with a pantomime limp, ignoring the snotty looks he was getting.

When we got to the gaff, I said 'it looks closed.'

'Nah,' Peter said, banging on the door. It was like a repeat performance of my entry into the hellhole I'd stayed at my first summer and I started to sweat.

'You sure this place is kosher?' I said.

'What's kosher?' Little Jimmy said. 'More bloomin' cockernee slang?'

'You know, decent, all right,' I said. 'It is, isn't it?

A young Majorcan girl who would have been gorgeous if it wasn't for her big nose, opened the door. 'Darling I'm home,' Peter said, kissing her on both cheeks and stepping inside. We followed giggling, while the girl – blushing and totally baffled – closed the door behind us.

'I'm not carrying that thing any more,' Peter said, kicking my suitcase. 'We've got a room booked for our mate here,' Peter said to the girl. I gave her my name, she checked the register where there was, of course, no record of the booking. But, the place was empty so that was no problem.

The girl took my passport details and I paid 50 pesetas for the first night in advance. It was a pretty good deal and I thought the girl could start to grow on me. She gave me the key but Peter snatched it out of my hand and vaulted up the stairs, bellowing 'walk this way, lads' while he exaggerated his limp even more.

The room was a definite improvement on last summer's cell. If I'd had a cat I could have swung it. Buddy went to the window and threw open the green wooden shutters which creaked suspiciously. 'Lovely view of the harbour you've got, Louie,' he said.

'And you know the best thing?' Peter said. 'We get a commission for every punter we drag here and we're sharing everything – of course – so you actually get paid for paying to be here. And it's half price till April anyway.' He scratched his head. 'So, thinking about it, if you'd paid full price we would have made more commission. Oh well, sod it. Great innit?'

'It is,' I said, sitting down on the hard bed. 'So, what's the SP? Where is David?'

Peter looked at the other two then at me. 'That's what we wanted to talk to you about, Louie Baby,' he said.

* * * * * *

'I know it looks bad,' Peter said. 'And, actually, it is. But we'll think of something.' We were propping up the bar at The Green Dolphin, one of our favourite places. It was a warm night with a light breeze from the sea. The moon shone on the water. The bar was full of chattering, smoking Spanish birds.

Everything should have been perfect. Only it wasn't.

The owners of the boats we used for the beach parties had rented them to a crew who organised trips to the Dolphinarium up the coast from Palma at Portals Nous. We had no boats and no boats meant no beach parties, so the only money I could make, unless something came along, would be promoting La Babalu.

Even though the hotel room was dirt cheap and I was getting paid for paying for it, as Peter said, and booze, fags and food cost nothing, I was still worried about money. And there was no way I was slinking back to Bethnal Green with my tail between my legs.

I was trying to look on the bright side but it wasn't that easy. The lads had also told me David wasn't coming back that summer. He'd decided to stay behind in the UK with a girl from Norway he'd met, settle down and run the family business. Why he'd want to do this was absolutely beyond me.

David was the coolest of the Beach Boys, I'd always thought, in a far less flashy way than any of the others. He had a really dry wit he didn't use often but when he let fly with one of his rare wisecracks it was always a blinder.

'What about La Babalu?' I said, unable to remember if I'd asked the question before.

Little Jimmy looked over at me, already a bit worse for wear. 'We told you, we had a meeting with the owners and they're trying to find a solution. They like us and want us to carry on doing the beach parties. No way do they want to deal with people they don't know. Maybe things will change. Let's just wait and see. Now, get 'em in, lad, it's your round.'

I signalled to the barmen. Slowly a grin slid across Jimmy's face. 'I've got it,' he said, raising his voice. 'Why don't we go to Ibiza?' We all looked at each other. Behind the beer fog, Peter's mind started slowly to move.

'Why not?' Peter said. 'There are tourists in Ibiza, like here. If there's no beach party, we can start one up.' He grabbed one of the fresh beers that had just arrived, handed the others to us and stood up, holding his bottle like the Olympic torch, and said 'we're off to Ibiza, lads.'

We stood up, clinked our San Miguels together and shouted 'Ibiza!' Of course, that was the moment everyone in the bar went quiet for some reason and turned and looked at us. We grinned at each other stupidly and sat down.

'San Antonio's meant to be where the action is, boys,' Buddy said 'and, let's face it, we've got nothing to lose.'

'Christ, I'm glad I thought of Ibiza,' Peter said. 'Saved our sausages again didn't I?'

'Oi, it was my idea!' Little Jimmy said.

Peter shrugged. He looked at me. 'You're a bit quiet, Louie Baby.'

I didn't want to say to Peter and the other two that, as I was only a ticket seller who worked for the Beach Boys, I felt I should keep my opinion to myself. 'Nah,' I said, 'I'm just...'

Peter looked at Buddy and Little Jimmy, winked. 'I think now's the right time to tell him don't you?' he said.

I looked from one face to another. 'Tell me what?'

'We've made a decision – a very tough one, as it goes,' Peter said. 'We want you to take David's place on the beach parties, whether it's here, Ibiza or, I don't know, anywhere. So you get an equal share in everything we do. How does that sound? You in?'

'Is this a wind-up or what?' I said.

'Course not,' Peter said. 'David's not coming back so it makes sense.'

'We want you with us,' Buddy said. 'Don't we, Jimmy?'

'Sure,' Jimmy said. 'We wouldn't be asking otherwise, would we?'

'So?' Peter said.

'What do you think?' I said. 'I'm in!'

'Perfecto!' Peter bellowed, scaring the life out of everyone in the bar. He leapt to his feet, picked me up and whirled me round so fast I nearly sent a couple of Spanish birds flying. He put me down, Little Jimmy and Buddy hugged me and we did the Beach Boy knee wobble, laughing hysterically.

For some reason, officially becoming a Beach Boy meant more to me than anything else that had happened in my life so far, even getting signed to a contract by Tito Burns back in Tin Pan Alley.

* * * * * *

I couldn't quite believe I was on the night boat to Ibiza from Palma. It had all happened so fast.

We'd told the owner of La Babalu - a Londoner called Peter Newman who'd built the reputation of the club by being the first to bring over live bands from the UK, mainly soul bands - the morning after we'd decided to go to Ibiza, so we couldn't back out. Newman wasn't happy but understood that we'd have to start making money for ourselves. 'Just keep in touch, boys' he said, 'and if the boat situation turns round we'll let you know.'

By that time other ticket sellers had started arriving and were looking forward to the summer season. When they found out what was going on, they were pissed off at the thought of maybe having to go home. Like I'd been. Peter suggested that, until the situation sorted itself out, they could earn a few bob handing out propaganda for La Babalu or perhaps sell tickets for the Flamenco Show at Los Rombos in Can Pastilla. The ticket sellers didn't have much choice but they understood it was every man or woman for themselves and none of us had a safety net of any kind.

It was a case of either find some way of making money or go home. And, for the Beach Boys, Ibiza was now the only option.

We owed the hotel money, and there was also the little matter of the arrangement we had with them to steer punters in their direction so we smuggled our cases out one at a time and did a bunk.

Now, the night boat was chugging slowly away from the lights of Palma, heading towards Ibiza and due to arrive around nine in the morning. Cabins were too expensive so we made a place for ourselves on deck, along with a bunch of hippies who were heading for Ibiza and, in some cases, to the smaller island of Formentera, a short ferry ride beyond.

Formentara had been a favourite beatnik and hippy destination since the 1950s. For the hippies, it had a sort of magical significance. A cute English hippy girl I got talking to on the boat told me that it was the place where all the witches in the Balearic Islands, of which Majorca was one, had often been exiled. The island was also hollow, apparently, because it was filled with caves where the hippies had all night parties, especially at full moon. According to the girl, the island actually changed shape.

The list of rock and roll people who'd hung out in Formentera was pretty impressive. Jimi Hendrix, Joni Mitchell, Bob Dylan and Pink Floyd all spent time there.

'You should come, man,' the girl said as we got to know each other a little better. 'It'll be a trip.'

'No doubt,' I said, 'but me and my pals are going to Ibiza to try our luck organising beach parties for the tourists.'

'Cool,' she said, but I don't think she meant it. As I got to know more hippies, I could feel that although we were looking for freedom, sun, sand and sex we were seriously different. For one thing, my pals and I took it for granted that we had to work for our freedom and liked the hustle. The hippies took freedom as their right and seemed not to care if they had money or not.

Probably because they seemed to pretty much all come from a nice background. And good luck to them.

The only one of us who was really on the hippy wavelength was Peter. He was sat in the middle of a bunch singing Beatles songs and smoking dope while a guy played the guitar by moonlight. With Peter involved the singing inevitably got louder and more raucous, which pissed off the Spanish people for whom this was a routine trip not an adventure.

I settled back next to the hippy girl, both of us a little stoned, put my arm round her and, as she nestled into me and fell asleep, looked forward towards Ibiza. A flying fish caught the moonlight as it jumped and I was sure

I saw a dolphin leading the boat. I didn't say anything in case it was the grass.

* * * * * *

'Thar she blows!' Little Jimmy's shout woke me up. The arm I had round the hippy girl had gone to sleep so I had to use my other one to lift it away from her shoulders. She was still spark out, her mouth slightly open. When I stood up, I discovered one my legs had also gone to sleep. I limped over to Jimmy, who clutched a bottle of red wine. By the looks of him he hadn't slept a wink.

As Ibiza appeared out of the mist, Buddy and Peter came up to join us. Across the water, we could hear the engine thump of the first fishing boats heading back to land with their catch. Soon, we could see a narrow beach, cliffs and the curling wall of the old part of Ibiza Town as it led up to what looked like a church and a tower. We sailed round past the headland on which the old part of town perched and eased into the docks.

It wasn't that different from Palma, just a lot smaller. But, we were on an adventure and we couldn't wait to haul our cases off the ferry and go explore.

We said our goodbyes to the hippies. The pretty little girl I'd snuggled up with as we sailed across the Med told me her name and invited me to look her up if I made it to Formentera. I promised I would even as I knew it wasn't going to happen.

Standing on dry land, waiting for our legs to get used to the sensation, rubbing our bare arms and taking in the sounds and smells of the busy docks, we had one of those 'what do we do now?' moments when time seems to stop.

Then Buddy broke the silence. 'Get lucky, Louie?' he said, jerking a thumb back in the direction of the boat.

'Might have,' I said.

'She have hairy armpits?'

'Um...'

Buddy chuckled. 'They all do, the hippy birds. The French are the worst. Like beards.'

While we were looking at each other, a long-haired, scrawny guy with a beard, wearing a pair of stained flares strolled up to us. 'Just got here, guys?' He said, in a whiny Midlands accent.

We looked at him without saying anything, freezing him out. Flustered, he tried to hand us flyers for cheap hotels in Ibiza Town but we strolled off.

* * * * * *

After a ride across Ibiza, which looked like a flatter, smaller Majorca with more trees, we got to San Antonio. The hotel workers who'd been on the bus with us chattering loudly trooped off and we stood looking at each other and scratching our heads. It was very quiet.

'Did we get off at the right stop?' Little Jimmy said. There were a couple of big white new-looking hotels and the bars and restaurants that ran along the strip but these were closed. We couldn't see a beach.

And, apart from us and a couple of stray dogs, there was no-one around.

'Blimey,' I said. 'Where's all the people?' By this time of year, the beaches we worked in Majorca – Arenal and Can Pastilla – were buzzing. It was unreal, a bit like one of those sci-fi movies when aliens land and everyone's vaporised apart from some astronauts who've just got back from a long space voyage or a western when the bad guys walk into town. I wanted to scream.

'Let's head for the centre,' Peter said. 'We might find intelligent life.'

We crossed over the road and started to head towards what we hoped was il centro. A couple of bars along the strip, we heard a creak and a head popped round the door of a bar called Las Vegas.

'Ey oop, lads, had your breakfast yet? Tea's on the brew. Been waiting long, 'ave yer?'

We stared at the geezer, looked at each other, then back at him and burst out laughing. The tall, fat man who opened the door and stepped into the street wasn't at all bothered by our hysterics. He stood rubbing his hands and beaming, the sun shining on his slicked back hair, adjusted his bow tie and shook the creases out of his incredibly loud check suit.

'Why not?' Peter said. We were starving. We followed the guy into Las Vegas and ordered full Englishes all round.

After we'd demolished breakfast, which didn't take long, had lit up and were sipping strong English tea, Peter told the owner why we'd washed up at San Antonio.

'I have to tell you, lads, there's no such thing as a beach party over here. And there isn't a natural beach at San Antonio, as you can see. Why don't you boys go down where the boats take tourists to the other beaches for a day out and ask one of the owners? I'll look after your bags. I'll also see what I can do about finding you somewhere to stay.'

We strolled down to a wooden jetty where touts for the three boat companies tried to tempt the very few tourists who were actually knocking around by shouting the names of the beaches they were going to as loudly as they could. They fell on us like starving cats and we took a leaflet from each of them.

'See that,' Buddy said, as we walked away. 'There's no beach parties.'

'Fan-bloody-tastic,' Peter said.

* * * * * *

I was dying. We were up on the stage of a San Antonio hotel singing The Everly Brothers 'Bye-Bye-Love' for the third time that night and I was nowhere near drunk enough not to care. It was one of two songs that Jimmy knew the chords for on the guitar all the way through – the other was the Everlys' All I Have to Do Is Dream - and the room was emptying, much to the hotel manager's disgust. We limped to the end of the song and I said 'thank you very much ladies and gentlemen, we're going to take a short break and we'll be...' I looked over at the hotel manager drawing his index finger slowly across his throat and switched the mic off.

We stumbled over to him. 'You were never at the London Palladium,' he said, 'and he's drunk!' He pointed at Jimmy, who giggled.

'What about our money?' I said.

'He's drunk it all, you owe *me* money!' the manager shouted before turning and walking away.

'Up yours,' Jimmy shouted. 'We're too good for this place, anyway.' The manager waved goodbye with the back of his hand.

I burst out laughing and we staggered off to find the others.

It was three weeks since we'd arrived in San Antonio and our money was running out. We'd found a quiet beach perfect for the parties, done a deal with a boat owner and sworn him to secrecy about what we had planned – the last thing we wanted was some other firm nicking the idea – and recruited a couple of Scouse salesmen to help us. Our interpreter was Charles, a poof from Cheltenham who had the hots for Little Jimmy – it must have been the blonde hair. But, we couldn't make our move until there were enough punters to make it worthwhile.

At night, we did the rounds of the bars, which were still pretty much empty, getting drunk on cheap red wine and always finishing up at a grim disco called Nito's which stayed open late.

Although the pension we were staying in had given us a special rate on two rooms, they'd told us that the price would go up in the high season, which was the beginning of June, about a week away.

One of the ways we made the money we had last was to hit the tourist beaches, which were gradually filling up and go fishing for sandwiches. We'd hit a beach, fan out and find easy targets, usually girls, and give them a sob story about how we'd been stranded in Ibiza and were waiting for money to arrive from our parents and bail us out.

This worked a treat, almost embarrassingly well. By the end of each day we were usually overloaded with goodies including money, cigarettes, things like toothpaste and shampoo and, of course, hotel packed lunches in brown bags. 'We should open a bloody shop,' Buddy said one night before he disappeared off into the night on a promise with a girl he'd cadged sandwiches off.

The problem with this was, although we weren't starving, we weren't actually making any money. The singing gig for Little Jimmy and me could have been a lifesaver if it hadn't lasted a week and we hadn't drunk up all the profits.

Just when things were looking really desperate, the Playboy club in San Antonia came to our rescue. They wanted us to bring punters from our beach parties to their club which was why they gave us a job painting tables and chairs. Like the one in Istanbul, this Playboy club had no connection with Hugh Hefner's empire. There was probably a Playboy Club in Kathmandu.

That worked out fine and we got paid. The only problem was Little Jimmy winding up the people at Nito's by telling them that when the Playboy club opened we'd be taking all our punters there, leaving Nito's empty. Why he did that, none of us could figure out.

So Little Jimmy got us barred from Nito's, leaving us with only the two bars with which we had tabs to go to at night.

Time was running out.

* * * * * *

We'd guessed right. About a hundred and fifty punters were filling up the owner Antonio's boat. Between us, we'd actually sold close to 200 tickets but it was always the case that about a quarter of the people didn't turn up because they'd got lucky or were too hungover.

Bronzed, wearing our new Playboy Club t-shirts and back in our element, we moved among the excited kids promoting the Beach Party they were about to go on and promising them the best day out of their lives. We'd all stayed off the sauce the night before, even Little Jimmy. It was our big day, a lot was riding on it and we wanted to make sure everything was a success.

And it was. We all knew the parts we had to play and Peter Bloss pulled out all the stops to entertain the punters and make sure they'd tell everyone how great the beach party was.

Exhausted but on a high, we swaggered into the Playboy Club for its grand opening as the conquering heroes. Everyone from the owners down to the salesmen we'd recruited was over the moon. The Beach Boys comeback had worked like a dream.

* * * * * *

For the whole of June we were the toast of San Antonio. Everyone knew the Beach Boys and, as the town was a lot smaller than our home turf, we became faces a lot quicker.

Splashing money around – even making a little dent in our huge bar tabs – and occasionally dining in San Antonio's posher restaurants, we felt the business. We forgot all about having to cadge sandwiches.

Ibiza – called the White Island, either for the white Arab style houses or the salt which made its fortune in Roman times - was reckoned to be far more tolerant than Majorca for some reason, which is maybe why it became more of a magnet for hippies from all over Europe, including Spain and draft dodgers from the States.

It was also a lot closer, easier and cheaper to get to than Morocco or India, the other destinations on the hippy trail.

The cops seemed to be far more laidback than Majorca, although we were all still living under Franco's Fascism so you had to be careful.

Because San Antonio was so small, we soon got to know some of the hippies, or freakies as the Spanish called them, who were hanging out.

Although I'd winked knowingly when Buddy had asked me about the hippy bird on the boat, nothing had really happened. It was in San Antonia that I had my first tumble with a hippy chick and it was great. Penelope was a daddy's girl from a well-off background. Daddy was a rear admiral in the navy or something. She was beautiful in that 1960s Bardot way – tanned, slim, long blonde hair, always wearing a bikini top and cut-off jeans.

Penny really was determined to live as a free spirit. Even though she always knew she could be bailed out at any time, she was sincerely trying to live a different way, which involved getting by on as little money as possible.

I'd grown up living on next to nothing and it wasn't romantic for me at all. I was proud of the cash I earned by hustling.

Apart from the obvious, part of the fascination for us was just how different our backgrounds were. Penny had been born and grown up in St John's Wood – like the heiress in the Stones song 'Play With Fire' – so she was as much of a Londoner as I was but she'd never been down to Bethnal Green. Our different worlds back home were only separated by a few miles.

I even went to a Full Moon Party in the woods outside San Antonio with Penny. It was a weird experience, not as different from our beach parties as you might think.

One of Penny's friends drove his jeep up a long windy track into the woods. The moon was so bright it was almost like day.

Screaming guitar music blasted from speakers on the trees. People, some of them naked, danced in a clearing in the middle of the woods. There were all kinds of drugs circulating. I'd bought my own beer because there was no way I was going to get spiked with LSD.

Penny dropped acid but I palmed the tab she gave me. I didn't fancy tripping at all. I followed her around as she stared deeply into people's eyes – some of them blokes with long straggly beards who looked like they hadn't washed for weeks – and stroked trees.

At one point, Penny dragged me into the woods and we had the most amazing sex. It was mind-blowing for me without having taken acid so Christ knows what it was like for her.

A couple of times I decided to leave Penny to the party and walk home but the strange thing was that I couldn't leave. I'd start to walk off down the track, the rocks like bits of white bone in the moonlight, and something drew me back.

It wasn't Penny. I knew she'd be absolutely fine. It was another thing else altogether.

Next day, as we lounged around on the beach, Penny with her head on my chest, I told her what had happened and she said it was something everyone she knew experienced. Once you were at a Full Moon Party it was impossible to leave until the sun came up.

Even though our fling never amounted to much we would always say 'hi' when we bumped into each other and I'd sometimes slip Penny a few pesetas. I'd never before experienced the feeling that sex could just be a bit of nice fun with absolutely no expectations on either side. With the straight birds I knew, I always felt like I had to spin them a line and then I'd feel bad.

One day Penny just disappeared, as the hippies usually did. She'd moved on to Formentera or even further, perhaps.

Observing the hippies at close quarters also had an effect on Blossy. He'd been fascinated by the travellers we met in Istanbul and took to smoking dope like he'd been born to it.

He also discovered Bustaids in San Antonio, incredibly strong Spanish diet pills that were freely available over the counter. When we were on Bustaids, we felt like we could do anything. We weren't just Beach Boys, the life and soul of any party. We were Gods!

* * * * * *

Buddy cracked first. Although we'd got off to a blinding start, there simply weren't enough punters in San Antonio for us to move up from one beach party to two and more dosh. So there wasn't enough money and we were getting worried.

'Sod this, boys,' Buddy said. 'I'm heading home.' We were shocked but understood. It was a sad day when we saw him off at the airport but we were sure we'd see each other again. 'It's been a great ride, lads,' he said before heading off into his own future.

As we headed back from the airport, Little Jimmy took his mouth away from the bottle of beer that had become his constant companion and said 'he's got some bird. Betcha.' He burped and went back to looking out the window.

Blossy was the next one to go. He convinced Little Jimmy and me it was a good idea to pop over to Majorca and see what was happening there. We said this was fine as long as Peter promised to be back in time for the next beach party.

With only two of us on the firm now, the pressure was on to sell tickets and make the party a success. One morning, when I knocked on Jimmy's bedroom door to get him up, there was no reply. I banged on the door for a while then gave up.

The night before we'd been in the Playboy Club and he'd started to get really loud and stroppy. Being a little guy, he could get like that sometimes and the combination of Bustaids and booze was pretty volatile. I left.

No matter how bombed he'd had been, Jimmy always turned up to punt tickets. I was worried. I went looking for him.

I finally found Jimmy at the Las Vegas, run by our Northern friend. He was sitting by himself at the bar with a glazed, far away look in his eye. He stank and obviously hadn't been to bed. I tapped him on the shoulder, pissed off and relieved at the same time. He turned round. 'There you are, mate,' Jimmy said too loudly. 'Come on, we'll have a drink and we'll go blast out some tickets.'

He was in no fit state and would have been an embarrassment so I said 'no ta, mate. You go home and get some kip and I'll see you tonight at the Playboy.'

Although he'd let me down badly we were mates – Beach Boys – and in my mind it was one for all.

That night, when I stopped by the Playboy Club, Jimmy was nowhere to be seen. I had a couple of sherberts and waited for a bit but, after a day punting by myself, I was wiped out and needed my bed. Badly. I started to walk home.

'Louie!' A voice called to me from the crowd sitting at tables outside one of the bars. I looked up. At first I thought it was Jimmy but when the guy called my name again I realised it was one of the ticket sellers from Liverpool. 'Over here, boss,' the guy said.

Wearily, I picked my way between the tables. The Scouser stood up, put his hand on my shoulder and said 'I just saw Little Jimmy. He wasn't looking good.'

'Why?' I said.

'I couldn't get much out of him but he was covered in blood and his face was coming out like this,' the guy mimed a balloon blowing up.

'Oh Christ,' I said. 'Is he all right? Where is he?'

'He's OK. He could talk, anyway. He got into some bother with a bunch of local lads outside Nito's and they gave him a pasting.' I could hear the relish in the salesman's voice and it pissed me off. I was about to have a go at him but I realised that he just saw Jimmy as a bit of an irritating liability. Why should he have any loyalty?

I took a deep breath. 'Ta, mate,' I said. He put his hand on my shoulder again, trying to look sympathetic. I resisted the urge to shake his hand off and stalked off into the hot, still night air.

I thought I'd have to spend another night searching for Jimmy when I was dog tired but when I got back to our pension his bedroom door was open and he was snoring on the bed. One of his eyes was almost closed. There were scratches on his forehead and dried blood around his nose and mouth. I shook my head, closed the door softly and went to my room.

I lay awake all that night trying to figure out what to do. Part of me wanted to disappear to Majorca and leave Jimmy to it but I couldn't. We were pals and I wasn't made that way.

When I left to sell tickets the next day Jimmy was still out for the count on his bed. There was blood all over his pillow and I saw that he'd pissed himself in the night. He was a mess. I thought about waking him up but what was the point? He couldn't sell tickets in that shape.

All that day, I threw everything I could into blasting tickets, wisecracking like a maniac, chasing giggling girls down the front to strong-arm them with charm into buying and promising the gangs of lads a world of crumpet if they took the trip.

I didn't want to have to stop and think about what was happening to our Ibiza dream.

Jimmy never showed but I was glad he didn't. Not with his face the way it was.

* * * * * *

I was lying on the bed in my room back at the pension still trying to figure out what to do when there was a knock on the door. 'Si?' I said, half expecting to hear

Jimmy asking apologetically if he could come in. It was day two of him having gone AWOL and I was sick of it and worried to death.

'Telefono, senor Louie.' It was one of the sons of the hotel owner. 'Senor Peter for ju.' The kid idolised Peter.

I leapt out of bed, opened the door and limped downstairs to the phone on my sore feet.

The phone receiver was hanging down from the wall-mounted box. I picked it up. 'Peter?' I said. I'd never been so relieved to be deafened as when I heard his voice come blasting down the crackling line.

'All right, Louie Baby,' he said. 'How's it going?'

'OK, I said.' I thought about not telling Peter about Little Jimmy's antics but I couldn't keep it to myself. 'But Jimmy's losing it, I think. He's...'

'Calm down, Louie Baby,' Peter said. 'Jimmy's always been a bit of a nutter. He'll snap out of it. But, listen. Harry the Horse has got all the boats now – Christ knows how he got them away from the Dolphinarium boys – and he's taking punters to Sloopy's disco in Palma. All our old sales guys are working for the Horse now.'

Harry was the guy who the Beach Boys worked for when I started in 1967.

'So where does that leave us?' I said. I was gagging to get back to Majorca. 'What are you doing?'

There was a pause before Peter said. 'I'm working for Harry too.' Sensing my disappointment, he said 'but, listen, San Antonio's burnt down for us anyway. You know that. There just isn't enough business for us.'

'So, what do I do?'

'Get through this next Beach Party. You can do it. And you'll have some wongah. Get your arse back here pronto. We can plan our next move. Don't worry, Louie Baby. I got you into this and I'm getting you out. Shit, running out...' The phone went dead. Peter had run out of money.

I put the receiver back on its cradle and walked away. Part of me was pissed off at Peter for leaving me with Jimmy but I also understood. And I trusted him. But I didn't know how long I could stand the situation with Jimmy.

* * * * * *

I was collecting money and steering punters on board the boat to go to the beach party next morning when Little Jimmy finally turned up, held up by two slightly less drunk Swedish birds. He had a patch over his battered eye and was swinging a nearly empty bottle of cognac. 'Beach part-eh' Jimmy shouted. 'Come on, people, it's beach party time.'

'Not for you it isn't, mate,' I said, hopping on board and pulling up the gangplank. Jimmy stood swaying on the dock, his mouth open, the two Swedish birds looking confused.

I'd had enough.

* * * * * *

Two of my salesmen were standing outside the entrance to the Playboy Club smoking and laughing as I walked towards the door. 'All right, Louie,' one of the guys said. 'What's the story with Little Jimmy. He finally lost it or what?'

'What do you mean?' I said.

They looked at each other. 'We just saw him dressed up like Batman – really, like Batman with a purple cape and all that – and he was jumping into a cab with his suitcase' the other guy said. 'We figured you'd had a bust up after today and told him to get lost.'

'Nah,' I said. And then something flashed through my mind. 'Catch you later, boys,' I said before turning and running off in the direction of our pension.

Jimmy had left the door to his room open and I could see that his suitcase was gone. I looked behind the radiator, where we hid our stash of cash along with our passports. The envelope and Jimmy's passport were gone. He'd done a runner.

'You little sod,' I shouted. I hurtled out of the room, down to the street, hailed a cab and we headed for the airport. I just hoped I could get to him in time.

I was in luck. When I got to the airport he was sitting in the departure area – he hadn't checked in and gone through customs – drinking a beer. He was wearing a purple cape, had his eye patch on and was chatting up the barmaid.

'Oi, Jimmy!' I said as I walked across to him. It takes a lot to get me mad but I was boiling. 'Going somewhere without your partner? Not very nice is it?'

Jimmy stood up. He looked ready to fight his corner but confusion flooded his face and he crumpled. 'I'm so sorry, Louie' he said. And he broke down and sobbed like a baby. The barmaid disappeared to the other end of the bar and made herself busy straightening packets of crisps. When Jimmy began to get his breath back he said 'I didn't plan any of this, mate. Honest. I just had to get away.'

'Why did you take *all* the money?' I said.

'I don't know. I really don't. I didn't even want it. I was going to send you your half from home. Here.' He handed over the envelope stuffed with thousand peseta notes. I stood up and trousered it.

'Why?' I said, thinking he might have done it as revenge for me not letting him on the boat.

'I can't explain,' he said. 'I'm so sorry, mate.'

I stood up, looked down at him and I wasn't angry any more. I just shook my head and walked away. I couldn't believe what had happened.

After I got a cab back to San Antonio, I went in need of a stiff drink. Funnily enough, it was Penny I really wanted to see but she was long gone. I felt truly alone.

I was sitting with my third cognac, slowly beginning to stop shaking when one of the girls who worked for me came in. I poured out the story of what had happened with Little Jimmy and she told me that he'd gone to bed with a friend of hers and had burned her arms with a cigarette when he was drunk. I was horrified. Jimmy must have been in a far worse way than any of us had realised.

Later that night, when Peter called to give me an update on the situation back in Majorca, he was also gobsmacked. 'Right,' he said. 'Get yourself back over here tomorrow. There's three flights a day.' He gave me a number to call him and we arranged to meet by the ticket sellers stand on the hill at Arenal. 'Don't worry,' he said. 'I'll fix you up with Harry the Horse and you can go back to entertaining like before.'

'Thanks, mate.'

'No sweat.'

'I've been thinking,' I said. 'Two months ago there were four of us. The Beach Boys. Best pals. The world was our oyster. All that and look what's happened.'

'Yeah,' he said. There was a pause. 'You know what it is, don't you, baby?'

'What?'

'You're a bleedin' jinx!' He started to laugh and I joined in. Soon we were both screaming with laughter. It was all we could do.

The girl who sold tickets for us met me in the bar and she took me to see her mate who Jimmy had burned with the cigarette. She was a big, sweet-natured girl who worked in one of the Brit bars and didn't deserve what Jimmy had done to her. No-one did. After that I did the rounds tracking down the other salesmen. I explained to them that I'd had enough and was going back to Majorca. They were gutted. All I could say was that my heart wasn't in it. The truth was that these people were not my mates.

I thought about telling Antonio, the boat owner, that I was leaving but by that time it was late at night and I figured it didn't matter that much.

And I couldn't wait to get off the White Island and back to Majorca.

* * * * * *

'There's a job for you in Majorca any time you want, love,' I said to the girl who Jimmy had burned with the cigarette. She'd stayed the night with me and was now seeing me off at the airport.

She smiled, said nothing. Kissed me on the mouth, turned and walked away.

I thought about what Little Jimmy had done to her and was glad I hadn't known about it when I'd seen him in the airport bar I was heading towards at that moment.

HANG ON SLOOPY'S

Standing at the ticket sellers' stand at Arenal, I looked out to sea and thought back over the events of the last month in Ibiza. I gave up trying to make sense of them. Everything had just happened so fast. And it was still 1968. But I was on my territory now, the Rock as we called it. I got myself a café con leche and sat in the shade watching the ticket sellers do their thing. I was ready to get stuck in myself. I had the money I'd bought back from Ibiza but I had to make that last. In any case, I wanted to get back to blasting out tickets. It was what I did best.

Down the street, a jeep pulled up and Peter jumped out. I ran down to him. Under the tarpaulin roof, the driver was a big shape behind the wheel. Peter hugged me, we did a quick knee wobble. He looked into my eyes, shook his head and said 'and then there were two, hey, Louie baby?'

'I know,' I said. 'I am a jinx.'

'Peter!' The voice from the jeep was London, grating and pissed off. Harry the Horse.

Peter winked, put his arm on my shoulder and walked me over to the jeep. I leant into it, offered my hand to Harry and he shook it. His own was fat, very white and wet. He looked up at me, inscrutable behind round, very dark glasses, face bloated and red. Sweat trickled down his forehead and behind his shades. His huge belly strained at the buttons of a shiny pale blue Hawaiian shirt with pictures of islands with palm trees sprouting out of them, guitars and flowers all over it. A gold Star of David nestled in his thick black chest hair.

On the seat beside Harry in the jeep was a half-eaten cheese and chorizo bocadillo and a stained bag of strawberries. As he talked, he popped strawberries in his mouth, the juice dribbling down his chin.

'Nice to see you again, Louie,' Harry said. His voice was London and gurgled as if he needed to clear his throat. It sounded a bit like he was taking the piss. 'All I can say is if you want to help my man Peter sell tickets and do the entertaining with him, the job's yours.' He looked at his watch. 'You can start with those four punters over there. All right?'

'Sure,' I said. I'd taken an instant dislike to the man but needed a job pronto and this was the only game in town for me.

'Good. *Now*. This ain't a tea party. Let's get to work.' Harry started the jeep, slammed it into gear and drove off in a cloud of stinking black smoke muttering to himself.

'Nice to see you again too, Harry,' I said to the cloud of exhaust smoke.

'He's 'orrible, of course,' Peter said, 'but he's the big man now, Louie. He's got the boat company all sewn up and he's taking the punters to Sloopy's in Palma. Thinks big. It's two beach parties and four hundred bodies a week.'

'Wow,' I said. The fat man certainly did think big.

'And his missus, Beauty...' I laughed and Peter grinned. 'No, she's all right, as it goes. Definitely no beauty, though. Speaks four languages and has got the sole rights to sell for boat trips tickets on Illetas beach, where the Scandies all go. But balls to all that business stuff. Let's get you to Palma and my gaff. You'll love it.'

'What about those four?' I jerked a thumb at the potential punters.'

'No sweat,' Peter said. 'Oi!' His shout made everyone in the whole street turn round, including the salesmen hanging out at the ticket booth. 'Them four!' One of the salesmen saluted and headed across the street with a big grin on his face and a handful of beach party leaflets.

* * * * * *

Peter's apartment was in a little square called Plaza de la Mediterráneo in a part of Palma called Terreno, opposite Sgt Peppers, the disco owned by Animals and Jimi Hendrix manager Mike Jeffery. Hendrix had played there in the summer of 68 and rammed his guitar through the ceiling.

Terreno and especially Plaza Gomila was the centre of all the nightlife in Palma. Back in the nineteenth century, when the city hadn't yet spread out to swallow it up,

Terreno was one of the first places people from Germany and the UK came to live. It wasn't too far from where the cruise ships touring the Med docked, for a start. Between the end of World War One and the beginning of the Spanish Civil War there were a few hundred of these people and they'd begun to change nightlife in Palma. The first settlers, if you want to call them that, were bohemians – artists, writers, musicians, remittance men paid by their rich families to stay away because of some terrible vice or addiction, black sheep, what have you – and this part of town still had that kind of vibe about it.

It was the area of Palma where hippies, Arabs, lowlife and larger than life characters mixed with the fresh-faced, tanned Brits, Germans and Scandie tourists all out for a bit of innocent fun.

You could easily score grass, hash, speed, LSD or even heroin in the tiny, funky bars on the side streets that ran up the hill towards Castle Bellver, a grand medieval castle that overlooked the huge bay of Palma. I was always fascinated by how new these castles looked. I guess it was something about the climate that preserved them and they'd never been bombed.

No wonder Peter loved the place. It was right up his dark alley.

Peter shared his apartment with two other salesmen so I had the small, lumpy sofa. He'd only been gone from Ibiza for a month at the most and cash was already pouring in. I was impressed.

We sat on picnic chairs on the tiny balcony, a line of brightly coloured y-fronts and t-shirts flapping in the breeze, looking out to sea and sipping ice-cold beers. For the first time in ages, I felt a little bit of calm but I also knew it wasn't going to last. It never did, especially around Peter. After a bit, Peter said 'look, I'm really sorry for leaving you in the shit with Little J. To be honest, I bottled it a bit. When I got back here I just couldn't face going back. I feel bad about it.'

'I'd have done the same,' I said. I wasn't sure if I would have and he didn't sound that sorry but I really didn't blame Peter. I was just so glad we were back together on our island. 'Don't sweat it.' The truth was, I felt like I'd screwed up.

We clinked bottles. 'Great,' Peter said. That's got that sorted.' He turned to me, his eyes lit up. 'We're really on to a winner here, man,' he said. 'Harry's got more than sixty salesmen blasting out tickets all along the strip from Arenal to Palma and the Palma boys – under the leadership of yours truly – get an extra bit for pushing Sloopy's. Like we used to with La Babalu. It's the same set up really, just on a big scale.'

* * * * * *

Next morning I felt better than I had in ages. Peter strolled into the front room around nine, rubbing his hands and said 'fancy breakfast? Ensaimadas, café con leche do ya?'

'Great,' I said, stretching. 'That's a first. You having stuff in for breakfast.'

'You're joking,' he said. 'It's room service. Watch this.' He drew back the curtain that covered the French window, strolled out to the balcony, leant over the edge and gave out a whistle so loud it echoed round the buildings of the square.

'Hola, senor Petair,' a girl's voice called up from below. 'Desayuno?'

'Si, Maria. Ensaimada, café con leche para dos. Bien?'

'Bien. Todo bien.'

I looked at him. 'So, what happens now?' I said. 'We go down and get it?'

'Nah.' He picked up a yellow bucket and lowered it over the balcony on a rope made up of old flowery kipper ties and bits of string. I went to the rail and peered over. A pretty girl with a mop of dyed blond hair was looking up at us. As the bucket came closer to her she pulled it on to a table where two of the spiral pastries dusted in icing sugar the Majorcans called ensaimadas and steaming cups of coffee waited. The girl placed our breakfast in the bucket, looked up at Peter, stuck up her thumb and he began slowly to reel it in.

'Fishing for breakfast,' I said. 'I like it.'

'Works a treat,' he said as he pulled the bucket the last few inches and over the balcony rail.

It certainly did. We sat in the morning sunlight munching on ensaimadas and sipping the hot, strong coffee and, for the first time in weeks, it felt great to be alive.

* * * * * *

Sloopy's was the perfect setting for a disco. It was a converted windmill on a high bluff that overlooked the buzzing Paseo Maritimo – the strip that ran along the edge of the harbour – with an amazing view out to sea. Next to it was another windmill that had been converted into a nightclub called Jack El Negro, named after a 1950 George Sanders movie called 'Black Jack' made on location in Majorca with scenes shot outside the windmill. Black Jack was about an American who smuggled drugs across the Med. Not much had changed.

Sloopy's could hold up to 600 people and the owner, a guy called Steve Kline, was bringing over big name acts from the UK and America.

Although Steve was the owner of record, he had a couple of silent partners. One of these was Bernie Bloom, the brother of John Bloom, the launderette king. Bernie was rumoured to know certain people in Manchester.

Behind Sloopy's was the barrio of Santa Catalina, a scruffy gypsy district. Some of the houses looked like they came straight out of the Middle Ages – no glass in the windows, blankets for doors.

The beach party had been a great success. Peter and I had slipped back into our entertainer roles no trouble and Ibiza was a rapidly fading memory.

Now we sat in a little bar called the Pisces across from Sloopy's, showered, shaved and Old Spiced right up, glowing from a day in the sun and feeling like proper

Beach Boys again. The jukebox in the bar played 'Young Girl' by Gary Puckett and the Union Gap.

The smell of fresh bread drifted up from the all-night bakery. Perfect for the 4AM munchies.

As we sat and enjoyed our beers, taxi after taxi pulled up at Sloopy's to deposit its cargo of bronzed, blonde, beautiful, giggling Scandie girls who, as we well knew, were up for anything. 'Young girl, get out of those pants,' Peter sang.

'Christ, I said, my voice full of admiration. 'Old Harry's really got it sussed, ain't he?'

'More than you think, Louie Baby,' Peter said. 'He gets a kickback from Zorba's in Arenal too. He's coining it.'

'Do you like him?' I said.

'What do you think?' Peter said. 'Do you? He's horrible. But we can learn something from him, Louie Baby. One day,' he spread his arms out to take in the whole of the glittering night, 'all of this will be ours, my boy.'

We sat back, grinned at each other. Peter's teeth and eyes were very white in the darkness. 'Why not?' I said. 'Why not indeed? Shall we repair to Sloopy's and grace the chicas with our presence?'

* * * * * *

After a few days of hustling on my own turf and long, wild nights with Peter I'd forgotten all about the events in Ibiza. But the White Island wasn't done with me yet.

It was a beach party day around the middle of September. I was on board the Santa Maria, one of the boats we used for the beach parties, waiting for the other, the Corbetta, to arrive from Can Pastilla when I saw two nasty-looking Guardia Civil police officers looming over Julian who owned the boats.

Things got worse when the two cops were joined by a third man who started throwing his arms around and shouting at Julian. He looked familiar. When I realised who the other character was, I was stunned.

It was Antonio, the boat owner from Ibiza. What the hell was he doing here?

I panicked, thought seriously about diving over the side of the boat or hiding below decks. But I decided to front Antonio out. Whatever he was after, there wasn't much chance of me doing a runner.

It looked like Julian had managed to calm down Antonio and the coppers. He walked over to me and when he came close I could see he was worried. 'This man, Antonio,' he said. 'He is from Ibiza. But you already know that. He says you owe him money for the boats you hired in Ibiza. He is very angry. Of course. I would be.'

The blood drained from my face. I'd completely forgotten about ducking out on what we owed Antonio. Ibiza was a world away to me now and it had never crossed my mind that there would be repercussions for what we did. 'What d-does he want?' I managed to get out.

'If you don't pay what you owe him now, they will arrest you.'

'How much do they want?' I squeaked. Julian showed me a police order with an astronomical figure written on it and I nearly fainted. 'What do I do?' I said.

Julian shrugged. 'You need to talk to the man,' he said.

I walked over to where Antonio stood with the cops, making sure to keep Julian and the police between me and him. I tried to explain to Antonio that this wasn't my fault but he wasn't having any of it. If looks could kill, I would have been dead several times over.

In the middle of all this, Peter came sauntering up. He took one look at Antonio, put two and two together and went white. But, in one of the most astonishing displays of persuasion I've ever seen, he managed to get Julian to agree to pay Antonio back with a cheque there and then and to take the money out of our wages.

Thank Christ, Julian came through. All the while, Harry the Horse sat and watched, a little smile on his fat ugly face.

After Antonio got his cheque, cursed us for being sons of whores for one last time and was escorted away by the cops, I turned to Julian and shook his hand with both of mine. I would happily have kissed his feet and he knew it. But he also knew he was going to get his money back.

* * * * * *

The last beach party of the season was always special. And we were determined to make this the mother of them all.

It was late October, still hot but nowhere near as fierce as high summer. There were occasional days of light rain and blustery winds. Both boats had sold out and all the salesmen had been invited. It was time for us to make the Beach Boys special sangria. Only today there would be something with more of a kick than brandy in it.

We cackled to ourselves as we poured crushed Bustaids from five bottles into the deep purple mix. Since Ibiza, we'd become Bustaids connoisseurs and had a good idea how potent the diet pills were. Two of the little buggers with your morning coffee would keep you yacking all day. But, even we didn't know what around 300 pills mixed with brandy and cheap red rotgut would do to 150 people.

We soon found out. Punters were dancing like crazy in and out of the water. Complete strangers yakked to each other nonstop, whether they could speak each other's language or not. Couples disappeared into the trees or swam out to sea for a bit of privacy. One guy dived into the water and just started swimming as fast as he could in the direction of Sa Dragonera, the tiny uninhabited island off the coast of Majorca.

Julian, the boat owner, decided he was in his own Elvis beach movie. He couldn't stop singing and doing the Twist.

The people manically making the barbeque couldn't understand why no-one, including themselves, was hungry. The grub was usually devoured.

Peter and I sat in the shade sipping our San Miguels watching the madness as if it was a spectacle purely put on for our entertainment. Which, in a way, it was.

Next morning we were woken up by a loud banging on the door of our apartment. I looked through the keyhole. It was Julian. I opened the door a crack. 'Meet... me... in... café,' he croaked. 'I must speak to you both.'

We scrambled into our clothes, dropped a couple of Bustaids to wake ourselves up and hurtled down the stairs.

Julian sat at a table on the terrace sipping a cognac. Maria bought us out a café con leche each. As she left, Julian followed her plump bum with his eyes. He probably didn't even know he was doing it. We waited for him to speak, pretty sure there was no way he could have figured out we'd spiked the sangria with Bustaids. 'I am sick of that fat pig, Harry' he said. We looked at each other, said nothing. 'I want you to run the beach parties next year. You can find all the salesmen you need, no?'

Peter and I grinned at each other. 'Of course,' he said. 'Fantastico. But what about the clubs? Harry has Sloopy's in his pocket.'

'Forget Harry,' Julian said, making a dismissive flicking gesture with his hand. 'We are future. Steve Kline at

Sloopy's say we can bring all the punters to him and not back to Arenal. He 'ates Harry. And it's easier for all of us. Shorter boat trips. I double your money and you get something from Sloopy's as well.'

'What about Harry?' I said. 'He ain't going to take this lying down.'

'I'll take care of Harry,' Julian said. I thought of how he'd stared down Antonio from Ibiza and believed him. He drained his brandy, massaged his throat and said 'I tell Harry later today. You in?'

We looked at each other. 'Abso-bleedin'-lutely' Peter said.

'Good,' Julian smiled wearily. We shook hands. Peter went to hug Julian but he held up his palms in warning. 'I go now. See you next year.' He stood up, winced and rubbed his back. 'That sangria, boys? It was special, no?' He said.

'A secret recipe,' Peter said, keeping his face straight.

'I hope so,' Julian said. 'I hope so.' He limped off to his SEAT 600. Peter stood up.

'Watch this,' Peter said. He threw his head back, opened his arms wide and belted out 'Wise men say only fools rush in…!' Everyone in the square turned and looked at Peter. Except for Julian. He wasn't going to give us the satisfaction. He just kept grimly hobbling on.

'What a result!' I said. Peter looked at me, punched the air, threw his arms open and we did a brief, elated knee wobble. Maria came out of the café to see what was happening and stood laughing as we capered around. 'Dos San Miguel,' I called out to her. Shaking her head she went inside.

We slumped down into our chairs, weak with laughter but high on the moment. 'We're on our way, Louie Baby,' Peter said. 'We're really on our way.'

THE MADNESS OF KING BLOSSY

The summer of 1969 built and built. It got hotter every day. Fresh tanned beautiful faces flooded the streets, bars and clubs of Terreno. Money poured in. And Peter Bloss became more and more outrageous.

When he wasn't dressed in our regulation beach party uniform of swimming trunks and a Miami Surfside Beach Party t-shirt, which was the name we'd given our parties, Peter had started wearing a long white kaftan. Sometimes with flip-flops, occasionally without.

I don't know exactly when he got the bright idea to ask people to write their names and messages on the kaftan but by the height of summer it was covered. Peter couldn't wash the thing so, along with the signatures, it accumulated layers of food, booze and God-knows-what stains. He was 23 years old and walking around in the Turin Shroud.

And as this was the year Peter really got in to growing his hair long…you get the picture?

Terreno was filled with characters and Peter had become one of them. He was up there with Lady Docker, Ted Cassidy - the 6 foot 9 inches tall Yank who played Lurch in the Adams Family - 103 Charlie and all the rest. People called his name in the street, and he loved it.

103 Charlie had got his name from another larger than life character by the name of Ricky Lash.

Ricky had been on the radio in LA, his hometown and had his own radio show on the Rock, along with Birmingham Sue and Tipsy the Talking Hound. He interviewed anyone famous who was on the island from his bar – Ricky's MOP which stood for My Own Place - people like Freddie Laker whose budget airline Laker Airways had revolutionised air travel to Spain and indirectly helped create work for so many of us. Ricky was always suited and booted and sported a jazzer's goatee beard. He talked like a hipster too. 'Hey man…what's up, baby? Cool. Far out.'

The Daily Bulletin, the English language newspaper which had been going since 1962 and was sold on the beaches paid Ricky to promote them on his show.

When he wasn't pouring honey down the radio, Ricky drove around town in a Cadillac coupe. It was rumoured that the Caddy had once belonged to Sinatra but, knowing Ricky, he probably started that one himself.

Ricky was terrific at giving people nicknames. 103 Charlie got his because 103 Cognac was his tipple. He did the rounds of eight bars every night and drank large 103s in all of them. We were convinced he drank more of the stuff than anyone else in the whole of Spain.

103 Charlie was an ex US fighter pilot in his late 50s with a ginger beard.

I don't know where the Charlie came from but there was a famous ad for 103 Cognac featuring Roger Moore looking all suave with a bird holding a bottle over his shoulder. Roger, Charlie, maybe?

Or, Charlie's name might really have been Charlie. He was always so pissed no-one ever got a sensible word out of him.

So Ricky writes to the factory where 103 Cognac is made telling them that 103 Charlie had drunk however many bottles it was in that particular year and suggests the company would like to reward him for his loyalty. They send an inscribed medal which 103 Charlie wears ever since. With pride.

* * * * * *

One hot night Peter and I were sitting in Loa's, our favourite bar, killing a slack hour before the cinema that showed English language movies opened.

I don't know why we'd chosen Loa's for our hangout. For a start, you couldn't sit outside. There must have been a couple of hundred bars in Terreno and we'd done them all. Actually, it did make the best pancakes in town and maybe that was what swayed us.

Carousel was the unofficial HQ of the US navy, with a cap from every division in the 6th fleet nailed to its nicotine-yellowed ceiling.

Palma was a refuelling stop for the navy and Terreno would fill with sailors on shore leave every couple of weeks. It was called a Liberty Port, a place where the sailors didn't have to wear uniform when they went on shore leave.

Texas Jack's was another Yank bar which sold American style burgers, fried chicken and booze.

Locals and yachties preferred Rustic, on the corner of Plaza Gomila, which never closed. Also in Plaza Gomila was the Piano Bar owned by John Bloom, the legendary launderette king. Choti's Bar, run by Bert was where people in the know went to score dope. Big Mo stood behind the bar of Africa on Callé Robert Graves where the real bohos and hippies did whatever it was they did surrounded by Zebra skin patterned wallpaper. Big Mo was big and her name was Mo. She ran the place with Little Helen. Helen was tiny anyway but next to Mo she looked like a midget or ventriloquist's puppet.

The night before we'd been to a Popper Party in a weird castle type place with a round turret outside a town called Portals Nous, just up the coast from Palma. I never found out who owned the joint but we were dragged along by our friend José Maria who knew everyone in the Majorcan night club scene and always had poppers.

Poppers were little glass vials of Amyl Nitrate originally used to revive people with heart problems like angina. They relaxed your muscles. They also made the blood rush to your head so hard you thought you were going to fall over, laughing like a madman the whole time. Poppers were great if you were having sex. You just broke the glass thing under the bird's nose and it was like riding a bucking bronco.

We loved poppers and they made Peter even more outrageous. He just didn't give a monkeys.

He was out of control at the Popper Party, shouting and singing at the top of his voice, bursting into groups of Spanish people, dancing with other people's birds, breaking poppers under the nose of complete strangers.

He'd put his arm round the neck of some little middle-aged lady who was just standing there minding her own business sipping her wine, got her in a headlock and shoved a popper up her hooter. He didn't let go until she'd breathed in, gone absolutely bright red like her head was going to burst and stood there reeling with her eyes popping out of her head.

Amazingly, the woman just cackled with laughter and spent the rest of the night following Peter around like a puppy.

'Why are you, you know, so soddin' outrageous, Blossy?' I said, peeling the label off my beer bottle. 'If you don't mind me asking, of course.'

'Not at all, Louie Baby,' he said. 'I've decided I'm Peter Bloss and everything's always going to be all right.'

'Fair enough,' I said. There was no answer to that.

'Nah,' he said before bending down under the table and taking a long hit of the joint he held between his fingertips. 'Did I ever tell you how I got here?'

'Something to do with boats?'

'I got a job on a boat when I got here but, no, that wasn't how I got to Spain.' He stuck a tanned thumb into the air. 'I hitched, baby,' he said. 'From Calais to Barcelona. Without a safety net. Like our European Tour. Only way to travel.' He sipped his beer. 'And, whatever happens, Louie, I am not going back to the UK as a failure. I walked out of a job back there and they told me I'd be back. Wankers. No chance. I'm here to stay. Another one?'

I squinted at my watch. Loa's was always really gloomy. 'The movie starts in fifteen minutes. Shall we do the off?'

'Nah, we've got time for a quickie,' Peter said. He threw his head back and shouted 'Miguel! Dos San Miguel, por favor.' Several miles away, on the other side of the island, a small dog raised its head.

* * * * * *

Moments of peace and quiet become precious when you're working and partying as hard as we were. One of the places where we went to truly relax was the Sala Regina cinema on the ground floor of a church on a side street that led down the hill to Plaza Gomila.

The Sala Regina wasn't a proper cinema but Don Pepé, the owner, ticket seller and ice-cream vendor had sloped the floor so he could get in as many rows of folding wooden chairs as possible.

Pepé was a lovely guy. On his birthday he invited all his regulars for a free drink and piece of cake. Not something you could imagine happening at the Leicester Square Odeon.

Don Pepé showed British language movies twice a week and all of us Brits and Yanks in Terreno and beyond, including Lady Docker and Ted Cassidy, went to every showing.

Lady Norah Docker would swan around Terreno in a Bentley. She was the notorious wife of Sir Bernard Docker, a director of Thomas Cooks, the travel company, and for a while their antics had been splashed all over the UK press. This was until one night in Monte Carlo. Lady Docker who liked a tipple and had been a dance hall hostess, got pissed and danced on the national flag of Monaco. After that, she and her husband were ostracised by what they call polite society. I have no idea what she was doing in Terreno but I guess it had some connection to Thomas Cooks.

When Ted Cassidy was in the house we did everything we could to avoid sitting behind him. If he was sat in front of you it was like being in the shadow of a lighthouse. The view was blocked for several rows behind him. And he wasn't someone you'd ask to move, especially as he liked a drink.

Most of the time, us and the guys who sold tickets for the other clubs like Barbarellas and the Craisy Daisy were fierce rivals. We would do anything we could to lure a punter to our place and win the commission. There had been punch-ups.

A gang of ticket sellers put together by a little Northern bloke named Gary was our particular rivals. Not because they were a serious threat to us – Gary's crew were our rejects – but because, like Gary himself, they were always looking for a scrap.

Without anyone coming right out and saying it, the Sala Regina became neutral territory. None of us wanted to start any bother in the place and get us all kicked out. But, there were times when Pepé had to do a bit of an Officer Krupke, using his big torch as a truncheon.

* * * * * *

The Sala Regina was showing Planet Of The Apes and it was jam-packed with people when we got there. Lady Docker sat in her favourite seat with her big straw sunhat still on. Lurch swayed like a tipsy statue off towards one side. Cigarette smoke drifted through the dusty light thrown by the projector. The movie had already started. We walked over to our side, where our ticket seller boys and girls all gathered and crept back to about halfway up the hall. One of the guys had saved seats for us on the end of the row and we slid into them. As I sat down I kicked over a bottle of beer and it rolled slowly down the hall towards the front. Around us, people shook with laughter. Pepé shone his torch in our direction and we slumped down into our seats snorting.

We watched as Charlton Heston, another bloke and some bird went across the desert in what we could only assume was Ape planet, found an oasis, took off their clothes and dived into the water. When they came out they saw that their clothes had been stolen. They discovered the thieves, some scrawny looking herberts wearing their stuff looking for food in a cornfield. Some gorillas on horses appeared out of nowhere, waving rifles, snares and nets and started rounding up the humans. One of the blokes, the one who wasn't Charlton Heston was killed, the saucy bird was knocked out and Charlton was shot in the throat. And then the screen went black. There was jeering and cheering while Pepé changed the reels and a few minutes later the screen crackled and flared back to life.

Now two monkeys in clothes were looking at each other. The girl monkey says 'what will he find out there, doctor?'

'His destiny,' the bloke one says.

OK, talking monkeys. Fair enough.

Cut to Charlton riding a horse along a beach with another sexy bird in furs behind him but not the astronaut girl. There was an explosion and some wooden thing fell on a load of gorillas on horses. Charlton saw something in the distance and rode towards it. The music went all moody. Something was going to happen.

Charlton got close to an object sticking out of the sand and the camera shifted so it was behind the thing, which had big spikes. Charlton looked up, fell to his knees and started banging his fist in the surf and shouting: 'Oh my God, I'm back, I'm home. We finally really did it. You maniacs! You blew it up!' The camera pulled back and we saw that he was looking at the burnt top of the Statue of Liberty. The bird in the furs watched, confused. I felt like she did.

Peter and I looked at each other. 'What's going on?' he said in what he must have thought was a whisper. 'Where did the bleedin' Statue of Liberty come from?'

'Don't ask me,' I said. 'I...'

'Christ that dope is strong,' Peter said. He leaned over to the guy next to him on his other side and said 'ere, is that the Statue of Liberty?'

'Course it is,' the bloke said.

'What's it doing there?'

'No idea, mate.'

We looked at each other and then back at the screen. Now the credits had started to roll.

'Stone me,' I said. 'That's the shortest movie I've ever seen.' All round us people were looking at each other. Some were standing up. Lurch hauled himself to his feet, a lamppost that could fall over at any minute.

The credits shuddered to a halt, the screen flashed back into life and we were in a city filled with monkeys in clothes throwing rocks at Charlton. One threw his rocks like a girl.

'What just happened?' I said as we settled back into our seats.

'I think Pepé just showed the film in the wrong order.'

'So we know what happens in the end?'

'Yep.'

'Why are we still sitting here?'

'I don't know. Shall we knob off?'

'Might as well.'

We got up, walked out and down the steep hill to Plaza Gomila and the sweet sounds of honking horns, the clip-clop of horses hooves from the carts that took the tourists around and thumping music.

'Thought I was losing it there for a minute,' Peter said.

* * * * * *

It was late September in that last summer of the 1960s, around 5AM and Peter and I were standing outside Sloopy's watching the sun come up on the bay of Palma and sharing joints with a motley crew that had formed when the club finally threw us out.

A lone fishing boat chugged back home to land, passing a yellow ferry steaming out to sea in the direction of Barcelona. An early bird Laker Airways plane came into land at Palma airport.

The air was deliciously cool and still.

'Who'd have thought, Louie Baby,' Peter said.

'Thought what?'

'Sitting here with this lot, watching the sun come up over the bay, kings of all we survey.' Peter shook his head. 'Who'd have thought. Proves my point, don't it? You can't sleep in case you miss out on the action.'

'True.'

'Mind you, the amount of Bustaids we've necked tonight, there'd be a fat chance of us hitting the sack in any case. How many?'

Somewhere along the line I'd become the Bustaid dispenser. 'Lost count.' I sipped from my warm beer, trying to soothe my dry throat. 'Going to be a scorcher today.'

'It always is.'

'Wanna go home?'

'Nah. Something will occur.'

'It always does.'

The gang showed no signs of moving. Pauline and Sally were two London girls who worked for us as ticket sellers. Pauline was small, blonde and quiet and Sally a tall, slim redhead with plenty of front, dusted with sexy freckles. They were from Peckham in South London and had come out to the Rock together for an adventure.

One of the very few rules Peter and I had was that we didn't get involved with the female ticket sellers. It wasn't that we had principles or anything like that. We'd learned that a certain kind of girl went all out to bag the boss and when she did practised her own brand of divide and rule.

And it wasn't like there was a shortage of tasty birds willing to have a no-strings tumble with us. We had our hands full with the punters.

Now that we'd taken sex out of the equation – kind of - it was easy for us all to be friends and Pauline and Sally were a right laugh.

Somewhere in the night a couple of black Yank marines had latched onto the girls. Charles was a very cool guy from Chicago, an amazing dancer and his pal Syl, who obviously worshipped him, was so laidback he was almost horizontal. Both wore the latest black street style from the US – huge flared jeans, tight ribbed vests that showed off their gleaming muscles and flip-flops. All night they'd had the local whores hovering round them but they'd zoomed in on Pauline and Sally.

The girls knew what was going on and were obviously flattered by the attention but they weren't in a hurry to hop into the sack with the two Yanks. Or, at least, they wanted to make it a fair fight.

The awe we'd all felt when we met our first Americans was kind of fading now.

Plenty of Yanks had washed up on the Rock. Draft dodgers and deserters drifting round Europe worked on the yachts moored in the bay of Palma for the summer while they waited for the Vietnam War to end. Not that it showed any sign of doing so.

Paul Smith, alias Smithy, who was also hanging out with us this morning, was one of our ticket sellers. He had a nice sideline selling Bustaids to the Yanks. His blonde hair was cut in a way that made him look like a debauched choirboy.

Charles, Syl and Paul leant up against a wall in the sunlight, rapping while Paul rolled a never-ending string of joints.

Two other black guys formed part of our circle. Preston and Chris were the singer and drummer in a tidy little soul and ska band called The Fantastics that played at Sloopy's. Preston was Jamaican but was bought up in London and could shift effortlessly backwards and forwards between Jamaican patois and Cockney. Charles and Syl were fascinated by Preston's accent and kept asking him to say something 'in your language.'

Chris was an American from Detroit and dodging the draft.

Sally, the redhead, clearly had a thing for Preston and had made sure she was sat next to him.

'So when do you guys report back to the ship?' Paul said.

'We got all day, dude. Shore leave.' Syl drawled, his voice rhythmic syrup.

'Any plans?'

'Naaah, man. Hang out, I guess. Be cool. Maybe go to the beach.'

'She-it,' Charles said. 'He always say that. We never go. Ain't seen nothing of this island but the bars, man.' He laughed, shook his head.

'We should go to the beach,' Peter said. 'Illetas or one of those.'

'No way, Blossy,' Paul said. 'What we should do is *really* go to the beach.'

'What do you mean?' Peter said, passing him the joint.

'You know, somewhere on the other side of the island. And I know exactly the place. Why not?' Unlike the rest of us ticket sellers, Paul was really into exploring the island. On his free day, he would take himself off on his Vespa in search of out the way beaches.

'Blimey yes,' Peter said. He never needed persuading.

'Why not?' Syl said. 'You got wheels?'

That stopped Peter in his tracks. All we had was the Vespas we whizzed around on and a SEAT 600 we had the keys for but that wouldn't fit seven. Seconds later he'd rallied. 'Got it,' he said.

* * * * * *

Paul took us to a beach I was never able to find again.

Peter had remembered that a bloke in our block, a German, had a VW camper van. The guy didn't seem at all bothered by nine raving maniacs rolling up at six on a Monday morning. He'd probably been up all night himself. We had a whip round, paid him 2000 pesetas for the day – Charles and Syl holding out fistfuls of money, as excited as children to be going to the beach – and went lurching and rattling out of Palma and onto the road that led eastwards down the coast.

Our first stop was a bar in a small dusty town, a weirdly large cavern, its walls lined with wine barrels and the usual bulls head mounted filled with old geezers smoking, drinking coffee and cognac. They did their best to avoid looking at the seven of us when we fell through the door and into the gloomy, smoky air, chattering and whooping. I'd handed round more Bustaids in the camper so we were rattling again.

Peter looked up at the bulls head and said 'Christ, he must have been running fast to get through that wall.' It was our favourite joke, always cracked us up. No-one else laughed.

We ordered bocadillos – the long sandwiches made out of French sticks – some slices of coca, a Majorcan pizza made with onion and pepper, spinach and sometimes salty fish but without cheese that someone told me dated back to the Romans, and ensaimadas to go and Smithy, whose Spanish was pretty good, organised a takeaway of a case of beer, another of Coca-Cola and a few bottles of wine. Charles and Syl had to be stopped from paying for everything. To them, pesetas were funny money and they either had no idea of the value of the notes they were waving around or didn't care.

While we were waiting, Smithy ordered coffees with a shot of this drink called Ron Amazona in them. 'Sounds like a wrestler's name, don't it?' Peter said. Usually, barmen gave you the bottle of cognac, whisky or whatever to pour into your drink yourself. We'd learnt that most bottles of spirits in the bars were refilled over and over again from a barrel in the back – whatever it was, the spirit was called carafe – and it was ridiculously cheap and they didn't really care how much you drank. So I was surprised when the barman held onto the bottle and poured shots of the drink into our black coffees.

I soon found out why he wasn't letting go of the Ron. The stuff was rocket fuel, especially on top of the Bustaids. Pretty soon we were jabbering away so fast it was hard to keep up with the words that tumbled out of our mouths. If there was even the slightest pause it was filled by someone saying 'and, yeah, have you noticed how...' And we were off again.

Walking out into the street, blinking in the fierce sunlight, I felt like a vampire. And judging by the scowls of the little old ladies dressed in black with big crosses on their shelves on their way to the vegetable market I looked like one.

The difference between the laidback cosmopolitan everyday madness around Plaza Gomila and this sleepy sunbaked town felt like centuries. Even the air seemed old.

Back in the VW, Preston and Syl swapped a guitar back and forth as they alternated between Motown and Blue Beat, one harmonising behind the other, Chris tapping out a rhythm on his bottle of beer with his lighter. The Jamaicans often did reggae versions of Yank soul songs so they knew loads of the same stuff – My Girl, Gypsy Woman, Tracks Of My Tears. Hearing those soulful black voices together sent shivers up and down my spine. I could see the girls' resistance was beginning to melt.

Peter drove, with Smithy giving him directions and me

jabbering away about nothing as if what I had to say was the secret of the universe.

After about an hour of driving up the coast, passing beaches that all looked fantastic because Smithy said where we were going was 'out of this world, babies', he shouted to Peter to stop at the entrance of a bone-white dirt track that ran between two stone walls. 'Found it,' he crowed. We turned right and bounced down the track.

We came to a halt at a stone wall about ten minutes later. The sea glittered in the distance but it was impossible to say how far away it was and how long we'd have to walk. Hauling the drink, food and ourselves out of the van, we climbed the wall and set off following a rocky, dusty path as it dropped down into cool air between sweet-smelling pine trees.

After maybe twenty minutes walking we began to follow the rocky bed of a dried out stream through a valley with a low red cliff on one side and trees on the other. We turned a corner and saw before us a deserted beach with sand so white it hurt my eyes.

'Wow,' Syl said. 'Now this is a beach, brother.'

'Right on,' Charles said. 'Truly a beach indeed, man.' They gave each other a complicated soul brother handshake.

'Let's show 'em the beach boys knee wobble, Louie,' Peter said.

And black knees and white knees joined together in a melting pot knee wobble till Sally fell over laughing, Charles making sure he collapsed on top of her. Not that she minded.

* * * * * *

The shadows were getting longer as the sun went down behind the hill. I lay on my sunburnt back, a towel over my face, watching the red swimming pool behind my eyelids, listening to the others talk.

'What a day, man,' Syl said. 'I'm going to remember this. Boy, that cave out there is something special.'

'Especially where we're going, right, brother man?' Charles said.

'Where's that?' one of the girls said.

'Next stop Vietnam, baby,' Charles said, grim humour and something else in his voice.

'You're kidding,' Peter said.

'Would I joke about something like that?' Charles said. 'You had the right idea, Chris, my man,' he said. 'She-it.'

'Why don't you guys, you know...?' Chris said.

'Where would we go, man?' We can't exactly fade into the woodwork. And we're marines, shore patrol would come looking for us.'

'But, Vietnam...' Peter said. I knew what he was thinking. We never read newspapers on the Rock and only watched TV when there was a big football match or Bonanza was on. Vietnam was there in the background but it had nothing to do with us. It didn't seem real.

'It's real, brother, bet your ass.' Syl said, as if he'd read Peter's mind. 'Way too real.'

For a while the only sound was the sea sliding up and down over the sand. Then one of the girls started to sob quietly. 'Hey, baby,' Charles or Syl said. 'What are you crying for? It ain't like you have to go.' Underneath his attempt at a joke, I could hear his fear.

'It's just...' and she lost it. Pauline started Sally off, so she was bawling too. And then, out of nowhere, we were all weeping. Like children. The deep sobs of the men became wild, unashamed wailing, howling and cursing. Our cries echoed round the empty beach.

I wept with the rest, until the towel on my face was wet through.

And when I was finished, when we all were, it was cold and time to go.

PART TWO

A PARTNER IN THE MIST

I thought selling tickets for the beach parties and disco nights at Sloopy's couldn't get much better. Blossy and I had our deal going with Julian, the boat owner and we were coining it. Harry the Horse was long out of the picture.

I was no longer Louie Baby. Ricky 'The Lash' Lazar had christened me 'Louie The Lip'. In Ricky's world, everyone had a nickname.

The new mature Louie The Lip was no longer playing the field. I was living in a great apartment in Can Pastilla with a beautiful Swedish girl, as much in love with me as I was with her.

I'd first spotted Gun, who I'd now been living with for a year, at a beach party the year before. Somehow, in and among 300 punters and sunbathing as if she was back home in her garden in Southern Sweden, she'd caught my eye from our ramshackle stage. Gun wasn't just blonde and beautiful, there was something special about her for me. On a bright summer afternoon, lightning struck.

After we'd finished our madcap entertainer routine, I dragged Blossy with me over the burning sand to chat up Gun and her friend. We sat down next to them, turned on the charm and found out they were going to Sloopy's that night.

We double-dated a few times while the girls were on holiday, until Gun's friend went off Blossy and hooked up with another Swede.

Gun and I stayed in touch and I realised that this Scandie flicka had got into my head like no-one else had before. That winter I schlepped over to Southern Sweden and spent Christmas at Gun's parent's house. We got on great. Gun shared my crazy sense of humour but she also had a down to earth way of looking things I didn't have but thought was fantastic.

We decided to give living together in Majorca a go and moved into an apartment in March 1972.

Like I said, Gun was really practical and when I met her she had a great job working for a guy in Lund, a university town in Southern Sweden. He'd set up a company called EF which sent students abroad to study, mainly English in the UK. Business was excellent so the guy was disappointed when Gun said she was going off with a nutty Englishman to live in Majorca. While she was trying to figure out what she'd do on the Rock, the guy called her up and told her he'd just bought a travel company on the island and wanted her to run it. Of course, she leapt at the chance and pretty soon had six reps working for her while she dealt with the hotels, managed the contracts and all that.

So, for the first time in my life, I had money coming in and a lovely bird to go home to. Unlike Blossy.

* * * * * *

One night, as the sun was setting behind the mountains, I was round at Blossy's having a beer, a smoke and a relaxing Bustaid, the diet pills we popped like they were sweets, before heading off back to Gun when the doorbell rang. 'You expecting company?' I said.

He stood up, took a deep hit of the joint that had been glued to his hand for the past half hour before finally passing it to me, scratched his balls through the pair of horribly tight swimming shorts which was all he was wearing. 'Interviewing this Swedish bird, see if she could bang out tickets.' Turning, he goosestepped across the floor and flung open the door. 'Come in, come in,' he said in a deep voice.

A very pretty but obviously shy girl almost crept into the room. Blossy shook her hand violently and waved in the direction of the table where there were two chairs. She sat down. Blossy didn't bother to introduce me so I said 'Hi, I'm Louie, Peter's partner.' The girl gave a little smile, pushed her hair back behind her ears, said 'Petra'. I walked over and shook her tiny, boneless and slightly damp hand, then waited for Blossy to start.

Blossy looked up at the ceiling for what seemed like five minutes, snapped his head down, stared at the girl and said 'Like it here?' Long pause. 'On Majoooorcahhhh?'

'Yes, very…'

'Sold tickets before?'

'Um, no…'

Blossy leant back in his chair. I heard it creak. He stared at the girl, a glint in his eyes. Her stomach rumbled loudly. She blushed. Blossy reached a hand into his pocket and, after a minute of wrestling, pulled out a jar of Bustaids and slammed it down hard on the table. Petra jumped as if she'd been shot. 'Know what these are for?' he barked. Petra shook her head. 'These sell tickets,' Blossy said, grinning. He stood up, still grinning like a sick wolf, and walked slowly backwards out of the room, closing the door behind him.

The girl looked at me, her mouth open. I shrugged. 'So have you been…?' I started to say when the lights went out. I flicked on my lighter, went to the kitchen and found the stub of a candle which I lit and carried back into the room. By its light, the girl's eyes were big and round, the whites very white. 'As I was saying, I…'

The door flew open so hard it banged against the wall. The girl and I both jumped. She squeaked. Blossy stood in the doorway wearing a bed sheet with eyeholes cut in it. He let out a long, gurgling moan, then a shriek, ran wailing round the room, shot back out the door. Petra and I sat looking at each other. I could feel a laugh building. Blossy hurtled through the door again, ran round the room, shrieking like a lost soul. This was too much for Petra. She screamed and headed for the door.

'Where are you going?' I shouted. 'The interview's not over yet!' No reply, just the sound of wooden clogs click-clacking rapidly down the stairs. I sat back in my chair and waited.

The lights came back on. Blossy strolled in through the door, without the sheet. He went straight past me and into the kitchen. I heard the sound of the tap running. He reappeared carrying a bucket filled with water, stepped out through the French windows and onto the balcony. I went to stand next to him. We looked over the balcony. Petra stood looking up at us, her mouth open. I think she was trying to say something. Blossy looked at me, his face blank and, without a word, tipped the bucket of water over the edge. We heard an outraged squeal followed by a string of vile Swedish swear words I recognised from when I pissed Gun off.

Blossy looked at me, shrugged and said 'wrong sort, never would have cut it.'

* * * * * *

Even though Blossy was becoming even more Blossy than ever, it didn't get in the way of us making money and having a right laugh most of the time we were together.

On the business side, if you can call what we did business, our only real competition was a guy called Curly and his partner. Curly was stocky, walked like he could handle himself and sported a massive Afro. Bernt, his partner was a cocky blonde German who was the best ticket seller I'd ever seen. The guy was a machine. He would sometimes hustle our English punters for the sport of it, without actually selling them a ticket. Just to freak out our PRs.

Even then, Curly and Bernt weren't really our rivals. For a start, they mainly sold to Krauts, running a couple of boat parties from Arenal to a Bavarian 'oompah oompah' beer hall called the Crazy Daisy.

I didn't know much about Curly, other than that he'd been headed for the West Indies but washed up on the Rock after an argument with the skipper of a boat he was working on.

Curly rode up and down the strip every day with Yvonne, his Swedish girlfriend on the back of his Vespa. The combination of his huge Afro and her blonde hair, which flowed down to her waist, was weird to say the least.

Whenever we saw each other, we'd nod but that was it so I was surprised when Curly pulled up in front of me one morning and waited for me to make a sale to four punters. As I pocketed my 400 pesetas commission, Curly said 'could we have a meet, Louie? I've got something I want to put to you.'

'Sure,' I said, 'why not?' That night we arranged for Curly and Yvonne to come round to the apartment I shared with Gun and Curly roared off in a cloud of blue smoke, Yvonne's hair flying in the breeze behind them.

I wondered what Curly wanted to talk to me about but I didn't really have a clue. Maybe, I thought, he wanted to be mates.

* * * * * *

I left Gun to look over the figures Curly and Yvonne had bought to show us and went out on our balcony to smoke a cigarette and think over the offer Curly had made me early that evening. They'd left an hour before. The night was hot and still, with just the faintest breeze from the sea. The moon was low, heavy and nearly full, moonlight shining on the inky Med in what looked like a path.

And I was being shown a path that could take me in a potentially fantastic direction if I chose to take it. I would really be my own boss and make ten times the amount I was now. My stomach was fluttering and my cigarette hand shook. I took a large gulp of my rum and coke.

Curly and Yvonne had arrived at our apartment on the dot of seven. He'd refused a drink, saying he'd stick with Coca-Cola, and then it was down to business. The figures Curly had whipped out showed what he made from running the boat trips himself, paying for the use of the boats rather than taking a commission, as well as providing buses to take punters from the Crazy Daisy back to Arenal afterwards. He paid the Crazy Daisy a commission per punter, rather than the other way round. I couldn't argue with his bottom line. And then he made his pitch.

'I want us to join up, Louie,' he said. 'You've got Sloopy's, a great team of ticket sellers and there's you, yourself. You're great at what you do.' I was flattered, which was obviously Curly's tactic.

Curly went on to explain that, if we joined forces, Julian would be fine because he'd be getting a double commission from the boat trips I already organised and the night ones full of Krauts Curly did. My salesmen would be employed by Curly's company, Cruceros Palma, which was owned on paper by a smooth, friendly Filipino named Ricardo. It was really Curly's company. Cruceros Palma didn't own any boats and made a loss every year for tax purposes.

What Curly was proposing made total sense from a business point of view. I'd have to be crazy not to accept his offer but I asked for the night to think things over and discuss it with Gun.

'One last thing,' Curly had said before he left. 'I don't want Bloss. I just want you. Bloss is a loose cannon. A liability. If you decide to say yes that's how it's got to be. He's out.'

I said nothing. I was stunned. I hadn't even thought about where Blossy would fit. I'd just assumed he'd be with me. 'Right,' I said. 'Of course. And Bernt?'

'I've had enough of that berk,' Curly said. 'It'll be auf wiedersehen pratface if we join forces. Don't worry about that.'

I finished my cigarette, slapped at a mosquito that had just bitten my ankle and stepped back into our living room. Gun looked up from the figures Curly had left. 'You have to do this, Louie,' she said. 'It's a fantastic opportunity. You can't lose.'

'I know,' I said. 'But what about Blossy?'

'What about him?'

'He's my partner and my mate. We're the last two beach boys standing.'

'Beach boys?'

I'd forgotten she knew nothing about the original four of us who'd met and had such great adventures five years before. 'Never mind. Look, I really want to do this. It is a great idea but I can't walk away from Blossy.'

'Curly's right,' Gun said. 'Peter is a liability. He's crazy. You never know what he's going to do next. No, Louie. You can't carry him any more.' I looked at her. Her voice softened and she held out her arms to me. 'I know you're great mates, Louie, but this is your future. Ours.'

'I know,' I said. And, really, my mind was already made up. 'But how am I going to tell him?'

* * * * * *

Next morning, I headed for Loa's to meet Blossy. It was where we always planned our day. He grinned when he saw me coming towards him and I felt worse than I had before. His eyes were glassy and he had a fresh scratch on his left cheek, just below his eye. I didn't ask. I took a deep breath, knowing that the only way I was going to find the guts to tell him was to get it out as fast as I could. I told him what I'd decided.

'Sorry?' he said. 'Say that again.' I repeated what I had to say. 'Don't beat about the bush, Lou, give it to me straight,' he said. I started to repeat myself. 'I was joking,' he said, no laughter in his voice. 'I heard you the first time.'

'I'm really sorry,' I said.

He looked at me, shrugged, smiled a sad smile. I didn't know if it was the light but his eyes looked a little more glassy than before. 'Oh well,' he said, 'that's showbiz, buddy. But, Curly…He can't even do a Beach Boy knee wobble.'

'I know,' I said. 'But you can still do the entertainment on the beach parties with me. And we can do the wobble whenever we like.'

'Won't be the same, Louie,' he said, shaking his head with cartoon sadness. 'It just won't be the same.' He looked up. 'No, mate, I'm made up for you. You deserve it. I'll be fine. Don't worry about me.'

Which all made me feel even worse, if that was possible. 'Right then,' I said, standing up. 'Best go find Curly and tell him the good news. See you later?'

'Sure, later,' he said. 'You know where to find me.' I didn't ever know where to find him but I knew what he meant.

I walked through the gloom of Loa's towards the sunlight that crept in through the curtain of metal strips shifting in the breeze. Just before I stepped out, Blossy called ''ere Louie Baby.' I turned. 'Watch him, son,' he said, 'watch him'.

* * * * * *

My partnership with Curly was a blinding success from day one. We each had what the other didn't. I was Louie The Lip, the entertainer and front man. Curly was the business brains, happy to stay in the shadows.

We ran four trips a week and switched from Sloopy's to Barbarella's, a much bigger club in the thumping, bustling neon heart of Terreno, done out in the shape of a bull-ring, which – when it was rammed – was pretty appropriate.

Gun and I had moved to a great place in Terreno which had its own little garden filled with orange and lemon trees. We got engaged and invited all the salesmen to the party. I passed the word that I really wanted Blossy to come. If we were going to get married he would be my best man, no question. I couldn't find him to invite him myself but I knew he hung out with the salesmen, popping Bustaids, getting plastered and cadging money so I asked them to get word to him. He didn't come.

One morning a few days after our engagement party I was driving down the Paseo Maritimo in a rented car when someone leapt out in front of me. I screeched to a halt, just in time. Blossy walked round to the drivers' seat and stuck his head in through the window 'got 25 pesetas for a boccadillo?' he said.

'I could have killed you,' I said.

'But you didn't, did you?' he said. 'Did you?'

GOING GOING GUN

April 1973. The days started to heat up and become longer and I was looking forward to another fantastic summer. I felt like I had just about everything I wanted in my life. I can't say it was what I'd dreamed of because nothing could have prepared me for the life I was living now.

Most of the salesmen Curly and I had recruited in '72 came back and we took on more as we continued to build our island empire. Gun was doing really well with the travel firm. We were both coining it. Everything was hunky-dory.

So we decided to try for a niño.

I don't know whether the spring air put a spring in my you know what or if it was the garlic in the alioli but by May Gun was pregnant and we were both over La Luna.

We saw out the season, she handed the reins of the travel company over to her second in command, and headed over to Sweden to be with her parents, Nils and Inga.

I'd last been in Sweden when the Beach Boys, Blossy, Little Jimmy, Buddy and me, did our European tour back in 1968 and I hadn't really seen much of the place.

Southern Sweden, where Gun was from, was all farmland – covered with a layer of deep snow - and they lived on an estate of neat, newly built houses. Nils and Inga were very friendly towards me. Inga didn't speak a word of English so we just smiled at each other most of the time.

We spent Christmas and New Year waiting for our big day and Maria, our angel, came into the world on January 8th. Both sides of the family were in heaven.

I stayed in Sweden all the way through the winter, completely wrapped up in my new family but come March I had to tear myself away and get back to business on the Rock.

Back on the Rock, without my family, I threw myself into work and making plenty of cash to send back to Gun and Maria. They came over twice that summer and, when they were around, it was pure heaven.

Summer 1974 was another blinder for Curly and me and we started to pull punters out of Magaluf and Palma Nova, up the coast to the north of Palma. Our patch was getting bigger all the time and we were streets ahead of the competition.

So, when I went back to Sweden for the winter of '74, I was exhausted and spent my time quietly bonding with Maria. But, I also kept in touch with Curly as we made more plans to expand on the Rock.

One night, after dinner, Gun and her mother went to the movies, leaving me and her old man to look after Maria.

We were sat watching TV, each of us sipping a Carlsberg, when I began to feel he was trying to find the right moment to say something to me. Sure enough, out it came: 'Don't you think it would be better if you stayed in Sweden and made a life here with your family? The life in Majorca, it seems crazy, especially for a baby.'

I was shocked. I went outside for a cigarette to calm my nerves, slipping on my clogs as I did so. We weren't allowed to wear shoes in the house, which was alien to me. It hadn't occurred to me that Gun's mum and dad thought this way, although it was logical that they would. And I realised that they'd obviously had this conversation with Gun, and she'd agreed. So she'd gone out to the pictures with her mum to leave the way free for Nils to try and persuade me to see sense and stay in Sweden.

I stepped back inside and, as politely as I could, said 'I'll think about it' and we went back to watching TV in silence. Which was how Gun and Inga found us when they came back from the cinema, their faces pink from the freezing night air.

Now that the subject of staying in Sweden had come out in the open, I was truly torn. I was devoted to my daughter and loved Gun to pieces but there was no way I could see myself settling in Sweden. It was beautiful, especially where they lived but it was also horribly quiet and regimented. The Swedes had a particular way of telling you what to do with a smile on their face and an oily way of speaking that was somehow worse than being shouted at. You felt like you'd done something wrong most of the time and usually had, without you knowing about it. I'd always seen myself as a free spirit, which was why I was at home on the Rock. It was the reason I'd come to the island in the first place! Gun and I talked and I thought I'd managed to keep her sweet by neither saying yes or no.

I went back to the Rock in March 1975 as planned and Gun promised to come and see me. She brought Maria over twice and, while it wasn't easy because we were a family in two different countries, I thought we made the best of it and, of course, little Maria loved the sea, sun and sand.

* * * * * *

As the season wound down, I began to really look forward to getting back to Sweden and being with Gun and Maria. I was still very much in love with Gun. I'd made plenty of money so we could relax and take it easy until the next year and, I hoped, Gun and Maria would come back with me to the Rock. I carefully avoided thinking about what her old man Nils had said to me.

Nils and Inga came over to Majorca for a short holiday towards the end of the summer and, once again, he gave it to me straight over a cold beer. We were sitting on the terrace of mine and Gun's little apartment, enjoying the slightly cooler evening air when he cleared his throat and said 'Gun does not want Maria brought up in this way of life'.

'What way of life?'

'The...This,' he said, waving his hand vaguely around. 'Whatever, it doesn't matter. She wants to bring up Maria in Sweden and, if you will not live in Sweden, it has to be over between you. She is sorry but that is the way it is.' I looked at him open-mouthed. His face softened. 'Look, Louie, I like you. We all like you. And you're a great father. But that isn't the problem. It's this place. Why can't you give it up and make a life in Sweden?'

I looked down at the floor, then back up at him. I was in shock. There was nothing I could say. He shrugged his shoulders, drained his beer, stood up. Patting my arm, he said 'I'll get us two more beers. I'm very sorry, Louie. Very sorry.'

As soon as I could that night, I called Gun. 'Why didn't you tell me how you felt, instead of getting your father to do it?' I said.

'I tried to tell you, hundreds of times but you didn't want to listen. Isn't it obvious that I don't want to be in Majorca? I'd be there right now if I did, wouldn't I?'

That stopped me in my tracks. Gun was always more logical than me. 'But...my life is here,' I said. 'It's what I do. I don't want to do anything else.'

'Even if it means being separated from me and your daughter?'

'I love my daughter, you know that.'

'I know you do but obviously not enough to make a life with her in Sweden.'

'That's not...' But I didn't know if it was true or not.

The truth was I wanted it all and couldn't see why life on the Rock, endless summer, bucketloads of cash and barrels of laughs couldn't be enough for anyone.

'I love you, Louie,' Gun said. 'And I know this is hard,' she started to cry, 'it's awful for me too but I will not bring my daughter up in Majorca. It's as simple as that. Please, take some time to think about what you want to do. If you want to come to Sweden, there's always a place for you.'

'I'll think about it,' I said. But there was no way I was living in Sweden.

Gun's mum and dad went home. I never blamed them. They were lovely people who only wanted to do the best for their daughter and grand-daughter. And, of course, they thought Sweden was paradise on earth. I called Gun a few times and begged her to change her mind. I didn't have a rational argument. I just begged.

But Gun's mind was made up. I could see Maria whenever I wanted but we were never going to be a family living on the Rock, as I'd pictured it.

THE STORY OF ALEXANDRA'S

From day one, the partnership between me and Curly worked like a dream. Between us, we packed the party boats and filled Barbarellas. And, when there were no parties, our crack team of PRs pulled in the punters for Barbarellas with Curly and yours truly taking our piece off the top too.

For Curly and me, the only problem was that we were making a fortune for Barbarellas and not for ourselves. So, when Curly stopped by my apartment one night saying he had some interesting news I was all ears.

'I've just left His Nibs,' he said over his shoulder. He was looking out my window at the bay of Palma, the sun going down behind his massive Afro. I lay on my back on the sofa giving my feet a well-earned rest. When I heard what he said I sat up abruptly, spilling sticky San Miguel all over my bare chest.

The guy we called His Nibs was the disco king of El Arenal and in his late 20s, our age. He'd been a pro tennis player before getting into the disco business, represented Spain and even played at Queens Club in London. So he was a hero to the Majorcan people, who, let's face it, didn't have many. His Nibs' first disco was a joint called Mach in El Arenal, an 'all you can drink for 100 pesetas' club. It had taken off like a rocket and, since then, he'd had his golden fingers in all sorts of pies.

'And?' I said. Curly was a great one for making you wait for good news. Bad news you knew about right away.

Curly turned to face me. 'You've got beer all over yourself, Louie,' he said.

'I do know that,' I said. 'His Nibs?'

'Right, he asked me for a meet.' It crossed my mind to ask Curly why he didn't tell me about that. We were partners. As if he was reading my mind, Curly said, 'it came out of the blue. I tried to find you but you were off on a party and I figured you wouldn't mind. You don't, do you?' He started to nod his head.

'No,' I said, nodding my own head. 'Tell me what His Nibs said.'

'He's going to buy Sergeant Peppers. You know, the place in Terreno and he's going to turn it into a super-club. Tear it apart, redesign it and...now comes the interesting part...he wants us to be his partners.'

I stood up, my head spun a little. 'Why us?' I said.

'He's got eyes and ears all over the place hasn't he? Must have seen what we were doing for Barbarellas, I guess. But, listen, we don't have to put up any money right away. He's going to finance it all. We've got three years to pay him back out of our share of the profits and we get 49% of the club between us. So...'

'We become club owners and don't have to pay a penny to do it,' I finished for him.

'Exactly. We've got nothing to lose and for His Nibs to make an offer like that means he really wants to work with us. So, what do you think?'

I held out my hand to Curly and, in a booming cowboy voice, said 'shake pardner.' Curly laughed. I moved towards him to give him a bearhug.

'Steady on, Louie,' he said, backing away. 'You've got beer all over you.'

* * * * * *

Sergeant Peppers was just down from Plaza Gomila in Terreno, a great location for the thousands of party people who packed Gomila every night of the summer. It was where Blossy had his flat before he lost it, somewhere near the end.

It was most famous for being the place where the legendary Jimi Hendrix played on 15th July 1968. So how did Hendrix end up in Majorca?

Sergeant Peppers was owned by a guy named Mike Jeffery who was Hendrix's manager. Plenty of members of the London music scene came to Majorca to play and just hang out and I guess Jeffery must have come with them.

They'd go to Deia, on the rocky north-west coast of the island, where the hippies went to sit at the feet of the writer Robert Graves, the I Claudius guy who lived up there. Graves was friendly with a woman who was the mum of the drummer in the Soft Machine, Robert Wyatt, the band that had supported Hendrix on a tour across America and they'd all become friends.

Maybe Mike just followed Hendrix out and realised Gomila was a good place to open a club. Perhaps it was a good way to launder money without paying UK tax.

Majorca was also just across the water from Ibiza and especially Formentera, the beautiful, tiny island a short ferry ride away from Ibiza which was a magnet for hardcore hippies. It was where Penny, the posh bird I had a tumble with in Ibiza back in '68 was headed for when I met her.

Apart from Hendrix, Bob Dylan, Joni Mitchell and Pink Floyd all wrote songs and recorded in Formentera.

To be honest, unlike Blossy, I never really had anything much to do with that hippy world. It was sort of like a weird parallel to our life of sun, sea and sand.

Peter may have well been there when Hendrix played at the opening night of Sergeant Peppers but he never mentioned it. By all accounts, Hendrix tore the place apart. Literally. He rammed his guitar up into the ceiling above the club's low stage.

Now, some people might say Hendrix doing that was part of his act. He was known for doing all kinds of crazy things like smashing up his guitar and even setting it on fire.

But, there's another way of looking at it. It was well known that Hendrix was seriously pissed off at the management deal he'd had with Mike Jeffery which worked him like a slave and left him broke. So, Hendrix could have taken one look round the club, realised that he'd helped pay for it whether he liked it or not and taken a chunk out of the ceiling in anger and frustration.

Mike Jeffery was dead by the time by Sergeant Peppers became Alexandra's. Jeffery's death was as dramatic as his life. On March 5th 1973 the Air Iberia plane he was travelling in back to the UK collided with another plane over Nantes in France.

So was Jeffery a complete villain? He certainly screwed Jimi Hendrix, as he had done the Animals when he managed them.

It was rumoured that Jeffery worked for MI5 and British Secret Intelligence and was connected with organised crime in Europe. And, of course, the most damaging accusation has always been that Jeffery was somehow involved in Hendrix's death on 18 September 1970. Hendrix was sick and tired of getting ripped off by Jeffery. Jeffery had also taken out a $2 million life insurance policy on Hendrix's life.

But, according to Trixie Sullivan who was his assistant and a lovely woman, Jeffery was stranded in Majorca because of a freak storm and, before he died, Jimi had been trying to reach him on the phone. Apparently, Mike had been very upset that Jimi had not been able to get through to him.

Since Jeffery's death, Sergeant Peppers had stood empty. His Nibs negotiated the deal to buy the place from Trixie Sullivan and, knowing him, probably got a bargain.

Trixie was great and she'd never had a bad word to say about Jeffery. Years later, up in Deia, I met an American guy who used to supply Hendrix with grass when he was recording at Electric Lady, his recording studio in Greenwich Village, New York. He said Mike Jeffery came across as a proper English gent and always paid for the dope, no questions asked.

So who knows?

For me, Jeffery is just one of the amazing, colourful characters who've swaggered around Plaza Gomila over those amazing years.

* * * * * *

I soon found out that when His Nibs decided to do something, it happened. And fast. There was no 'mañana' for him. He had the club ready to open in six weeks flat and, after me and Curly signed the paperwork His Nibs' lawyers drew up, we were officially partners. We had 49% between us because, under Spanish law no foreigner could own more than that. Mind you, there were two of us – Curly and me – so we could have had 25% each. As it happens, Curly had 25% and I had the rest. This crossed my mind but I didn't mention it. His Nibs had made one of my fantasies come true so I wasn't about to ruffle any feathers.

His Nibs had spared no expense doing the club out and it made all the other joints around Gomila look well shabby. Except Tito's of course.

To get into the club, punters walked over a triple thickness glass floor filled with brightly coloured tropical fish and, once they were inside there were three more huge aquariums.

Just so you know, the way we got the fish in and fed them – and cleaned the glass - was like this. We stuck two big industrial rubber suction plungers to either end of each glass panel. Next, we attached a metal device to the rubber which you could tighten by turning until it had enough resistance to lift out the glass.

Curly loved the fish. They were his pride and joy. Until they started eating each other.

The club was done out in black and white. There were four long bars and each of these had an oil-based wave machine on it that we'd shipped over from London, where they were all the rage.

We called the club Alexandra's on the advice of Yvonne, Curly's missus who said that was the top disco in Stockholm. Named after a woman called Alexandra Charles, the original Alex's was the place where stars and famous people like Mick Jagger and Tom Jones went when they came to Stockholm. Abba shot an album cover there.

By calling our place Alexandra's we wanted to pull in the Swedish punters who thought there was some connection.

Alexandra's was the centre of my life from 1975 to 1992, my girlfriend and mother rolled into one. I loved that place.

Our opening night was a massive success. We took our places: Curly greeting people on the door, Yvonne taking tickets and Louie The Lip acting as Master of Ceremonies and all-round life and soul of the party.

His Nibs had made sure all kinds of Majorcan dignitaries and famous Spanish people came. But, for me, the guest of honour was my old man, who I'd flown over especially. I was thrilled to be able to show him what I'd made of myself on the Rock.

From then on, for years to come, Alex's really was the number one disco in Majorca.

To give you some idea of just how big a hit the club was, me and Curly paid off His Nibs in 18 months instead of three years.

My first rented cell, El Arenal 1967

Sloopy's Disco, Palma, Salesmen 1967.
Louie - top row 2nd from right
Peter Bloss - bottom row far right

Party night! A coach tour flyer, late sixties.

With Ricky Lazaar & 'Birmingham' Sue,
Ricky's Bar, Palma, 1970.

The Sun reports my runaway bride, 1981.

One of many 'Miss Wet T-Shirt' winners, 1981.

All aboard! Boat to the beach party, mid seventies.

Fun and games at the beach party. Mid seventies.

Boarding the coach for the evening party. Mid seventies.

Bodega (wine cellar) party. Mid seventies.

RIP Arthur Donaldson.

With Jose Feliciano, outside Alexandra's, early eighties.

GOMILA GLAM

Picture this.

It's coming up for ten o clock on a sultry hot August night in Palma. The Paseo Maritimo is a necklace of neon lights. A cruise ship, looking like a lit up office block on its side is docked at the ferry port. Blinking red lights of planes taking off and coming into land. The air smells of traffic fumes, bougainvillea, frying fish, suntan lotion, cheap perfume and, as always, sewage.

I'm leading 150 giggling, frisky sun-kissed and slightly squiffy Scandinavian party people up this alleyway that goes from behind Tito's club through to Plaza Gomila. The pavement is polished almost to glass so it must have been there for years. To get to the alleyway from the Paseo Maritimo you have to climb up a few flights of stone stairs.

I love this smelly little alleyway because it helps me act out one of my favourite party pieces.

I'm the Pied Party Piper of Plaza Gomila. Heels click-clack on the ancient stone. We've been out on a night disco champagne cruise around the Bay of Palma and now we're heading for Alex's for the next stage of my party mission. I'll give them an unforgettable night and we'll part them from the rest of their money.

Like my loyal followers, I'm very merry after a few hours sipping cheap but chilled champagne on top of a couple of Bustaids to get the patter flowing and the plastic platters spinning.

Just before we get to the top of the alleyway, which opens into the middle of the plaza, I stop and blast my people with a sharp wolf whistle. They stumble to a halt and stand looking at me. I feel my power. I explain what I'm going to do. There are a few giggles. I put my fingers to my lip and let out a long, slow 'shuusshhh'.

I turn and step out into Plaza Gomila while they wait in the shadows. I stop for a moment and take in the square in all its glittering glamorous glory.

* * * * * *

There are about twelve cafés all round the tiny square, each with tables and chairs set out in front and waiters dressed in black trousers, white shirts and bowties buzzing around tables groaning with glasses, bottles of champagne in ice buckets, jugs of sangria, plates heaped high with saffron-coloured paella – mussel shells sticking out of the rice like mouse ears and bright orange lobster claws. At this time of night every chair is taken and people are hovering close by tables where others have called for 'la cuenta', the bill, or are making a writing motion in the air in the hope of attracting a waiter's attention.

Women wear long elegant evening dresses in blacks, purples and golds, plenty of makeup and their hair either piled up or immaculately coiffed and suited and booted geezers mingle with tourists fitted out in the latest trendy gear.

Some of the people taking the night air in the square will have moored their luxury yachts in Palma harbour and strolled up to Terreno. Others may have a house in the quiet streets that head up the hill to Castle Bellver.

Still others will have come just to look.

And, in among the crowds, you'll find a fair sprinkling of stars and the occasional superstar, not to mention Eurotrash princes and princesses, buccaneers of industry and, no doubt, all sorts of dodgy characters. They love hanging out in Plaza Gomila because no-one bothers them.

I've seen Engelbert Humperdinck, Shirley Bassey, the singing duo Nina and Frederik, Peter Ustinov and, back in '68, Blossy and me were sure we saw Sidney Potier strolling down the street.

Mainly, the stars come because they're performing at Tito's, a jewel in the crown of Mediterranean nightlife and up there with the Lido in Paris and the Casino in Monte Carlo. Joe's Bar was one of Errol Flynn's favourites when he was on the island. I'd been told the story of how Tito's was given its name by a waiter in Joe's Bar on the square who used to serve a Mr Tito his morning coffee back in the early 1930s when he came to the island.

According to the waiter, Mr Tito was from Sicily by way of Chicago. For some reason, Al Capone had told him he had 24 hours to get out of Chicago but had also given him some money to help him on his way.

Mr Tito opened the original bar on the spot where Tito's night club now stood. But, he was only on the square for a couple of years before moving on to Sicily. The club itself opened in 1957.

I never went to Tito's myself but, some nights, you could hear the music from the famous open air roof terrace. Apparently, the terrace was big enough to take 800 tables round a six-metre wide stage with a red carpeted floor. The Bay of Palma and the Med were the stunning backdrop.

Over the years, Tito's played host to stars that included Tom Jones, Shirley Bassey, Sandie Shaw, Lulu – who climbed up on the bar of one of the other clubs and did a few numbers the amazing tap dancing Clarke Brothers and Ray Charles, who was paid half a million pesetas for a night's work.

Frankie Vaughn, who also played Tito's, liked Majorca so much he became part owner of Mario's, just up from the square towards Palma proper. This was Majorca's first ever Italian restaurant and a huge success until the square started to die and Mario did a runner to Venezuela owing a fortune.

I never met Ray Charles but one time the management of the singer José Feliciano asked if he could plug his latest record down at Alex's. José was a tiny blind Peruvian who'd had a gigantic hit with 'Light My Fire', the Doors song, in the summer of 1968. That was a few years before and José's star had slipped a bit. He was booked to perform at Barbarellas Disco that night and, after that, he wanted to take in the local – well, not the sights but you know what I mean.

Somehow, after José had finished at Barbarellas, I was delegated to walk him down the road to Alex's. 'No problem,' I said, grateful for a chance to take a bit of a breather.

As we're walking back in the direction of Alex's, José says 'I want women and coke.' I tell him I'll do my best.

So we set off through the streets of Terreno. People are laughing, clapping and, depending on whether they know my real or stage name, they're calling out 'all right Tom Brown' or 'how's it going, Louie?'

What José doesn't know is I'm wearing white clogs, pink trousers, a frilly shirt, a bright pink jacket and to top it all off a huge pink Afro wig that looks like someone's stuck a giant dollop of candyfloss on my head.

* * * * * *

Now, while I'm taking in the splendour of Plaza Gomila, I look behind me and realise my natives are getting restless. I pick out a couple dining at a table who look well oiled and in a mellow mood and approach them. 'Excuse me,' I say, 'could you tell me where the famous Alexandra's disco is?'

'Sorry, we're here on holiday,' the man says.

'No, no,' the woman says, pleased with herself. She stands up and points across the square, past Big Pepé the policeman who stands watch in case any lowlifes are about. I follow her pointing hand and see the bright neon sign of Alex's which, obviously, I already know is there.

'Thank you,' I say. I turn to my gang still waiting in the shadows. 'ALEXANDRA'S FORWARD HOOOOOO!' I cry.

And I charge off across the square in the direction of Alex's, with my 150 gleefully whooping followers in hot pursuit.

As I hurtle pass Big Pepé, he shakes his head and says 'buenos noches, Senor Louie.'

He sees my routine at least once every week of our long summers.

EASTER CHARADE

Once we'd decided to keep Alex's open all year round the question was how to get the punters through the door in the months before the boat parties started again towards the end of May.

Tourists started coming to the Rock from about late March. Hotels and all that were cheaper then and, although the weather was changeable it was usually good for three or four days at a time. The sea was always freezing, though.

As far as we were concerned, we had everything in place to start up some sort of party with punters ending up at Alex's. Our ticket salesmen began arriving around the end of the month to find somewhere to live and, of course, they'd be looking for ways to earn some loot.

Our brilliant idea was to come up with what we called 'Wine Cellar Parties' held in a bodega – a Spanish wine cellar. We found one called El Cocodrilo in Palma that looked the business – barrels along the wall, faded bullfight posters, wooden ploughs hanging up. I have absolutely no idea why the place was named after a crocodile.

Our salesmen hustled punters to persuade them to come along to a 'genuwine Spanish bodega' for all they could drink and eat as well as great live entertainment. After the Wine Cellar Parties we'd bus them to Alex's.

The first Wine Cellar Party was a complete disaster. Only six punters showed up, outnumbered by the twenty salesmen who dished out the grub, kept the wine flowing and organised an international drinking contest using the leather Spanish wine flasks called porróns with a spout that squirts wine into your mouth in theory but mostly all over your face and shirt.

The highlight of that first party, the 'great live entertainment', was yours truly in a glittering new persona. I stood with my back to the crowd of six - Miguel the confused, disappointed bodega owner and my salesmen – as Mike Pinker from Brighton shouted 'you've all heard of Gary Glitter, you've heard of Alvin Stardust. But there's a star who's bigger, brighter and shinier than all of them put together. Live, and at great expense, tonight, let's hear it for SIDNEY SPARKLER!!!' And off I went.

Camping it up as Sidney Sparkler, backed by a couple of salesmen with guitars, I led the six punters and Miguel the confused bodega owner in a sing song before introducing my mock marriage routine. I grabbed a couple of punters, stood between them and, pretending to read from the bible, I said 'I hope that, when you return to your hotel after Alexandra's, in the words of my dear, close, personal friend Winston Churchill, it is hard and long, with plenty of comings and goings and with no withdrawals. Now, you may kiss the bride.'

After this we all linked arms and I started the newlyweds, the four extra punters, Miguel the confused bodega owner and my salesmen singing creaky old chestnuts like 'My Bonnie Lies Over The Ocean'.

Sidney Sparkler was obviously a joke but it made me laugh to think I was the same age as Gary Glitter and Alvin Stardust, who'd both been around and trying to make it big since the early 1960s. I may well have rubbed shoulders with them schlepping in out of Tito Burns's office back when I was a hot young songwriter.

* * * * * *

It was Good Friday 1976 and we'd finally managed to sell out a Wine Cellar Party. Four bus loads, two each from Magaluf and El Arenal, were set to meet outside the new, much larger bodega I'd found in central Palma. This place really fit the bill. Muy autentico. Along with the barrels, the posters and so on, it had three or four bull's heads mounted on the wall. Every time I walked in I thought of Blossy's 'must have been running pretty fast to get through the wall' joke and chuckled. You could almost smell the bullshit.

The day before Good Friday I'd phoned the bodega and spoken to one of Juan the owner's waiters and told him to get ready for 200 ravenous, thirsty tourists to clean him out of red wine, pigs legs and lamb.

So, I was more than a little baffled when we rolled up outside the bodega and there were no lights on in the gaff. I smiled a weak smile at the excited busload of punters – feeling not at all like Sidney Sparkler – climbed down and under the arch that led into the bodega. Pinned on the huge ancient oak door was a hand written note that said something like 'cerado para semana santa....abierto martes...'

My Spanish was not that great – I obviously hadn't managed to make myself understood to Juan's waiter – but even I could understand that the joint was closed. The waiter must have thought I meant the following Friday or something.

Heart beating like a jackhammer, I took a deep breath, turned on my heel and walked back to where my salesmen had gathered ready to show the punters into the bodega and get the party started.

'The place is closed,' I hissed.

'Are you sure?' one bright spark asked.

Taking another deep breath I said 'yes, I am sure, thank you very much.'

Panic started to ripple through the salesmen, most of whom had already spent the commission they'd earned on the party and were having visions of being torn limb from limb by an angry, thirsty, starving mob.

I watched like a sweating zombie as a couple of bottles of Bustaids were passed round and for once I didn't help myself. All the speed would do was accelerate the panic and I really didn't want my heart beating any faster than it was already.

I looked up the night sky. It had started to rain. I sent up a silent prayer. And then, unbelievably, a brainwave! El Cocodrilo was just round the corner. I hurried my jabbering salesmen onto the buses and told the lead bus driver to head to El Cocodrilo. Sending a prayer up to any saint that was listening, I clutched the Star of David I always wore round my neck and crossed my fingers and toes.

Through the rain, which was now falling steadily, I saw the shining neon jaws of a crocodile. I only realised I'd been holding my breath when I let it out. Salesmen started to cheer. Some may even have cried.

I rushed inside. Miguel was sitting behind the bar reading a newspaper. Three tables were occupied by couples having a quiet, candlelit dinner. One pair were billing and cooing, the other two were ignoring each other and having a hissed argument, in that order. 'Miguel,' I cried as I scurried up to him, fixing a weak grin to my skull. He looked up, not exactly pleased to see me. I'd not thought twice about shifting the Wine Cellar Parties to a rival bodega, don't think I'd even told him I was going to do it. I figured my only option now was to give him no chance get a word in edgeways and throw myself on his mercy. 'Look, Miguel,' I said, 'I've had a disaster. Do you have lots of cheap vino, even cheaper Spanish champagne, chicken or beefsteak?'

'Si,' he said slowly, raising an eyebrow. 'Why?'

'I have a group waiting outside who've been promised a Wine Cellar Party and...'

'The other place isn't open?' He said this very softly. I nodded. 'And now you want me to help you?' I nodded again. Miguel chuckled, then started to laugh. He shook his head. 'What if I said no?'

I shrugged, gulped. 'You can double what you charged us before,' I said.

'Thank you,' he said. 'I will. How many people?'

'150 más o menus.'

'You are doing well, then?' I nodded again. I could see exactly where this was going. 'I'm sorry...', Miguel said, shaking his head. I looked up, forced myself not to fall on my knees and beg. 'I only have chicken,' Miguel the sadist said. 'No beefsteak. It's OK for you?'

'Anything, anything,' I squeaked. I could have kissed him.

'Vale,' Miguel said. He smiled at me, put a hand on my shoulder. 'You move the tables like we used to have them and I'll start with the food.'

I shot outside, gave my salesmen the thumbs up. They hurtled in, fizzing with Bustaid energy and rearranged the tables into long rows in seconds. The punters filed in and took their places, the vino started to flow and the games commenced.

The three Spanish couples wolfed their meals down pronto and left. At least we'd given the arguing couple something they could agree on.

I have to say, Miguel did us proud. He rang round his family and friends to rustle up some waiters and waitresses and managed to serve every punter a small plate of chicken, chorizo sausage, chips, a lettuce leaf, half a tomato and some of that funny tinned white asparagus stuff that looks like dead man's fingers, followed by ice-cream or crema Catalan in plastic pots.

Sidney Sparkler started his sing-song early that night and married four couples instead of one. The international drinking contest went on way beyond the limits of sensible boozing, fuelled by gallons of plonk that Miguel had probably despaired of ever shifting. But, a disaster was averted.

After the last punter had wobbled out the door, I downed the chopito of Hierbas, the Majorcan aniseed liqueur, Miguel put in front of me on the bar. Without saying anything, he filled the shot glass again. I downed that one too. He filled it again. 'What can I say, Miguel?' I said.

'Nothing,' Miguel said. He licked his pen and looked back down at the bill he'd been working out. He did a final calculation and slapped it down in front of me, grinning. I held it up to the light, pretended I was going to faint and theatrically threw my right hand over my heart. Miguel laughed. I pulled the wad of notes my salesmen had collected from the punters and passed on to me out of my pocket and began the long, slow process of counting out money for Miguel while he kept me fuelled with shots of medicinal Hierbas to numb the pain.

When I'd finished, Miguel looked at the money then up at me and said 'you learned something tonight, Louie, no?'

'I did,' I said. We shook hands and I walked out the door.

* * * * * *

I was surprised to see Curly waiting outside Alex's as the coaches pulled up and vomited out tipsy, happy punters ready to strut their funky stuff, chattering, relieved salesmen and a well-oiled Sidney Sparkler.

Given Curly's boat race it was hard to tell when he was more pissed off than usual but I was sure I could see steam escaping from his ears and into the wet night air. As our salesmen led punters down the stairs into Alex's, he pulled me to one side and said 'there's a problem. We can't play any disco music until after midnight'. I looked at him, blinked, burped and then down at my watch. 10.30.

'Why?'

'It's the law isn't it? It's Easter Friday so there's no pop music allowed. Even the radio's only playing religious stuff.'

'Who's going to know?' I said.

'The cops come round checking.'

'What are we going to do, then?' I said.

'I don't know,' Curly said. 'You're Louie The Lip, Sidney Sparkler. Think of something.'

'I can't,' I said, burping again.

'Right,' Curly said, 'we'll get 'em inside, give 'em a free drink and tell them the sound system's broken down until you can think of something.'

'Jesus Christ,' I said. 'Nobody told me.'

'Nobody told me either,' Curly said. It was one of those times when we were reminded we lived and worked in a foreign country which, at that time, was under the control of a fascist dictator.

I looked up at the sky, thought of my prayer outside the bodega, shook my head and repeated 'Jesus Christ. Thanks for nothing, mate.'

'It's not my bleedin' fault,' Curly said.

'I wasn't talking to you,' I said over my shoulder as I trudged down to the club. Oh, what a night!

* * * * * *

After twenty minutes or so of silence, the punters' complaints began to get louder. I knew I had to do something. 'Have you got anything suitable in your box we can play?' I whined to Eddy, our resident DJ from Luton.

'I've looked,' he said.

'Look again,' I said. 'Please.'

Eddy sighed but bent over his record box and started flipping through discs. After a few seconds, he said 'Jesus, I don't believe it.'

'What?' I said.

He turned to me, grinning, and handed me the record he'd found.

'Jesus Christ...' I said.

'...Superstar,' he finished for me. 'I didn't even know I had it. Wasn't there when I looked before. But the cops can't make a fuss about this, can they?'

'Just play it,' I said. 'Play it now!'

He slipped the record out of its sleeve, put the needle to the vinyl and the overture to Jesus Christ Superstar blasted out. I saw one punter jump out of her skin.

Right away, Curly came running over. 'What are you doing? You want the cops in here? Get that shit off now!'

Eddie and I smiled at each other. The band began to play the famous 'Jesus Christ Superstar' theme. Curly looked at us and, unbelievably, started to laugh until tears were running down his cheeks. I'd never seen him laugh like that. I thought he was going to burst something.

For the next hour, Eddie switched between 'I Don't Know How To Love Him', the slow one, and 'Superstar'. Thankfully, the punters really got into it, throwing themselves around the floor madly.

But when the clock struck midnight, there was only one superstar in the place. Tom Brown AKA Sidney Sparkler AKA Louie The Lip got the party started.

With more than a little help from his friends upstairs.

WOULD YOU LIKE A KNUCKLE SANDWICH WITH THAT?

Ever since I'd been on the Rock, a character called Gary had been knocking around. He was a little Northern bloke, pushy and likely to flare up for the slightest reason.

Gary had been a rival to Blossy and me, heading up a team of PRs who worked for different clubs to us and now he was always nipping at Curly and my heels.

Mind you, as Gary was trying to build up his empire he didn't have a lot of luck. At one point he ran party boats to the caves at Cap Falcó, just up from Magaluf where there was a disco.

As with all the caves in Majorca, there were stalactites hanging down from the roof that had built up over thousands of years and the disco punters danced beneath them. One party night, a young lad was dancing away and a stalagtite fell from the ceiling onto him. He wasn't killed outright but died of his injuries later in hospital. I guess the loud, thumping music must have sent out vibrations that weakened the stalagtites. What a way to go!

The Old Bill wanted to know who'd bought the group into the disco and Gary had to lay low for a while.

* * * * * *

The English people who started coming to the Rock from the early 1960s onwards with the arrival of cheap flights and mass tourism were often going abroad for the first time.

Many of them only came for sun, sea and sand – and maybe sex – not to immerse themselves in Spanish culture. In any case, they saw Spain as hopelessly backward, a place where nothing worked, the water gave you the trots, food was greasy and stank of garlic – like the people – and everything was put off until mañana.

Carry On Abroad, set in a half-finished hotel on a fictional island called Els Bels pretty much sums up the cartoon version of Spain.

Because they had this perception of Spain, many British tourists wanted to eat English food, drink familiar beer and stick with tourists who spoke their language. So, it wasn't long before English people started coming out to the Rock, and other parts of Spain, to live and try their luck running English bars and restaurants.

It looked like an easy way to live the dream. Sometimes it was, often it wasn't.

First of all, there were conmen who made a good living parting dreamers from their money. It's terrible, but there was a time when me and my pals used to help an English guy who sold bars unload them onto unsuspecting would-be investors.

This guy, whose name was John, would look for bars that were obviously going under, do a deal, get them cheap and search for suckers. Once he'd found one, he'd ask us to fill up the place and make it look like the bar was a proper little goldmine. We'd get paid in free beer.

So, the sucker would buy the bar and be totally baffled when he opened the place and we were nowhere to be seen.

John sold at least six bars that I know of this way.

He sold a bar to a bloke called Jim in Can Pastilla. The bar was a dead loss and Jim's wife left him. His son kept trying to run away. The police would find him at the airport and bring him back.

We used to go into the bar to play pinball and we'd always win. So the only people who went in his bar used to win money off him.

Every now and then someone would come in asking for John. 'Jim's the name,' the guy would say. 'John's the bastard who sold me this place.'

Like I say, I'm not proud of what we did but I was amazed that people looking to buy a bar didn't do the obvious thing and rent an apartment in the area first to see how popular it really was before investing.

But that was so often the story on the Rock. People, often really smart businessmen, seemed to become idiots the minute they stepped out of the airport. Majorca was heaven for conmen. The place was full of bogus royalty and nobility from all the four corners of the globe.

Having said that, there were other people who did make it work.

* * * * * *

The Lotus was a restaurant just outside Can Pastilla run by three retired people from Liverpool who'd won the pools and gone to Spain.

Hilda took the orders at the tables. Jack was the chef. Steve, Hilda's husband served the drinks. And they worked hard to build up a reputation for serving the best Sunday roasts anywhere on the island.

Two of my salesmen stumbled across The Lotus and spread the word among us. For my mates, who were often homesick for good British cooking, the Lotus was a godsend. I, on the other hand, loved tapas and paella and could cheerfully have lived on them for ever.

Every Sunday, around 15 of us would whizz up on our scooters and tuck into a huge roast. The menu was always the same – you had four choices – but Hilda would insist on rattling off the options as if it was the first time we'd ever been there.

As well as roasts, The Lotus made delicious homemade pasties and puddings.

We became addicts and started going every day.

As soon as The Lotus had started getting more popular, Gary's boys found out about it and began to come in. We didn't like it but we couldn't stop them.

* * * * * *

It started with a bit of staring, face-pulling and the odd hand air-wanker gesture being exchanged between my table of 12 salesmen and roughly the same number at Gary's. Gary and me just nodded to each other. We never had a problem. The needle was between Curly and Gary.

A week before, Curly had flattened one of Gary's salesmen, a lad called Irish, for slagging off our boat parties to the punters.

Along with our two tables, there were maybe 20 Brits out to enjoy a quiet Sunday lunch.

So we're sitting there and Curly comes walking through the door with Yvonne. He's decided to join us for the roast. The place goes silent. Curly takes one look at Gary, grinning defiantly up at him, strides over and without saying anything starts laying into him.

Two of Gary's boys dive onto Curly, who's well ahead on points. We try to pull them off. And then the place erupts. Gary's boys start hurling chairs at us. We do the same. Plates of beautiful roast beef are going everywhere. The air is thick with gravy, apple sauce and horseradish. I set myself up to throw a punch but slip on a roast potato and go down. My white strides are covered.

Once they get over the shock, Hilda and Steve open the front doors to let out the other terrified Brits. Jack comes out of the kitchen carrying a huge carving knife. Gary's lot get thrown out, one by one.

When it's only our crew left, Curly makes a big apology to Hilda, saying he'll pay for the damage. But, it's already been done.

Hilda folds her meaty forearms on her bosom, says 'you're all barred. Don't any of you ever set foot in here again.' Her Scouse voice, usually so sweet, is trembling with anger.

And that's the end of The Lotus for all of us.

THE PR'S BIG DAY OUT

1977. Once Curly and I had made a roaring success of the boat parties it wasn't difficult to convince the clubs in Arenal, C'an Pastilla and Magaluf we were in a great position to steer punters in their direction.

We did a deal with the three biggest clubs – Zorba's in Arenal, Kiss in C'an Pastilla and Sir Lawrence in Magaluf - which meant our salesmen would hand out cards giving a discount on the door for their joint to whomever they stopped. Most people would only go on a beach party once during their holiday so this gave the salesmen an extra income. The salesmen put their names on the cards so we knew who to pay a commission to.

At the end of every month, we would pay out 25 pesetas per card to every salesman with his name on the cards collected by the clubs.

Naturally, Curly and I also got a kickback from the clubs.

* * * * * *

Curly and I ran our operations with the closest we could get to military precision, Curly because he couldn't stand the thought of missing out on a single shekel, me because I was a competitive sod and I wanted us to be the best.

We also knew that our people faced a parade of mouth-watering temptations every night from birds and blokes on holiday – some of our best salesmen were girls – free booze and the sheer pleasure of staying up till the small hours on those long hot summer nights.

If any of our PRs turned up late or didn't show at all they were docked a percentage of the money they earned from the clubs. Curly and I hung on to it. This money paid for our company treats.

One treat I came up with was a day trip to the other side of the island, to a place called Ses Covetes on the sandy south coast about thirty kilometres down from Palma.

* * * * * *

Come the day, our sixty salesmen and women gathered at the pick up points in Magaluf and C'an Pastilla and were collected by the bus. It made me laugh to see that some of the people who arrived first were the worst offenders for getting to work late.

The driver was an easygoing fat bloke with huge sweat patches under the arms of his pale blue short-sleeved shirt who was looking forward to an easy day out.

Curly and Yvonne took the pair of seats immediately behind the driver, like schoolteachers do but I headed for the back of the bus. Like naughty kids do.

I couldn't believe how excited my salesmen were to be going on a jaunt until it dawned on me that they spent their summer hustling for a living and their days off recovering from the ferocious pace of their life. Most of them hadn't left the resort where they worked since they'd washed up on the Rock.

Soon we were singing away. Some of us were sipping breakfast beers from the crates of San Miguel we'd bought along. A game of Pontoon started. A girl from Gidea Park in East London and a bloke from Brighton started snogging.

We had the windows open and as we went through the island towns and villages – collections of cardboard boxes leading up to a church spire in the middle – we'd whistle at any pretty girl we saw. We left a fair number of short, fat outraged old ladies dressed in black in our wake.

And all the while Curly sat ramrod straight, his Afro turning from left to right as he pointed things out to Yvonne.

From C'an Pastilla we drove inland through countryside baked dry and bone white by the summer heat to a biggish town called Llucmajor. Just outside town we turned right and began our drive towards Ses Covetes.

'Why don't we check out that place?' I don't know whose idea it was but it turned out to be a great one. Kind of.

'That place' looked a bit like a castle at first glance. A dirty big sign advertised Majorica pearls and traditional liqueurs.

Don't ask me how I know this but the only reason pearls came to be associated with Majorca is because of this. About 100 years ago, this German bloke invented a process for making pearls out of glass, mother of pearl and plastic which were much cheaper and easier to produce than the real thing. Obviously.

The German bloke moved to Majorca, outside a town called Manacor, and started a factory making the pearls which later became a big hit with the tourists as Majorica pearls.

So much for Majorica pearls. The liqueur place was what we were really interested in. Especially when the driver told us we could try free samples of all kinds of liqueurs at the fake castle. He should have known better than to tell us that.

* * * * * *

Forty-five minutes later, we fell out of Castle Piss-up into the blinding mid-day sunlight. Or, at least, sixty-one of us staggered out. It looked like someone had dropped a booze bomb and we'd been caught in the shockwaves.

Standing in the shade of a tree, tapping his foot but trying to stay calm, Curly still had his military bearing. He didn't drink and Yvonne wouldn't dare overdo it around him. 'It's not ladylike, Yvonne.'

Behind us, the bus driver was being given a bollocking in Majorcan by one of the owners of the liqueur place. He sounded like an extremely angry crow. All the driver could say was 'si, si'. Not only wasn't he going to get a kickback from the castle for steering us to them, he was going to have to wait a while before he bought any more coach-loads back that way.

The other owner just stood and watched us with his mouth open as we weaved in the vague direction of the bus. There must have been about a hundred barrels of booze, all different shades of brown, yellow, green and some colours that shouldn't have been allowed. We'd each been given a small tasting glass to make sure we only took a little snifter, a strategy which probably worked well with normal, polite tourists.

Not us.

We'd taken it as a personal challenge to sink as much as possible and managed to drain more than a few barrels dry. It was a heroic effort. I was proud of us.

And we hadn't bought a single bottle of liqueur.

* * * * * *

From Llucmajor the countryside rolled gently downwards towards the coast. Dry stone walls followed the road as it wound between more low hills of white earth. Off in the distance, a huge biscuit-coloured finca stood on a hill. Closer to the coast, the road ran between sea salt flats. After we'd been driving for about twenty minutes, someone called out 'I can see the sea' and there it was, glittering in the distance.

'Are we there yet, daddy?' another person shouted. Laughter all round.

'Piss off,' from Curly. More laughter.

And then we were parking up and bursting out of the bus into the shocking heat of the day. There was heat haze over the tarmac. A sandy track led down to Ses Covetes beach and the salesmen shot off down it. They were in the sea ducking and splashing water at each other in seconds.

Curly, Yvonne and I followed at a more genteel pace or with as much dignity as I could summon. My feet kept getting tangled up. I knew I shouldn't have had that last shot of Green Chartreuse.

'You'd think they'd never seen the sea,' Curly said, shading his eyes with his hand. 'They work next to it every day of their lives.'

I wanted to say that this may have been true but the salesmen had never seen an empty beach which wasn't ringed by tall hotels before. There was no-one else at Ses Covetes. We had the whole place to ourselves.

* * * * * *

I don't know how long I'd been out for the count but when I woke up I had a stinking headache and I could feel my face pulsing from the sun. Someone was kicking me, not too gently. Then I heard Curly's unmistakable nasal tones. 'Come on, Louie, time to go. Rise and shine or we'll leave you here. Shake a leg.'

I opened my eyes and sat up. Everything spun round a little before it righted itself. Curly held out a hand to me, I took it and he yanked me up so hard he nearly took my arm out of its socket.

Somewhere up the coast the sun was going down behind the mountains and we cast long shadows as we followed the exhausted PRs up the lane and back to the bus through the soft late afternoon sunlight. Looking around I saw that everyone had the dazed, sleepy faces of happy, if still slightly tipsy, kids.

I only realised that one of our guys was missing when we got to the outskirts of Llucmajor. 'Here, where's Lee?' I said to Johnny Kwango, lolling next to me on the back seat of the bus with his eyes closed.

Lee Dorrington from Crawley was a bit of a nutter. He was harmless but able to take anything to the land beyond the joke. If anyone could have been washed out to sea by a freak wave or dragged off by a rogue shark it would have been him.

I nudged Kwango again. 'Where's Lee?'

'Dunno.'

'Huh?'

'Ask Curly.'

I stood up and walked down the bus, holding onto headrests to steady myself. 'Curly,' I said, when I'd reached his seat, 'where's Lee Dorrington?'

He looked up at me, smiled his tight smile. 'No idea,' he said.

I laughed. 'Good one, Curl. Really, where is he?' Curly looked up at me. His smile got bigger. And I remembered Curly didn't joke.

'Tranquilo, Louie,' Curly said. 'He's a big boy. Well, he isn't – he's a little runt – but you know what I mean.' Curly started nodding his head up and down. 'You don't mind do you?' I started nodding myself. This was one of Curly's tricks to get you to think you'd agreed with him. He'd started nodding his head up and down. You'd get mesmerised and, before you knew it, you'd be nodding yourself. 'Thought you didn't. Lovely day wasn't it? Not that you saw too much. You crashed right out, didn't he, Yvonne?' Yvonne smiled sheepishly at me. 'You want to put something on that sunburn,' Curly said. 'You'll look horrible tomorrow. Trying for a Charlie Chin on the boat were you?'

I thought for a minute. 'Charlie Chin? Oh yeah. It's Charlie Chan, Curly. Charlie Chan suntan.' I walked off towards the back of the bus shaking my head.

* * * * * *

It turned out that Lee Dorrington had started getting out of order, like he always did and some of the other guys had found this old cave with a wooden door and a length of rope in it, used for tying up boats or something. They'd tied Lee Dorrington up, thrown him in the cave, shut the door and blocked it with big boulders.

Kwango was one of the culprits.

It took Lee two days to get back to Magaluf.

237

TURKEY TROT

I'd say summer 1977 was as good as it ever got for Alexandra's. It was blinding. But by the time October rolled around we were down to just one wine cellar party a week.

And, although Alex's stayed open all year round now, as we approached Christmas things got very quiet indeed, which was to be expected. Still, our crew of diehard salesmen who had absolutely no desire to go back to the UK or Scandinavia kept going, sniffing out punters wherever they could.

By now, I knew what winter in Majorca was like but the way the weather changed around the middle of November was still a massive shock to the system. The buildings went the colour of old cardboard boxes. People who'd had deep tans a couple of weeks before started to look like they had some incurable disease, their skin going like tobacco. The wind howled and it drizzled with rain for days on end, the damp getting right into your bones.

It was cold but never *really* satisfyingly cold like it was back home or in Scandinavia.

What amazed me was the way the Majorcans seemed to make no allowances for the cold weather. The bars were never heated, which made them just miserable. I don't think the Majorcans have a word for 'cosy'.

One winter, for some reason I've blotted out of my memory, the only way I had of keeping warm was a hair dryer!

Somehow, Christmas was made worse by the fact that the Majorcans didn't really celebrate it. Their big day was The Three Kings on January 6th, when the three kings bought Jesus their gifts. But, the Brits, Krauts and Scandies living on the Rock were programmed to start celebrating in the lead up to Christmas. So the so-called festive season went on and on.

On one memorable Christmas, I decided to buy a turkey and invite the boys and some Yank sailors we'd met the night before at Alex's round for a traditional British style dinner. We went out on the piss, leaving the turkey in the oven on a low heat. When we got back to my gaff, fire engines were gathered outside, sirens blaring. Smoke poured out the window of my apartment and onto the terrace. A crowd had gathered and people were pointing. I dashed upstairs, opened my front door, fought my way through the thick black smoke that smelt of burnt turkey and saw that the bird I'd bought was so big it had actually tipped over my oven and set fire to the fat it was cooking in. I'd also forgotten to take the plastic bag of giblets out of the turkey, which made the smoke even more toxic.

So now I had the winter blues and business was slow. But, worst of all I was missing my daughter Maria, now four years old and living with Gun and her grandparents in Southern Sweden.

* * * * * *

It was around 5AM on the morning of Christmas Eve when I woke up feeling utterly miserable. I lay under the covers in my gloomy bedroom and thought 'I can't stand any more of this'.

'Why can't you just take off for Sweden?' I said to my self.

'Why not indeed?' my self replied.

'Shall we go then?'

'Why ever not? Let's do the off now.'

'After you.'

'No, after you.'

Me and myself shot out of bed, retrieved cash from where I'd stashed it all over the apartment, found our passport, after a bit of searching, swearing and stubbing of toes, threw some clothes into a holdall and we were set to go.

There was no point telling Curly what I was going to do. He'd have muttered and complained, even though we were meant to be equal partners and he couldn't stop me doing what I wanted.

Sitting in the back of a cab heading down the Paseo Maritimo in the direction of the airport – the sea a horrible snot green colour – I saw Johnny Kwango, hunched against the wind howling off the Med and trying to blag a couple of punters. Unbelievably, they were wearing shorts and t-shirts, arms and legs a bluey-pink colour. I leant forward, tapped the cabbie on the shoulder. 'Parada aqui, por favor,' I said. He grunted something that might have been a question or insult. 'Aqui, por favor. Una momentito.' The guy stopped and I rolled down the window. 'Oi, Kwango, over here,' I shouted. He ambled across, leaving the punters to scuttle off down the Paseo.

'Where you off to, boss?' Kwango said.

'Airport, mate.' He raised an eyebrow. 'Going to see Maria in Sweden. At least, that's the plan. Depends on if I can get a flight to Copenhagen but, if my luck's in, I'm out of here.'

'Fair enough.'

'But, listen, if I don't turn up tonight, I'll have found a flight. So, if Curly says anything, keep schtum. I don't want him knowing. OK?'

'Sure. Good luck, chief.' He stuck his freezing cold hand through the window. I shook it. 'Merry Christmas,' he said.

'Same to you,' I said. ''Ere, your punters are getting away.' Johnny grinned, turned round and raced off down the

Paseo. 'Aeropuerto,' I said to the driver, 'muy pronto.' He grunted again and we were off.

The route to the airport took us through a neighbourhood called Coll d'en Rabassa, once a small town on the edge of Palma but now part of the concrete strip extending up the coast east of the city. As always, the street was clogged with cars.

We stopped at a set of traffic lights. I looked sideways and then I saw them. A row of ten of the biggest turkeys I'd ever seen in my life – even bigger than the one that had almost burnt my apartment to the ground. I had an idea. 'Parada, aqui,' I said. The cabbie twisted round in his seat to look at me. 'Parada, por favor.' His shrug said it all. I hopped out of the cab, the lights changed and he pulled forward and halfway up onto the pavement.

Inside the butchers, I unhooked the biggest turkey from the rail it hung down from, dragged it onto the startled butcher's counter and asked him how much he wanted for it. He looked at me, down at the turkey and at the little old lady who was next in the queue. 'Pardon, senora,' I said, 'aeropuerto, rapido, muy rapido,' she smiled, showing lipstick stained false teeth and waved me forward. 'Gracias,' I said, 'muchas, muchas gracias'. The butcher wrestled the turkey to the scales, hefted it on and weighed it. The thing probably weighed as much as Maria. The butcher gave me a piece of paper: 13 kilos = 2000 pesetas. I paid him from my wad of cash, danced out of the shop with the turkey, much to the little old lady's delight and got the beast into the back of the cab. Without saying a word, the driver watched as I stuffed the turkey into my holdall and covered it over with clothes. When I'd done the best I could, I said 'aeropuerto…'

'Muy pronto,' he said. 'Si, si, senor.' And we pulled back out into the traffic.

* * * * * *

The girl at the Iberia ticket office was very sympathetic. Especially as I'd told her, fingers crossed behind my back, that my daughter was very sick and I had to get to Sweden that day, no matter what.

'Sorry,' she said, looking up at me from where she sat. 'All flights to Denmark are full. It's Christmas.'

'Please check again,' I said. 'I'm desperate.' The wobble in my voice wasn't acting. I was getting more choked up and frustrated by the second. I looked at her name tag. 'Please, Silvia. I'll take anything.'

Silvia looked at a sheaf of paper on her clipboard. 'Wait,' she said. 'I've found a flight to Copenhagen but you have to go via Nice?'

'Great,' I said. Although I was going to Sweden, the easiest way to get to Gun's place was via Denmark. I would fly to Copenhagen then take the Flying Boat, as they called it, over to Malmo, which took about 40 minutes.

Silvia smiled, which gave her very cute dimples. 'Right. Your flight to Nice is at 12 – in two hours – you wait in

Nice for a couple more hours and you'll be in Copenhagen by four.'

I bought my ticket, gave Silvia a peck on both cheeks, took her telephone number and headed off to wait for my flight.

* * * * * *

The Danish customs officer looked down at the turkey he'd hauled out of my bag and back to me. 'So, you have no clothes but you have a turkey. Why, please?'

My bottom lip trembled. I crossed my fingers behind my back again. 'It's my daughter, Maria. She's very ill. The last thing she said before...' I gulped, tried to carry on, 'before...'

'Go,' he said. 'Now.' He stamped my passport. I shook his hand, caught the strong smell of alcohol on his breath and left before he had a chance to change his mind.

It was, of course, freezing in Copenhagen. And dark. The air was so cold it felt like someone had rammed an ice-pick down my throat every time I breathed in and the snow stung like shrapnel. I climbed into the back of the first taxi on the rank, shivering and blowing on my hands. 'The port, please. Rapi...quickly. Need to get to Malmo.'

The driver, whose breath also stank of booze, looked into his rearview mirror. 'There are no crossings, my friend,' he said. 'The ice is frozen too thick. Maybe in a few days.'

'You're kidding,' I said. He shook his head. 'But, I have to get there, my sick daughter is waiting for me. I've come all the way from Majorca in Spain to see her.' Now, I was close to tears for real.

'I'm sorry,' the driver said. 'I understand but there is thick ice. It's impossible. You want I drive you to a hotel?'

'No, no,' I said, opening the car and stepping out into the snow, which was getting heavier by the second. 'Thanks anyway.'

We stood there, the turkey and me. 'What do we do now?' I said. My face, fingers and toes were beginning to go numb. At least the turkey couldn't feel the cold. He said nothing.

I had no idea what to do, except to stand there and freeze to death. The taxi pulled away. I watched the tail-lights as they lit up the snow falling across them. The taxi stopped, reversed until it drew level with me. The back door opened. 'Get in,' the driver said. 'I have an idea.' I climbed into the boozy warmth, too exhausted and frozen to care about what was or wasn't going to happen next. I drank from the hipflask of schnapps the driver had given me while he told me his plan, the liquor scorching my throat as it went down. 'There's a boat leaving Helsingor, which is along the coast, for Helsingborg in Sweden in three hours time. And the ferry's running. I know, I took someone there earlier today.'

'Fantastic,' I said, through numb lips. 'Let's go.'

'I can't take you, my friend,' the driver said. 'It's Christmas Eve, I am expected home with my family in an hour. The drive from here to Helsingor and back to my home will take two hours. It is more than my life is worth.'

I wanted to scream and cry at the same time. 'Of course, of course, I understand,' I said. 'You go. I'll figure something out.' Slowly, feeling completely beaten up, I opened the cab door.

'Wait,' the driver said. 'Wait here. I have another idea.'

He thrust the hipflask of schnapps into my hand and climbed a little unsteadily out of the cab. I watched as he disappeared into the snowy night, took another drink of schnapps. 'What a day, mate,' I said to the turkey. He said nothing.

The driver appeared out of the snow, climbed into his seat which, I noticed, had one of those beaded things covering it, to protect against back ache. 'It is all arranged,' he said. 'You are coming home to my house where you will have dinner with my family. Then I will drive you to the ferry at Helsingor.' This time tears welled up in my eyes for real. I coughed. The driver turned round, slapped my knee, said 'the shnapps, it's good for the cold, yes? Must be a very different from

Spain,' I nodded, not sure if I could say anything, handed him back the flask. He took a long drink, corked it and we eased off into the snow.

Ten minutes later I was sitting round the table with Eric the cab driver, his confused wife and two wide-eyed little girls, stuffing my face with duck and herring washed down with strong Carlsberg beer and more schnapps. As soon as we'd finished, Eric handed me a huge cigar and said 'time to go'. I kissed the confused wife and girls, wished them Merry Christmas, picked up the turkey and followed Eric out the door.

At Helsingor, Eric dropped me off at the quayside. I hugged him, stuffed a wad of 1000 peseta bills into his hand, told him to look me up if he was ever in Majorca and slipped off across the icy road to buy my ticket for Helsingen. Before I went on board, I called Gun, asked her to meet me, not to ask any questions, and, above all, not to tell Maria I was on my way.

* * * * * *

I stood outside Gun's parents house, my feet blocks of ice inside my light Spanish shoes, hands stuffed inside the pockets of Gun's coat, which was too small for me but was stopping me from freezing to death. It was no longer snowing and the night was still. Lights twinkled. Smoke drifted from chimneys. The church bells rang. I wouldn't have been surprised if a sleigh pulled by reindeer hadn't come swooping out of the sky. The front door opened, light and warmth spilled out, and Maria, my own little angel, stood on the doorstep looking up at me, her brown eyes wide. For a second, she stood there with her mouth open then she squealed 'daddy, daddy!' and threw herself into my arms. I hugged her to me as hard as I could and we stepped inside.

* * * * * *

Three days later I was back in Majorca and getting ready for Alex's big New Year's bash. Curly had gone into one when I got back but I knew he understood why I had to go. He just couldn't show it, could he?

JASON AND THE PUPPETS

It was the end of 1977. We stayed open right up until New Year's at this point. If you've ever celebrated New Year's in Spain, you'll know that the big ritual is to eat 12 grapes at midnight, one for every stroke of the clock.

I was given the job of preparing the grapes, which meant bagging up 500 sets of 12 – 6,000 of the buggers. Talk about the Grapes of Wrath.

Still, the night was a huge success with the Spanish and we closed the club as the sun was coming up.

* * * * * *

February 1978 and gloomy, grey London was getting to me, like it always did. I recharged my batteries, ticked off the list of things I loved doing in the Smoke – catch up with my mates, go to football and eat my weight in bagels from the 24-hour shop on Brick Lane - and, after that, I got itchy feet all over again.

Peter DeLovely, one of my salesmen who'd become a good pal, was in the UK and kicking his heels. I got the feeling that, as he began to know me better, Peter was kind of intrigued by my eye for an outrageous scam, almost superhuman skills as a salesman and golden spiel. At that time, Peter was a nice middle-class boy from the home counties but someone who instinctively knew he didn't want a conventional 9 to 5 number.

Peter Ratcliffe AKA DeLovely was skinny, 22 and a good looking bugger with shoulder-length hair, the charm of the devil and the gift of the gab, which was why he got the nickname DeLovely. He was one of the best PRs I'd ever seen in my ten years on the scene.

DeLovely had been around since 1972, when he came over on holiday. He'd met one of my salesmen called Ginger Jason, who'd sold him a ticket for a beach party then invited him to one of our do's at the bar-b-q place in Arenal where we all hung out.

Me and DeLovely had got chatting when we'd met for a drink at a place near Barbarellas, after he'd been on another beach party. I liked him and offered him a job.

We'd become closer when Gun decided she wasn't coming back to the Rock. Peter had split with his girlfriend around the same time and we bonded in the way that guys going through that particularly joyful experience will. We were both good listeners but, most of all, we had the same zany sense of humour.

We were sitting in a pub somewhere around the arse end of the Kings Road one lunchtime, our rain-soaked winklepicker shoes steaming gently as they dried off in the smoky fug of the saloon bar, a barely touched pint in front of me, the last third of Peter's second before him. He drank faster than anyone I'd ever met. It was like he ate his beer. 'Christ, I'm sick of this place,' Peter said.

'We could always go to another boozer.'

'No, this country. The UK.'

'I know what you mean.' Even with the winter weather at its worst on the Rock, the days were mostly bright and sunny and it really made me feel alive. Most days in London, the sky looked like someone had spilt ink over it. After a few weeks, it felt as if there was grey ink behind your eyes. And, a lot of the time, I trudged around like a zombie. But, I didn't want to go back to the Rock, to Curly and Alex's just yet. I followed the blue smoke from my cigarette as it uncurled into the cloud hanging below the ornate London pub ceiling. I could feel Peter willing me to come up with a scheme. I said the first thing that came into my head. 'Why don't we go to Sweden?'

'So you can see Maria and Gun? Stangs that.' Stangs was our own private word that meant at least four different things. Here it meant 'leave it out'. 'I'm not going thousands of miles to be a gooseberry or Uncle DeLovely.'

'No, not to see them, that wasn't what I was thinking. Honest.' And it wasn't, which surprised me. But, now DeLovely had mentioned it, it wasn't such a bad idea. 'No, we could do a bit of promo for Alex's, hook up with some of the lads in Stockholm and have a laugh.'

Peter grinned, he nodded. 'Nice one, Senor Lip. It'll be brass monkeys all the way and I, for one, am skint, but it's a great idea. How we going to get there?'

'Did I ever tell you about the time me and the original Beach Boys bought a Bedford van and drove round Europe? Back in '67.'

'No, daddy,' Peter put his face into a cartoon of childish eagerness, 'but I'd thimply love to!'

'Sod off,' I laughed. 'Seriously…'

'Lou, you've told me that story Christ knows how many times,' DeLovely said. 'Bleedin' Beach Boys. But, if I understand you correctly, you're suggesting we buy a van and drive to Sweden, yes?'

'Si, senor,' I said. 'And, we'll cover our costs by loading up with these hat umbrellas I've found in a warehouse just off the Whitechapel Road. The Harris Tweeds in Stockers will go made for them.'

Peter looked baffled for a second. 'Harris Tweeds? Oh yeah, I get it. Swedes. OK,' he said, 'why not?' He necked what was left of his pint, stood up, looked down at my beer. 'Let's have another to celebrate. You going to drink that?'

'Eventually, yes. We're not all like you.'

'Drop of short?'

'Nah. I'm fine with this.'

'Fair enough. I'll be back in a mo and we can start planning.'

I watched as Peter almost bounced up to the bar. Within seconds he had a smile pulling at the corners of the mouth of the surly barmaid and by the time he'd turned round with his pint she was laughing and shaking her head. Peter was amazing like that and he was also a fantastic 'why not?' merchant, always up for anything.

Peter sat down on his stool, raised his glass. I touched mine to it. 'Saluté' he said before draining about a third of his lager in one gulp. Wiping his lips with the back of his hand, he said 'now, where do we find a van?'

* * * * * *

It was a good time to buy a VW camper van cheap. Someone had told me Australia House on the Strand was the place to go. This was where Aussies or Kiwis who'd bought a VW van in which to do their European tour flogged them. Because they either needed the money to get home or just wanted a quick sale – they weren't going to take the VW on the plane, were they? – it was the place to find a bargain. We picked up a van for next to nothing, me standing holding the folding while Peter looked the thing over and relentlessly beat the stoned Aussie selling the van down in price. I thought Shane was going to burst into tears by the time Peter finished.

As we pulled away and off into the rush hour I looked in the glove compartment. Tucked away to the back, behind the manuals, was a leather purse that looked like a kidney. I unzipped it. Inside were a pack of kingsize Rizla papers, a battered but shiny American Zippo lighter with '68–69. The more days you've been in the army the more hell you've gotten!' engraved onto it and a black tube with a grey lid. I knew what this was and what was in it. I flipped off the lid. The tube was filled to the top with grass. I held it under Peter's nose. He grinned. 'Perhaps we should turn round and give laughing boy his dope back,' I said.

'Absolutely,' Peter said, gunning the VW to overtake a taxi. 'Skin up, Lou.'

'Let's wait till we done the deal with the hat umbrellas,' I said, snapping the lid back down. 'Marijewanna and haggling clearly don't mix. The lighter's smart, though. Must have bought it off some GI in Nang Pang Dang or wherever.'

'Let's have a look.'

'No way. I know you, you'll trouser it.'

'Won't.'

'Will. Anyway, I baggs it.'

'You *what*?'

I could feel myself blushing. 'I said I baggsed it.'

'Baggsed it?' Peter was laughing now. 'Jesus, Lou, I haven't heard that since I was a kid.' He shook his head. '*I baggsed it.*'

I laughed. 'We played it all the way across Europe, me and the Beach Boys. All the way from Harwich to Istanbul.'

'No wonder Bloss went mad.'

'That was a lot later,' I said.

'Who knows when the curse of baggs will strike,' Peter said in a doomy voice.

'True.'

'So, I baggs I do the negotiation for the hat umbrellas. And, if I remember correctly…'

'…what is baggsed can never be unbaggsed,' I finished, solemnly. 'Fair enough.'

And so it was that the curse of baggsy tainted another generation and I watched while Peter got completely done up like a kipper by the Pakistani owner of the warehouse in the backstreets behind the Whitechapel Road.

The way Peter and I worked was that whoever handled the buy up paid while the other one did the heavy work and the driving. There's nothing worse than two people haggling with one – you always come off worst. As I humped boxes filled with 800 hat umbrellas into the back of the VW van, I swore to myself. I climbed into the van and waited behind the wheel for Peter to hand over the last of the folding to Mr Patel, who was grinning from ear to ear. Peter slipped into the passenger seat, turned to me and said 'all right?'

'He'd have gone a good fifty quid lower. You had him and you let him off the hook.' I shook my head, 'you've got a lot to learn, young man. I curse the day I told you about baggsy.'

Peter snorted, opened the glove compartment and started rolling a joint. 'I'd like to see you do better,' he said.

'You will next time,' I said. 'I baggsy that the next important financial transaction we make will be done by yours truly.'

'Fair enough. Shall I skin up?'

'If you want.'

Peter rolled a one-skin joint in seconds. 'Got that lighter?'

'No chance,' I said.

He laughed, wriggled around on the seat, raised a buttock and pulled out a box of matches, put the joint in the side of his mouth. 'Worth a try, wasn't it?'

* * * * * *

The moment we rolled off the overnight boat and onto Gothenburg dock, I was frozen like I'd never been before. And we discovered that the VW heater didn't work, or if it did I felt like it didn't. So maybe Shane had the last laugh.

From Gothenburg, we drove through the snow, pine forests and villages of wooden houses down to Stockholm, which took the best part of a day. The winter snow was still piled high by the side of the lake and we saw plenty of people ice-skating on the frozen lakes. The moose signs on the side of the road confused us a bit. There aren't too many of those in Bethnal Green. It was still absolutely freezing inside the van so we travelled bundled up in layers of clothing. We hit Stockholm long after dark and, with nowhere to stay sorted out, realised we needed to find a gaff to crash, rapido.

There was an English pub in Stockholm's Old Town where we knew there'd be loads of faces from Majorca. The Tudor Arms was the very first English pub in Sweden and opened in 1969. Quite why, I'm not sure. Whatever the reason, the Tudor was the place for British expats to party.

* * * * * *

'Christ, this is a bit surreal,' DeLovely said, as we stepped out of the bitterly cold, cobbled Stockholm streets and into a heaving mass of people necking pints surrounded by Union Jacks and traditional British pub mirrors. Many of the throng were lovely Swedish birds and both our eyes lit up right away.

As we stood, getting our breath back after dashing across frozen Stockholm, trying to force our numb mouths to work, I heard a voice calling our names above the incredible noise made by the people drinking. A figure burst out of the crowd. It was Jason, one of our salesmen. 'Louie, Peter, what the bloody hell are you doing here?'

We hugged. 'Never mind that, Jason, I'll tell you later,' I said. 'What we need is a place to crash tonight.'

'And fast,' Peter said. 'We don't want to die of hypothermia.'

Jason scratched his head. 'I'm staying with this bird I met in the summer. It's not all that but it takes good care of me, if you know what I mean.' He winked.

'Nice one, Jason,' I said. 'Can she put me and Pete up? It'll just be for a few days. Until we find somewhere.'

'I'll call her. She won't mind.' He grinned, turned, took a pint from behind the back of a giant Swedish bloke in a rugby shirt who was busy chatting up a blonde bird and walked off with it.

We thought about fighting our way through the scrum to the bar but couldn't find the strength. Peter pulled a half bottle of schnapps out of his pocket and we passed it backwards and forwards while we waited for Jason. We watched as his red, sweating face appeared in the crowd and he forced his way through. Just before he got to us, Jason lifted another pint almost from under the nose of a fat, ginger-headed bloke. 'Sorted,' he said, after he'd drained the beer. 'Let's go.'

We set off down the narrow, winding streets of the Old Town. The night was crystal clear. The masts of tall ships cut into the sky. Lights glittered on the water, where it wasn't frozen solid. Everything was still and we were in the heart of the city. 'Very quiet, isn't it, Jason?' Peter said.

'You're in Sweden now,' I said.

'What does that mean?' Peter said.

'You'll find out,' Jason said, 'won't he, Louie? So what's your plan, boys?'

'Sell hat umbrellas by day and party by night,' Peter said.

'Great idea,' Jason said. 'What's a hat umbrella?'

'What does it sound like?' I said. 'It's an umbrella you put on your head.'

'I only asked,' Jason said. 'I wish I had something to flog. I've got my ticket money back to Majorca and that's it.'

'What do you do for cash?' I said.

He shrugged. 'The bird, you know.'

Jason's bird was up and waiting for us. She was a skinny thing – blonde, of course. I could guess how she felt when the hero of her summer romance had arrived on her doorstep, how her delight had turned into the cold reality of having a penniless mooch on the firm. She offered us some schnapps, explained that she had a couch, the floor and some duvets. 'I baggs the couch,' I said, before DeLovely could open his mouth. I curled up undercover and drifted off to the sound of Jason and DeLovely draining the bottle of schnapps.

* * * * * *

It was around five in the morning when I was woken up by the horrible sound of a baby yelling. Jesus, I thought, where did that come from? I tried to get back to sleep but it was impossible. The screaming got louder and louder until it was like a drill going through my head.

The girl was in the kitchen, making the baby's milk, when I crept past so I peeked into the bedroom. Jason was spark out, warm and snug, a stupid grin on his face and slobber dribbling over the pillow. The room smelt of fart and old beer. For some reason, the sight of Jason so obviously cosy really pissed me off. I saw this big plastic blue toy crane on the floor and thought, if I can't sleep, he's not going to either.

I crept back to the front room, kicked Peter awake and whispered 'come and have a look at this'. His eyes lit up and, with the duvet still wrapped round him, he followed me back to the bedroom. He watched as I carefully inserted the plastic hook of the toy crane into Jason's nostril and pressed a button to start the thing. We kept quiet as the crane slowly pulled Jason's head into an upright position. Just when we thought we were going to pull the head off his shoulders, Jason woke up with a scream. By now, Peter and I were on the floor in hysterics. Jason kept shouting 'it's not funny, it's not funny, how would you like it?' which, of course, made us laugh even more. Even his bird was laughing.

* * * * * *

By mid morning, after a breakfast of coffee and Swedish cinnamon rolls, we were in the main walking street which ran down from the modern bit, which looked like Basildon in Essex, to the ancient gate which marked the entrance to the Old Town.

Within a few hours we'd knocked out around 70 hat umbrellas at a cost of 50 kroner each but were very close to dying of frostbite so we packed up and headed for The Tudor Arms. This was a very good morning's work.

Jason was waiting for us at the pub. He had cotton wool up one nostril and was holding his head at a funny angle. We burst out laughing all over again when we saw him. He still hadn't seen the funny side yet but we had high hopes. We got ourselves drinks and started counting out the morning's takings. Jason looked on miserably.

'Why the long face?' I asked. Peter spat beer everywhere and it was only then that I got the joke I'd accidentally made.

'I could really do with something to sell,' Jason said.

'Something will come up, mate. Meanwhile, I'm Hank Marvin. Let's eat,' I said. 'We'll buy. It's the least we can do. Where's a good, cheap place?'

Jason's eyes lit up. 'I've found this amazing joint,' he said. 'It's near here, ridiculously cheap and they have a different menu every day.'

We necked our drinks and followed him down the road to a big building, outside of which was a band playing instruments. Their uniforms looked familiar. It took a few seconds before I realised they were singing 'Onward Christian Soldiers' in Swedish.

'It's the Sally Army,' Peter said. 'We're not that desperate yet.'

'No, no,' Jason said. 'Trust me.' We followed him past the band, smiling like idiots, up some stone steps and into a long corridor down which wafted a delicious aroma. We turned a corner and were in a huge canteen filled with down and outs tucking into to mountains of hot food being served by scarily fresh-faced smiling blonde teenagers.

Because we didn't know yet how well we were going to do with the hat umbrellas, even though we'd had a good morning, and were watching our pennies we ordered the cheapest thing on the menu. I took a spoonful of what I'd ordered and slowly put down my spoon. 'What was that?' I said, resisting the impulse to spit my food out onto my plate. 'I can't eat that shit.'

Jason looked up from his plate of rapidly disappearing food. 'It's meatballs and peas, Louie. Delicious.'

'No it isn't,' I said. I buttered a bread roll and started munching. I was still starving and watched as DeLovely and Jason demolished their grub.

Seconds later, a very elegantly dressed chap who looked like he was a banker or something sat down opposite me with the biggest, juiciest steak I've ever seen in my life. I was really cheesed off by now. Turning to the others,

I said 'yeah, this geezer really needs salvation. I bet he's stockbroker.'

After he'd taken a couple of small bites, the bloke put down his knife and fork and started to read the paper. I couldn't stop staring at the steak. And then my angel must have heard the prayer I was sending up because the guy carefully folded his paper, put it down, stood up and headed off in the direction of what I guessed was the bathroom.

The temptation was too much. I leant over, speared the steak with my fork, placed it reverently on my plate before savagely attacking it while Jason and Peter looked on with open mouths. Just under a minute later, I let out a huge burp. It was like the steak had never existed.

When the Swede came back and sat down, he looked at his empty plate in disbelief then looked around in mild confusion before eating what was left, a potato and a slice of tomato I hadn't been able to fit in. Afterwards he carried on reading his paper as if nothing had happened.

I was actually in pain as we walked outside, a mixture of being stuffed with steak and laughing so much. I pulled a 50 kroner note out of my pocket, put it into the collecting box of a girl with a tambourine and a red, runny nose and said 'great food, love. It's so cheap here!'

* * * * * *

Delovely and I figured that we might as well wear out our welcome at Jason's bird's gaff. The only real downer was his constant complaining about money and how things would be different if he had a good line to sell himself.

One night back at the Tudor Arms, which had become our local, I was standing at the bar next to this guy who I'd seen plotted up near us on the street. He sold these really badly made hand puppets that I guess people only bought because they felt sorry for him. He couldn't believe it when I asked him if he was prepared to let us have 30 of them on a sale or return basis. He shrugged, said 'why not?' He popped outside and came back with a cardboard box full of the horrible things.

'There you go, Jason,' I said, handing the puppets to him. 'You've got something to sell now. The geezer wants 25 kroner a puppet. You sell them for 50 and make a tidy profit.'

Next day, all three of us were out on the street side by side, knocking our gear out to the passing crowd. As had happened every morning, Peter and I pulled in the notes. Jason had yet to get off the mark. Pretty soon he was complaining bitterly 'I'm freezing, let's go home,' he begged.

By that time, DeLovely and I had done pretty well so we agreed.

Back at the flat, I said to Jason 'you've got to improve your sales pitch, mate. You need to shout out what you're flogging. It's the only way. Do you know any Swedish?'

'No, I don't,' he said. 'The bird speaks English. Everyone does here.'

I glanced at Peter. 'Don't worry,' I said. 'I know what you can do. I'll ask Sven at the Tudor to write down a few good lines in Swedish for you to shout out. That's going to work.'

* * * * * *

As soon as we walked into the Tudor that night, Jason said 'Get 'em in, lads, I'm going for a slash,' and headed for the lav.

We shouldered our way to the bar and filled Sven in on the fast one we were going to pull on Jason. He roared with laughter and wrote down some phrases for us on a napkin.

When Jason appeared, I said 'there you go, mate, Sven here has kindly given you some things to say to help you with your sales pitch.'

'But you must remember to shout them out really loud,' Sven added. 'Swedes love that. Especially the children.'

'Cheers, Sven,' Jason said, taking a large gulp of his pint. 'I owe you one.'

'Got that?' I said. 'Especially the children. Back in the East End, we always pitched to them, because that's how you get their mums to buy.' I slapped him on the back. 'I've got a feeling your luck's going to change tomorrow, mate.'

'Me too,' Jason said, grinning from ear to ear. 'You're a real pal, Louie. I'll tell you what, let's have an early night tonight so I'm fighting fit for tomorrow. I can't wait.'

* * * * * *

It was a beautiful crisp, cold morning on the street where we pitched up. You could almost believe spring was in the air and that really put a smile on the faces of the punters. Peter and I watched as Jason took up his pitch on the other side of the street from us. He was brimful of confidence. He'd even put a clean piece of cotton wool up his nose. He reached down into the cardboard box he had at his feet, pulled out two of the puppets, put one on each hand, threw back his head, glanced at the crumpled piece of paper he held in one puppeted hand, took a deep lungful of breath and, in Swedish, shouted 'all right you f*cking Swedish sons of whores, buy my f*cking shitty puppets, you c*cks*cking pieces of shit.' Once he'd done this, he looked proudly over at Peter and I who were fighting to keep straight faces.

'Give it more,' Peter called out. 'Don't forget, nice and loud.'

'And the children,' I said. 'Target the children.'

Jason gave me the thumbs up with one puppet and repeated the torrent of vile abuse at ear-splitting volume. Peter and I had to turn our backs away from him so he didn't see us crying with laughter. All the way down the street, heads were turning. A crowd began to gather, much to Jason's delight. But, he started to look a bit confused when none of the people he was shouting at wanted to buy a puppet.

Mystified, Jason shouted louder and louder, thrusting the puppets in children's faces as he did so. A little girl burst into tears. Now the crowd was really beginning to turn ugly. 'Coppers!' DeLovely shouted to me. I looked down the street and saw two big cops heading in Jason's direction.

I nipped across the street. 'Time to do the up, Jason,' I said, picking up his cardboard box and marching him off down the street.

'What are you doing, Louie?' he said. 'I had a crowd.'

'I'll explain later,' I said as we ducked down a side street and into a café.

* * * * * *

That night, at the Tudor, it took around six pints of Carlsberg, on us, for Jason to finally see the funny side of things.

'Tell you what, mate,' I said. 'Stangs the puppets. We'll give you 100 hat umbrellas to flog.'

'50/50, mind,' Peter said.

A glint appeared in Jason's eye. 'So that means, I make...' he started to calculate his profit but soon gave up.

BOOTED OUT OF PARADISE

'I don't like it, Louie. Not. At. All. Not on our patch. It's got to be sorted.' Under his heavy tan, Curly's face was brick red. His Afro bobbed as he stabbed the desk with his finger.

Spit came out of his mouth and over the tall stacks of the cash he was counting, the club's takings from the night before. We took in at least 200,000 pesetas a night so there was a hell of a lot of money there.

A lovely sight.

It was June, the start of the season and Alex's was already on a roll.

Curly hit the table hard, with his fist this time. A stack of greasy peseta notes wobbled and fell over.

'Right, Curly, right.' I agreed without listening. Something I did a lot with him. Anything to shut him up so I didn't have to hear his booming voice, which sounded like it was coming out the middle of his nose. All he ever did was complain.

He was my partner in Alexandra's, along with our Spanish silent partner Curly had christened His Nibs, and we needed each other.

I leant back in my chair. There was no window in Curly's small office and, even though a fan was rattling away and the door was wide open, I was dripping with sweat. I wanted to be out on the street with my boys, my team of PRs.

What Curly meant by our patch was the narrow, steeply sloping side-street off Plaza Gomila where Alexandra's was located. As far as he was concerned, no other club had the right to be on our street, let alone do good business.

Which The Factory, the joint a few metres up the street towards the Plaza had the cheek to be doing.

Good luck to them, I thought. It was summer and there were plenty of punters to go round. Every night of the week.

What really got up Curly's nose was the way PRs from the Factory hustled the punters we brought up to Alex's from the boat trips we ran. It was like those westerns where some Audie Murphy rancher is trying to get his cattle to market to sell and they're being picked off by Indians or rustlers.

The PRs from The Factory would be trying to deliver their patter and stick tickets under the punters noses while we hurried them along as fast as we could, telling the other PRs to 'piss off' out the corner of our mouths.

But The Factory didn't really have much luck. Our crew of PRs, under yours truly, was the best in the Plaza and

Alexandra's was the top draw. Still, Curly just hated the thought of anyone spending money in another club – any amount of money.

Curly spun round in his swivel chair, grinned like a shark. 'I'll have a word with Paco, get 'em shut down on some technicality. Bung someone.' He leant back, powerful gut muscles stretching his Alex's t-shirt. 'That's what I'll do. Paco will help me sort it.'

Paco was the moonlighting cop who worked as our bouncer.

* * * * * *

One morning, a few days after Curly's rant about doing over The Factory, I lay in bed thinking about whether I could be bothered to go out or if I should just lower a bucket to the café downstairs and ask them to put a cup of coffee and a croissant into it so I could pull it up. This was a trick I'd learned years ago from my old mate Peter Bloss, now long gone and back in the UK.

The phone rang. And rang. Stopped. Started again. Whoever was on the other end wasn't going to go away. I picked up.

'Louie? What the hell are you doing? I was about to come round and knock you up' Curly said. The phone made his nasal voice even more nasty to listen to. I held the receiver away from my ear. 'We've got a major problemo. Get your arse to Alex's pronto.'

'Why?'

'Tell you when you get here.' Click. He'd hung up.

'Tosser,' I said.

I showered, threw on a t-shirt, shorts and flip-flops and hotfooted it to Alex's. Curly was sitting in his office, looking even more grim than usual, if that was possible.

'What's going on?' I said.

'I've just had a call from His Nibs to tell me that in 48 hours, you, DeLovely and Gaylord are going to be deported for working illegally.' I opened my mouth. 'Look,' Curly said, 'we know it's bollocks. You've all got your work permits but the fix is in.'

I swayed, felt dizzy. 'How...?'

'His Nibs heard a whisper from one of his boys, thank Christ, otherwise you'd have been out on your arse without knowing what had hit you. He's doing everything he can but you need to prepare yourself in case it's too late and the deportation order can't be stopped.'

'What happens then?'

'According to His Nibs, how it works is you're off the Rock for two years. The three of you. But we'll be doing everything we can to get you back here. Believe me.'

'But, we're all legal, we've got work permits.' It was all I could think of to say.

An edge came into Curly's voice. 'I know that, Louie. Don't you listen? You've been got at is all. And there's nothing we can do about it.' He took a deep breath. 'Listen, you know His Nibs. If anyone can get you back, it's him. You know that.'

Peter, Gaylord and I being deported spelled disaster for all of us. Which was putting it mildly. Those two were Alex's star PRs and I was Master of Ceremonies. Louie The Lip - the man who always got the party started. Putting us out of action meant a major handicap for the club that coming summer.

I looked at Curly. His mind was whirring and you could see it in his face. 'What do we do?' I said.

'If His Nibs's lawyers can't make the deportation order go away, you have to present yourselves at the cop-shop in 48-hours time.' Funnily enough, there was a police station right outside Alex's.

'But what do we do if we *are* deported.'

Curly got all businesslike. 'Right. You won't be able to take any money out of the country, apart from your train fare back to Bethnal Green. I suggest that whatever cash money you've got around, send it in envelopes back to your family and mates in Blighty. Anyone you can trust.' Curly rubbed his hands, warming up. 'Stick carbon paper inside the envelopes. That way no-one can see there's money in the envelopes and have it away.'

'Done this before, have you?' I said.

Curly scowled at me. 'This is serious, Louie. You won't have a pot to piss in otherwise.'

'OK.' The reality of being deported was beginning to sink in. 'Does His Nibs know who did us?'

'He does.' Curly tapped his desk with his lighter. 'It was La Sirena in Cala Major.'

Cala Major was just down the coast from Palma proper in an area that was mainly popular with Danes. It had a lovely long beach but there was a sewage outlet pipe in the middle of it so it always smelled a bit of sewage. La Sirena was one of maybe five discos in Cala Major.

We'd clocked that the PRs from the discos in Cala Major were a bit slack and didn't start selling to punters before one in the afternoon. So we'd been getting down there before they arrived, nicking their trade. We'd been at it for a couple of years and there was nothing they could do about it. We thought.

'There's this guy who goes to La Sirena,' Curly continued. 'Loves the place because of the birds and all that. The usual. And he's got friendly with the La Sirena lot. They start bending his ear about how we're coming into their turf, messing with their business. Which means that fewer of the foreign birds he's into are coming into the place. So, it turns out this guy works at the foreign office and he says he can do something about it. He goes to his boss and says he knows we're selling tickets down there without work permits. Matey's boss sends a telex to Madrid and it's done and dusted. The deportation order's signed. And we're screwed.'

I thought about how Curly had been scheming about who to bung to do over The Factory up the street. 'I suppose I better get on with it,' I said, 'tell DeLovely and Gaylord the bad news?'

Curly looked at me like I was nuts. 'PRs are ten a penny, Louie. You ain't. Who's going to run the show? I can't do it without you.'

I was surprised Curly said this but I guess he was desperate. He wouldn't have praised me up, otherwise.

Out on the street I looked up at the empty blue sky. I took a deep breath to get the stink of Curly's office out of my lungs and lit a cigarette. I was gasping for a sherbert after that.

I was also kind of in shock.

And I needed to break the news to DeLovely and Gaylord.

Gaylord, born Stephen Morris somewhere horrible up north, acted like he was Swedish. This was a smart move. Alex's market was the Scandies and, more than any other country, a Swede will always trust another Swede. So Gaylord wore these flared blue jeans you could only get from a Swedish boutique called Gul och Blu and smoked Swedish cigarettes called Prince. He wore white clogs and a white belt, even dyed his hair blonde. We were convinced he actually thought he was Swedish.

Although he couldn't read a word of Swedish, he used to walk around with a copy of Dagens Nyheter, one of the leading Swedish daily newspapers, in his mitt.

I walked up the street to the square. A few tourists who'd obviously just woken up waited for the bus to take them to one of the beaches just outside the city. The tables outside Plaza Gomila's twelve cafés were dotted with people having a late plate of tapas or taking a beer to see off last night's hangover and start the day right.

Peter and Gaylord were sitting inside Loa's, our favourite bar. Where I'd guessed they'd be. I went in and sat down.

'You all right, Louie?' Peter said. 'You don't look well. Fancy a little pick-me-up?' He waved a bottle of Bustaids at me.

'We've got a problem,' I said.

* * * * * *

While we waited to see if His Nibs could overturn the deportation order at the last minute, we got things in order in case we were kicked off the island.

I went to the two Spanish banks in which I had accounts and took out most of my money in the largest denomination bills they had.

Following Curly's expert advice, I put the money in envelopes with carbon paper separating the notes and sent about 50 of these back to the UK. It must have been about 20,000 quid. If it had been later in the season, there would have been a lot more.

I prayed that at least some of them would get there.

Gaylord resigned himself to his fate but Peter was mightily pissed off. His dad, who was pretty senior in The Rank Organisation, the huge British film company owned by J Arthur Rank, flew over and tried to clear Peter's name with the Spanish authorities.

Quite what he thought he could do, I don't know but at least he gave it a shot.

* * * * * *

It was 11.30 in the AM the next day. We were due to report at the police station next to Alex's at 12 sharp to be deported.

His Nibs had reached out to everyone he could but the deportation order couldn't be stopped. Madrid had decided and that was that. They had no interest in seeing whether we had work permits or not.

All His Nibs could do was promise he'd do everything in his power to get us back on the Rock as soon as he could. I had no doubt this was true.

The mood outside the Bally Jay Café, where we'd gathered with our overnight bags, was pretty black. Peter sat with his dad. Gaylord was saying goodbye to a tearful Swedish bird. A few of the PRs had gathered to give us a send off but we were all silent over our coffee and Soberano cognacs. Curly ground his teeth, plotting a hideous revenge, no doubt. His missus, Yvonne, tried to cheer us up at first but soon gave up. 'It's not fair,' she said. 'All those idiots in Madrid needed to do was look at your work permits.'

'Shut your north and west, Yvonne,' Curly growled. She looked confused. 'Your gob,' he said, making a zipping gesture across his mouth. Curly never did master Cockney rhyming slang.

A jeep pulled up outside the police station. The man from the foreign office, a good-looking young guy in a sharp suit, stepped out followed by two nasty-looking Guardia Civil with the shiny black plastic triangle hats. One of them recognised Curly and waved us over to do the formalities.

'Look at him,' Curly said, eyeballing the young guy as we walked over, carrying our grips. 'Cat who got the cream. Puts us out of business. Gets a promotion and a legover into the bargain, no doubt. Give me five minutes down that alleyway with the bastard and he wouldn't be smiling for a long time.'

We trooped into the police station where Peter, Gaylord and my passports were stamped: 'Two years deportation. Prohibited from entering the borders of Spain.' The foreign office guy held onto them. In case we decided to make a run for it at the last minute, I guess.

Throughout all of this, it was clear the guy who'd sent us on our way for something we hadn't actually done was loving it. As far as he was concerned, he was only doing his job and his patriotic duty. After all, we were foreigners and deserved everything we got.

And he was doing his bit to help bring the lovely Scandinavian birds back into La Sirena. He'd get a hero's welcome down there that night.

After we'd got our passports back, I was shocked when the cops whipped out handcuffs and slapped them on us. Even they looked a bit sheepish but apparently this was the official way of deporting someone. So bracelets it was.

They led us out to the jeep and we were told to hop into the back, which wasn't easy with the cuffs on. We waved to Curly and the crew. Yvonne, who was sniffling a bit, called out 'hasta pronto'. We went down the hill towards the Paseo Maritimo, trying to sit up straight without sliding into each other, headed up the bay towards the coast road and the airport, lights flashing and siren wailing.

All the while, the guy who set it all up, got us kicked off the Rock and put the boot into my business, had this horrible smug look on his face. We knew he understood English so we couldn't take the piss out of him. We started up in our own private language.

'Clock the barnet on the ice-cream,' Peter said. 'Dos mucho.'

'Si, si,' I said. 'Probablemente una syrup.'

'Definitivamente,' Peter said. 'Check the hooter. Derecho un boat race horrible.'

The guy wasn't entirely daft. He knew we were taking the piss out of him. He just didn't know how. Which clearly cheesed him off.

In your actual Queens English, what we'd said was:

Peter: Look at the hair on that geezer (ice-cream freezer, shortened to ice-cream).

Louie: Yes, yes, probably a wig (syrup of figs, abbreviated to syrup).

Peter: Definitely. Look at his nose. Right horrible face. (Cambridge and Oxford boat race, face).

It wasn't surprising other people didn't know what we were talking about. Half the time we didn't either. We just looked like we did.

But, having a go at matey and him not being able to do a thing about it gave us a little bit of sport.

When we got to the airport we hurtled straight onto the runway, everything flashing and blaring, and up to a plane waiting to go back to Gatwick. If the circumstances hadn't been what they were, it would have been pretty cool. Like we were the Beatles or something.

The cops undid our bracelets, did a quick search of our bags to make sure we weren't smuggling any money out.

I silently thanked Curly for his advice. If the cops had found money, the chances of it going straight into their pockets was pretty high. They gave us our bags back. The young guy from the foreign office handed over our passports and that's when I thought, I've got to get the last word in. Grinning at him, I said 'by the way, want to go to a beach party on Thursday?' Peter and Gaylord cracked up. Matey didn't.

We climbed the steps to the plane. Peter, me, Gaylord. At the top, I turned back and took a look at Majorca, the clear blue sky above the mountains. I wondered when I'd be seeing this place I loved again. I ducked my head and stepped into the plane.

Turfed out of paradise.

By the time I'd got inside, Peter had already made the stewardess blush. As she walked down the aisle, he reached out his hands as if to grab her arse. Gaylord sniggered. I envied Peter his ability to turn everything into a laugh. I was thinking about Alex's, what would happen to it. How long would I be away? Days? Weeks? Who knew?

It was actually pretty funny having 200 people looking at you, all trying to figure out what terrible crime you'd committed. A little boy said 'what have those men done, mummy?' She shushed him.

I tapped DeLovely on the shoulder and, in a stage whisper, I said 'well, let's hope they don't find the dough.'

He turned round. Out of the side of his mouth, he said 'or the bodies'.

We took our seats on the back row of the plane. I looked at Peter, started to sing. 'Leaving on a jet plane,' He joined in, so did Gaylord. 'Don't know when I'll be back again.' I stood up. 'Come on, everyone, join in. You know the words.'

People laughed. Some actually sang along.

PART THREE

MOTORS ACROSS THE POND

My first morning back on the Rock after a two year absence. I rolled over in bed and fell on the floor. I'd forgotten I was on the very narrow couch in the apartment of a pair of Swedish girl PRs who worked for Alex's. I lay on my back and chuckled before hauling myself up and heading out onto the balcony for the first smoke of the day.

Squinting in the bright sunlight, feeling the warmth on my back and smelling the sweet morning air, it was hard to believe I'd been away for almost two years.

The delightful Swedes were still sparko and snoring so I had a quick shower – it went from ice cold to scalding with nothing in between – and headed out for breakfast. It was only after I'd shut the door behind me that I realised I didn't have a key. Oh well.

Gomila was waking up as I strolled to the Bally Jay, the café next door to Alex's where we'd met before me, DeLovely and Gaylord were deported two years before. I got out of the heat and under the shade of an umbrella as fast as I could, inhaled the smell of coffee, toast, gas fumes and the Med and thought 'I'm home.'

Service was never rapido at the Bally Jay but I was happy to wait and soak up the scene. I was surprised when José the waiter came out with a café con leche and put it down in front of me so hard coffee slopped into the saucer. Just like he always did. José patted me on the shoulder and walked back into the Bally Jay, whistling. I sipped the tooth-rattlingly strong coffee and looked around me. The feeling nothing had changed was so intense it made me feel nervous. But good.

I half expected Blossy to come strolling down the street in his Turin Shroud kaftan fizzing on Bustaids and buzzing with plans for the day but there was no chance of him coming back to the Rock any time soon.

I'd last seen Blossy a few months before. After his crack-up he'd married a born again Christian called Rose and become one himself. I got the feeling he was hanging on to Jesus for fear of cracking up all over again.

Last time I saw him, Blossy was fly-pitching with some gypsies, selling handkerchiefs three for a pound. He'd do the markets all over Essex – Romford, Basildon, Chelmsford - striped handkerchiefs in one hand, open suitcase at his feet, booming out his spiel under grey skies, ready to do the off in a flash.

The gypsy guys were pretty heavy. One was a monster, strong as an ox and psycho with it. He had a weird squeaky voice. You always knew when he was going to turn because his voice got so high it was like steam coming out of a kettle. But Blossy had them all wrapped round his little finger. They loved him, like everyone always did.

And when Blossy broke the all-time record for selling handkerchiefs he was the bollocks. A thousand in a day. A thousand quid's worth of hankies!

But it wouldn't have been about the money for Blossy. He'd have been fired up by the challenge. What a waste, though.

I lit another cigarette, watched the blue smoke drift up into the air and grinned as I thought about my idea to revolutionise Alexandra's. The competition wouldn't know what hit them.

I really was going to pull out all the stops. Just like Curly wanted.

I'd been inspired by something I'd seen in Florida on an epic trip across the USA with DeLovely just a few months before.

* * * * * *

The epic trip was actually two, one following a week or two after the other.

I'd given up on trying to get back to the Rock before my time was up because the Spanish Embassy fobbed me off whenever I went in to try and get things moving.

Curly had come over just before Christmas with my share of the club's profits so I had a decent amount of cash.

Peter DeLovely and I were in touch and had tried out a few hustles together, like selling hat umbrellas to tourists up London's West End. This was more for the giggles than the loot.

One afternoon not long after New Year 1979, DeLovely and I were having a Turkish and a sauna at the old public baths in Bethnal Green, where I used to go for my weekly scrub up when I was a kid. The only other geezer in the Turkish was huge with a back so hairy it should have had 'Welcome' written on it. He was reading the Financial Times.

Fatso got up and waddled and wobbled off out, leaving the paper behind. DeLovely grabbed it and turned to the motors for sale section. 'Blimey, that's cheap,' he said.

'What is?'

'Bentley S3, six grand.' We peered at each other through the steam.

'Let's check it out,' I said.

Next day we schlepped out to where the car was, a scruffy industrial estate somewhere near Staines in Middlesex. It was a beaut, in great condition and a snip at six grand. The owner explained that ten other people wanted the car but he knew they were just going to sell it on. He only wanted to sell to someone who'd really value the Bentley, not some flash wheeler dealer who'd flog it in the USA.

'Heaven forbid,' Peter said, shooting me a look. 'This is our dream car.' He put his hand on his heart. 'It will definitely not be sold in America.'

DeLovely gave the Bentley the once over. It was as good as it looked and the papers were all in order. I handed over the cash in a bulging brown envelope.

As we glided away through the grey slush, I turned to Peter and said 'the States it is, then. Right?'

'Of course,' he said. 'Ever been?'

'Nah,' I said. 'But my sisters live there. They're due a visit.'

'They fit?' Peter said.

'DeLovely! That's my bleedin' sisters you're talking about. And they're both married, as it goes. Dirty sod.'

'Only asking,' he said. 'Keep your wig on. Here, what's this geezer want?'

A big guy in a sheepskin jacket was waving us down. Peter stopped and pressed the button that lowered the power window on his side. 'All right, lads?' the bloke said. He grinned, showing a missing tooth. Clear snot ran from his red nose. He patted the Bentley's sleek grey bonnet. Peter bristled. 'Got yourself a bargain there, boys. Lovely motor. How much do you want for it?'

DeLovely looked at me and back at the bloke. 'What you offering?' he said.

'Seven grand. Cash. Right now.'

'No thanks, mate,' Peter said. He pressed the button for the window again and it slid smoothly up, gave the gas pedal a slight touch and the Bentley roared quietly. The guy stood back, trying to smile as we pulled away.

'Seven grand,' DeLovely said. 'He must be having a laugh. We can get at least twice as much in New York. You do realise that don't you, Louie?'

'I do now,' I said. 'Nice one, DeLovely.' I lit up a fag and settled into the ridiculously comfortable passenger seat. 'Next stop the Big Apple, amigo.'

'Watch the upholstery,' Peter said, glaring at me. He looked in the rear view mirror. 'Hope that geezer doesn't follow us,' he said. 'The sooner we get this beauty on the boat to New York the better.' When he patted the top of the dash I knew he'd fallen in love.

* * * * * *

New York was, as Stevie Wonder said, 'just like I pictured it, skyscrapers and everything'.

We walked out of JFK airport into a bitterly cold night. We could see our breath in the air. The lights of the city glittered in the distance. The cars out front of the airport were huge. A bus for downtown was just pulling away. When it did, I half expected to see the wheels go backwards like they did in the movies.

It was weird but I immediately felt this incredible sense of freedom. I felt like I could go and go without stopping.

DeLovely and I looked at each other and grinned. He dropped his suitcase, threw his arms wide open and bellowed 'New York, New York, it's a wonderful town!' I joined in and we finished with a little tap-dance, bowing to the startled people heading towards the line of gigantic, muttering yellow cabs.

* * * * * *

New York really was just like I'd pictured it. And more besides. We stayed at the Taft Hotel at 51st street and 7th Avenue, just north of Time Square. It had about a million floors and our room had an incredible panoramic view of the New York skyline. We were so high up, the horizon seemed to curve.

That first night, we decided to head out for a beer. Like a couple of sailors on shore leave, we scuttled down to Times Square. I'd never seen anything like it. It was hard to act cool.

Neon signs for Coca-Cola, Suntory Whisky and Sony flashed and blinked. Rows of cinemas advertised porno movies with names like Insatiable and Little Girl Blue. Guys in silk shirts tried to hustle us into peepshows. Hookers wearing next to nothing in the cold night air grinned at us and licked their lips. One coffee-coloured chick winked at me and I grinned back until DeLovely said 'it's a bloke, Louie.' A pair of black kids wearing white gloves did this strange, jerky dance to music from a massive portable radio that ended with one of them spinning round on his back on a piece of cardboard on the road while his mate went round collecting shrapnel in a Burger King cup.

And in among this sea of mad babbling, drooling, bug-eyed humanity, a very straight looking middle-aged lady with those cat's eyes glasses walked around with a sandwich board that read 'Get rid of yours sins before your sins get rid of you.'

I could really believe sin could get rid of you in Times Square. 'Shall we find somewhere a bit quieter?' I said to DeLovely.

'And a little less hairy,' he added.

We beat it out of Times Square sharpish and had a couple of beers with whisky chasers to calm our nerves in a bar called the Blarney Rock not too far from the hotel, a long, dark, narrow place with a row of stainless steel tureens down one side filled with ancient looking cabbage, potatoes and ham like school dinner food. I was surprised at the way everyone left their change on the bar.

Walking home past steaming manholes, it felt like we were in a movie. And maybe we were.

Out of nowhere, what sounded like a nuclear bomb warning went off. DeLovely and I looked at each other, suddenly sober. The noise got louder as whatever was making it came closer. A fire engine hurtled up the street and shot past us. We were deaf for the next ten minutes.

That night I couldn't sleep. I lay smoking, listening to the city's soundtrack of honking horns, shouting and distant music. Just before I fell asleep, I was sure I heard the sound of gunshots.

Next morning we got a cab out to the docks at Newark in New Jersey to pick up the Bentley. Can you imagine how we felt cruising back into the city? Like kings.

Until we were heading back into the city by way of the Holland Tunnel and the Bentley died on us. *In* the tunnel. We opened the bonnet and, to the accompaniment of pissed off New Yorkers shouting 'get that fag car back to England, limey assholes' we discovered the battery was flat.

* * * * * *

We ran ads for the Bentley in the New York press, covered the car with luminous 'for sale' signs and toured the city.

While we waited for a bite, we explored Manhattan. I loved strolling the streets of Greenwich Village and Little Italy, wondering which of the no-neck guys hanging out on the street munching pizza was a gangster or not.

The closest we came to crime was when I bought some Bob Hope – dope – off a black guy in Washington Square. 'How much?' I said.

'It's a dime bag, brother,' he said.

'Ten cents for all this. That's cheap!'

'Ten dollars, fool.'

Exit Louie The Lip, feeling very stupid.

One Monday night, wandering Manhattan, we stopped in for a drink at a place called The Carlyle Hotel. A jazz band was playing. 'That clarinettist looks familiar,' DeLovely said. It was Woody Allen.

Another night, we took the Bentley down to Studio 54. All the stories we'd heard made it sound like we didn't have a hope in hell of getting in. But, we parked the Bentley in front and strolled straight past the beautiful people as their mouths dropped open. Somewhere that night we found ourselves chatting away to Steve Rubell, the owner of Studio 54. We tried to flog him the Bentley but he claimed he was broke. Looking round his amazing club, we found that hard to believe.

But, a couple of days later I picked up a paper and read that Steve Rubell was being charged by the IRS with tax evasion on a massive scale.

We finally sold the Bentley to a puffed up advertising executive who owned a company on Madison Avenue. 'He better worship it,' DeLovely said. 'Or I'll be back.'

* * * * * *

DeLovely and I had definitely caught the bug after our first mind-blowing trip across the pond. We probably spoke with Yank twangs for a bit, called each other 'buddy'. We started planning our return right away. If we could flog one classic motor, we figured three should be no problem this time.

We picked up a lovely old Roller, another Bentley S3 and a Vanden Plas Limo with a dividing glass screen which the driver could slide back if he needed to talk to his passengers. 'Caviar at the Ritz, modom? Of course.'

DeLovely found the motors, gave them the once-over and made the deals. I did the weighing in.

I was happy to finance the whole number, which came to about £18,000, including buying the cars, shipping them to Jacksonville, Florida and driving to Largo, on the Gulf of Mexico, where my sisters lived. After our result the first time, I was pretty confident we'd make a tidy profit.

We resisted the temptation to hang out on the white sand beach and soak up the rays – the temperature was in the mid 70s every day - ran ads for the cars in the newspapers around where my sisters lived and got bites right away.

The Vanden Plas went to a limo company in Tampa and we made $2000 profit. Next to go was the Roller. We got a call from a guy who lived in Melbourne Beach, a four hour drive away from Largo. In his booming drawl he told me 'the Franklins are sitting right here on my desk, buddy, and they're yours as long you can get that lil ol' Rolls Royce to me by mid-day tomorrow.' It was his wife's birthday and he wanted to surprise her.

I didn't know what a Franklin was but guessed the bloke was talking about wongah.

Next morning, we were up and ready at 6AM. I had a bit of dicky stomach from guzzling ice-cold beer and eating the mountains of rich American food my sisters prepared and the tension added to it.

Peter took the Roller and I followed in the Bentley. We turned a few heads as we rolled down Highway 4 across Florida before turning onto Highway 95, heading down the coast – two young lads cruising through these sleepy Florida towns in classic British motors, me in my Gatsby cap. Lord Louie The Lip and The Duke of DeLovely. I couldn't resist doing the royal wave a couple of times, freaking out a Red Indian guy who was sitting outside a liquor store sipping from a bottle in a brown paper bag.

I was feeling the business. The sky was an impossible blue, the sea turquoise and the strip of sandy beach blinding white. I had the aircon on full blast and I'd found a great radio station pumping out nonstop oldies but goodies. I sang along with The Beach Boys 'I Get Around' at the top of my voice. That song always reminded me of my heroes from back in 1967.

I thought of Peter flogging hankies in the drizzle at Romford Market. Jesus!

About two hours into the trip, I saw DeLovely's hazard lights flashing. My heart went into my mouth. Peter managed to limp to a garage. I pulled in behind him. 'What's up?' I said in a squeaky voice.

'Dunno,' he said. A drop of sweat dripped from his forehead into the open bonnet and sizzled. Peter was great at selling cars but he wasn't the world's most clued up mechanic. 'It's not over-heated or anything. Just losing power.'

'Battery?' I said, remembering our disaster in the Holland Tunnel, first time out.

Peter turned the key in the ignition. The aircon roared into life, as did the radio. 'Nah,' he said. 'It's not the battery.'

As we stood looking at the Roller, which almost looked a bit embarrassed – like an old lady duchess who'd farted - a black guy in filthy red Castrol overalls and a ball cap with the beak creased down the middle came out of the garage. He looked under the bonnet, at Peter and me, back at the sheepish Roller and squirted a thin stream of chewing tobacco juice onto the floor dangerously close to my feet. 'Sheeit,' he said, 'I ain't never seen one of them before, man. Rolls-Royce, right?'

'Yes,' I said in my most English voice. 'And we seem to have a bit of a problem.'

'I'd say you do, brother,' he said. 'Sheeit.'

'Can you help us?'

'Like I said, man. I've never seen one of 'em before, let alone worked on it.'

'If it's money…'

'It ain't that. Believe me, I wish it was. Naw,' he lifted up the bonnet and scratched his head. 'I truly wouldn't know where to start. All I can say is, wait a bit, see if she cools down.'

'How long?'

'A few hours, maybe.'

'We don't have a few hours,' Peter said in a strangled voice. 'This car needs to be in Melbourne Beach in,' he looked at his watch, 'ninety minutes'.

The black guy laughed. 'Sorry, brother. It don't look like you're going to make it.' Peter's face, which was already red, flushed dangerously.

My stomach gurgled and I had an overwhelming need to use the bathroom. 'Where's your khazi, pal?' I said.

'I'm sorry?'

'John? Bathroom?'

'Back through the office. Help yourself.'

Peter looked at me, his mouth open. 'Sorry, mate. When you've got to go you've got to go,' I said.

I dashed through the garage office, used the filthiest lav I'd seen in the States, made a note never to call Arlene for a good time. Walking back through the office, I clocked a calendar. Miss February was a soul sister with Bo Derek cornrows wearing nothing but a pair of crocheted bikini bottoms and a big smile. I started to grin too when I saw the business the calendar was promoting. It was a tow truck company. 'Peter,' I called out, 'in here, quick.'

He came in, followed by the black geezer. I pointed at the calendar. 'She's fine,' the black dude said.

'She is,' Peter agreed. 'But now's not the time.'

'It's for a tow truck company,' I said.

Peter scowled at me. 'We can't exactly tow the car to the guy's gaff, can we? He just might think there's something dodgy going on.'

'I know that,' I said. 'But we can get close and by that time the car might have cooled down.'

'Worth a shot,' Peter said. 'We've got nothing to lose, have we?'

I called the tow company and they came straight away. We hooked up the car and drove in the direction of Melbourne Beach as fast as the Dodge truck would go with a dirty big Roller in tow. Peter rode with the driver and I followed in the Bentley. No more royal waves. I was bricking it.

A couple of hundred yards before a sign saying 'Welcome To Melbourne Beach' the tow truck pulled off Route 95 and into the parking lot of a Dunkin Donuts beside a lake called Indian River Lagoon that stretched off into the distance and looked like it had alligators lurking. I'd seen a couple sleeping by the highway and they gave me the right heebie-jeebies. I tucked the Bentley in behind the Dodge and watched as the tow truck guy unhooked the Roller. Peter gave him some cash and the guy walked back to his truck shaking his head. It sounded like he was laughing.

'What did you say to him?' I asked Peter as the truck pulled out onto the highway, did a U-turn and with a blast of its horn rattled off into the heat haze.

'Nothing. Honest. I don't know what he was laughing at. My eck-sent, I guess. Yanks. All I did was ask him where the geezer's house was and he reckons it's a couple of hundred yards down the road. In the chi-chi part of town. Guy's rolling in it. Everyone knows him. Made a mint out of garbage or something. Right, fingers crossed, Lippo. Let's see if she starts.'

Peter climbed behind the wheel of the roller. When he touched the steering wheel he winced. 'Jesus, that's hot,' he said.

'Don't turn on the aircon again,' I said. 'It drains the power.'

'I know.' He turned the key. I sent up a prayer to the empty sky. The engine purred into life and I let out an almighty whoop. We grinned at each other. Leaving the window open, Peter pulled slowly away. We still had fifteen minutes.

We found the guy's house easily enough. Even from the road, it looked four times the size of the others on that strip. We followed the palm-tree lined drive through rolling lawns so green they didn't look real until we pulled up at a huge white wood pile with three levels of covered balcony running round it. Behind the house the Atlantic surf rolled endlessly in.

As we cruised slowly and carefully to a halt, a figure sitting in the shade of the porch stood up. The man who waited for us to come to him was very short. He couldn't have been more than five foot and was as brown and wrinkled as a sultana. A bright red polo shirt stretched over his gut, casting a shadow on his madras pattern shorts, black socks and deck shoes. His Japanese wife, who stood next to him was taller. 'I was beginning to think you boys wasn't gonna make it,' the guy said from the shadows. 'But you did. Good for you. Come on in. Your money's waiting for you.' He looked at an enormous Rolex on his wrist. 'Ten of twelve. You only just made it, fellahs. Let's have a drink to celebrate.'

Peter and I looked at each other. 'A very quick one,' I said. 'Then we've got to go. Get back to Largo and take it easy. We're leaving tomorrow and my sister's doing a special farewell dinner.'

We weren't but Peter caught on quick. 'Yeah and we want to check out Lauderdale.'

'Sure you do, boys. It's pretty wild. I guarantee you won't have seen anything like it. Stay at the Fairwinds Hotel on the beach. Party central, fellows.' The man winked at us and his wife smiled. She stood to one side and we followed him down a never-ending hall to a huge, gleaming kitchen with a giant General Motors fridge that made me feel like Jerry in the cartoons. The cash for the Roller was stacked neatly on the table. $19,500.

'Wanna count it?' the man said.

'I'm sure it's all there,' I said. I was desperate to get out of there and my stomach was starting to gurgle again. I looked at Peter and I couldn't believe how cool he looked. He was enjoying this.

The wife gave us two Cokes with white cotton napkins wrapped round them. We drained them. 'Right,' I said. 'Lovely meeting you. We'll be off then.'

The wife whispered something to the man and he looked at us. 'She wants to get the car signed over properly. Do things right. You know what they're like. We've got a notary standing by in town. Witness everything.'

'Is that necessary?' Peter said, his voice squeaking.

'It's what my wife wants.' Steel appeared in the little man's voice.

Peter shrugged. 'Fair enough. We'll all go in the Bentley then?'

'Hell no,' the guy said. 'She wants to try out the Rolls-Royce, buddy. Get a feel for it.'

I couldn't look at Peter. My stomach gave off a long, growling gurgle that said everything.

The Japanese lady drove slowly and regally into town, us following in the Bentley with our fingers crossed. 'How many cushions you reckon she's sitting on?' Peter said.

'Like the princess and the pea. Can you imagine if she meets someone who saw the Roller being towed into town?'

We started to laugh hysterically. My stomach mumbled and I stopped laughing sharpish. 'When we get through this, I've got to find a lav,' I said.

Peter chuckled. 'Pressure got to you has it, Lou?'

'Beer and barbeque sauce, mate. Fatal.'

The Roller made it to the notary's office without dying. We signed the papers and were out of there like a shot, $19,500 up.

* * * * * *

It was after we'd shifted the Bentley that I stumbled across the phenomenon that was going to change Alexandra's and Majorca nightlife forever.

We sold the Bentley from outside Houlihan's Stadium, home of the Tampa Bay Buccaneers. We papered the motor's windows with luminous for sale signs like we had in New York and sold the car for $25,000 in a day. Even we couldn't believe how easy it had been.

To celebrate, we decided to head down to Fort Lauderdale for the weekend. We checked in to the Fairwinds Hotel on the beach like the guy had told us to. That night, spruced up, we thought we'd check out a bar called The Candy Store, just off to the right of the hotel before heading into town.

It was only about nine but we could hear that the joint was jumping. We paid $10 to get in but this covered all we could drink and free pizza. Inside, the air was thick with the smells of perfume, suntan lotion, cigarettes, marijuana and frying. A very brown girl wearing a blue t-shirt that said 'Surf Naked' in big yellow letters smiled as she slid between me and Peter. 'Smells like Alex's,' DeLovely said, looking round him at the suntanned lovelies like a wolf on the prowl.

'Don't it,' I said. I stood to one side and let a guy pass. He was wearing a white hardhat with two cans of Coors beer strapped onto the side and a clear straw going from one of the beers into his mouth.

'Good idea,' Peter said.

'But that's even better,' I said, pointing at a hand-written sign that said 'Wet T-Shirt Contest Tonite! Sign up here! $100 first prize. $50 second prize. $25 third prize. Champagne 4th prize.' What do you reckon a wet t-shirt contest is?'

He looked at me and in his best 'duh' voice, said 'I'd guess it involves t-shirts getting wet and young women, wouldn't you? Get 'em in, Louie. I'm gasping.'

I fought my way to the bar. I was buzzing. I ordered us two margaritas and asked the blonde girl in the red and white candy-striped one piece swimming costume when the wet t-shirt contest was. She smiled, showing a row of impossibly white American teeth. 'About an hour, honey. Say, you English? I jest love yur eck-sent.' I paid her and gave her a couple of dollars tip which went in a jar full of notes.

While we waited for the contest, the bar, which had been packed when we came in, got insanely rammed. 'I wish they made them hats with margaritas,' Peter said, as he fought his way back from the bar to our table. Just as he sat down, a mic'd up voice boomed round the bar.

'Ladeez and gentlemen, it's time for the Candy Bar's legendary wet t-shirt contest. The first and still the best in the whole USA.' I jumped up and forced my way through the crowd to a low stage. The MC asked for girls to take part and six climbed up out of the audience. They were taken to one side, took off their bras, changed into Candy Stripe t-shirts and started jiggling around to Ladies Night by Kool and The Gang. The girls had obviously had a bit to drink and were really getting into the dancing, shaking their tanned bums in the faces of the guys in the front row. The MC introduced the six girls. The barmaid in the candy-striped swimsuit handed him a glass jug full of ice water and he tipped it over the first girl. Her t-shirt went see through and at the first sight of her nipples the crowd went wild. She grinned and started shaking her breasts. The MC did the same to the other girls and they began to shake their breasts, pretending to unbutton their cut-off jeans. What got me was the way they were having fun showing off but were really competitive at the same time. The whole thing was exciting and naughty but also strangely innocent.

The girl with the largest breasts won and, with a shriek of delight, she lifted her t-shirt all the way up and over her head. I looked at the guy next to me. His eyes were out on stalks.

The whole thing was genius. I knew it would blast the competition back in Plaza Gomila out of the water.

* * * * * *

After Lauderdale, we said goodbye to my sisters and headed up to New Orleans for Mardi Gras. We'd brought over 400 hat umbrellas from the UK in one of the cars to flog, figuring that whether it rained or was boiling hot, we'd be on a winner because, whatever happened, people would need either shelter or shade.

We found a room on Bourbon Street in the heart of the French Quarter, which the owner claimed was converted slave quarters. I could well believe him. Downstairs from us were a couple of cute black hookers who we came close to knocking up at least one drunken night.

New Orleans was like no place I'd ever been. I'd soon discovered that American cities either surpassed their reputation or failed miserably. Like New York, the Big Easy was every bit as amazing as its legend promised, if not more so.

It was hot and so humid your shirt was soaked through the minute you walked out the door. The mosquitoes had pilots. The whole place stank like a huge kicked over trashcan. But it was heaven.

The bars were packed night and day with people throwing back booze. They were nearly all hugely fat and proud of it. One morning, we went to a famous soul food café on the edge of the French Quarter and tried grits for the first and last time. They tasted like wet paper covered in butter. Mohammed Ali looked down from a signed photo. He was laughing.

And, of course, there was music everywhere. In a bar on Bourbon Street having a livener at about nine in the morning I listened to this black geezer singing 'When A Man Loves A Woman' to himself while he swept the floor. He sounded better than Percy Sledge.

For me, who had nothing but respect for the black people I'd met and a great love of soul music, the racism of New Orleans was a shock. One night, DeLovely and me went for a meal at an upscale joint called Antoine's on Rue St Louis. Black people bought our water and cleared the table but the actual food was served by whites. It was like a black guy couldn't touch a white person's plate if it had food on it.

The first time a black geezer said 'yassuh' to me I thought he was taking the piss.

Although there were parades every day, Mardi Gras proper kicked off on 18 February that year and DeLovely and I were at the head of the parade, dancing with the beautiful café au lait girls wearing next to nothing apart from the glitter on their faces and enormous headdresses and grooving to the music from the jazz bands that honked and wailed away.

What really blew my mind were the Indian Kings who danced through the crowd. These guys were covered in feathers from their ornate Red Indian headdresses to their feet – pink, blue, orange or purple. Faces and patterns were picked out in beads on their costumes. The things must have weighed a ton.

We sold the hat umbrellas that first morning at five bucks a pop out of a couple of shopping trolleys from a Piggly Wiggly supermarket, which paid for our plane tickets home. After a bit of hunting around, we found a shop which sold hat umbrellas, bought up their stock at $2 each and shifted these too. This covered the rent for a couple of weeks, along with booze, marijuana and po'boy deep-fried shrimp sandwiches.

Mardi Gras left me with a kingsize hangover. Once it wore off, I was itching to head back to the UK and then on to the Rock and get back to business now that my two years in exile were nearly up. Peter had met a beautiful Creole bird in, of all places, a shoe shop. His Southern Belle got him a job in her shop and, happy as Larry, he stayed on.

The only English guy ever to sell shoes in the Big Easy as far as we know.

* * * * * *

I found it when I was unpacking after that first trip to New York. I'd bought the cassette at a tourist place in the Big Apple. It was called 'Sounds of New York'. I put it in the player, expecting to hear Sinatra or some cool, smoky jazz.

At first I thought the tape was knackered. All I could hear was the sounds of traffic and car horns honking and blaring. Then I realised the tape was exactly what it said it was. Literally the sound of New York. Brilliant!

Roping in DeLovely, I decided to nick the idea and make 'Sounds of London'. We borrowed a professional mic with a big furry end and set off on a journey round London to record the sounds of the Smoke.

Our journey started at Heathrow with me getting into a cab and saying 'take me to Oxford Street' to the cabbie, actually a friend of ours who we'd hired for the day. Thinking about it, why we felt the need to actually go out to Heathrow and record there, I really don't know.

At one point we decided to record me on a bus. We bunged the conductor, a laidback Pakistani bloke, a quid to come up to me and ask me where I was going and what I wanted while Peter recorded our conversation. Before we started, I explained to the Pakistani guy what I was going to say: 'I'll ask for three singles to Buckingham Palace.'

'This bus doesn't go to Buckingham Palace,' he said.

'OK. The Tower of London.'

'It doesn't go there either.'

'Where does it go?'

'Elephant and Castle.'

'That'll do. So I say three for Elephant and Castle.'

'But there's only two of you.'

'Right,' deep breath, 'two tickets. And then you give me the tickets and ring the bell for the off.'

'Right. I've got it.'

I gave the guy the thumbs up. Peter, sitting next to me with the professional mic and headphones did the same. I said 'two to Elephant and Castle, please.'

The conductor turned the handle on his ticket machine, handed over the tickets and told me the price. I paid him and he stood smiling down at us. I looked up at him. He looked down at me. I pointed at the bell. 'Ding-ding' I mouthed. He looked confused. 'Ding-ding', I pantomimed ringing the bell, smiled at him. He looked blank and a big grin spread across his face. He gave us the thumb's up and said proudly: 'Ding-ding!'

Peter and I burst out laughing. The Pakistani guy looked bewildered. We got off the bus, stood on the pavement and laughed till our sides hurt.

Believe it or not, 'Sounds of London' was actually sold at WH Smiths at Heathrow and Gatwick for a bit and we made a few bob.

A FREE MAN

By October of 1981 I was back in London after my first summer on the island since I was kicked out, shoulders hunched up around my ears, dodging the dirty puddle spray from double-deckers and thinking about how to scam a crust until the following spring.

That winter, London was a tense city. The IRA had started planting bombs again. In October one went off in Chelsea Barracks killing an old age pensioner and later that month a disposal expert was blown to bits trying to defuse another, which had been planted in a Wimpy on Oxford Street.

I was in the West End that day and remember hearing the dull thump of the explosion.

A bombing campaign wasn't anything new for Londoners and people carried on with their lives. Nervously.

I didn't like to think of my life on the Rock because it seemed so far away from all this that it was a dream. My Rock wasn't exactly la isla de la calma – the island of calm as the Majorcans called it - but I seemed to have a ball, pretty much non-stop.

* * * * * *

While I was back in the UK that winter, there was one thing I wanted to sort. So, once I'd slept my way out of the total exhaustion that always flattened me after a season on the Rock, I took care of something that had been hanging over me for a couple of years.

* * * * * *

On 19 November 1981, the following article appeared in the London Evening Standard.

'Once bitten, twice shy...I've learned my lesson'

It was love at first sight for night club manager Louis O'Brien and the beautiful winner of the Miss Wet T-shirt contest at his disco on the sunny island of Majorca.

He even arranged for the Spanish beauty, Marianna, to fly to England for their wedding.

And he thought nothing of giving her £500 to go shopping in the West End after the registry office wedding.

Winner

But that was the last 36-year-old Mr O'Brien saw of his 26-year-old bride for she hot-footed it back to Spain and into the arms of a former boyfriend.

And today in the London Divorce Court Mr O'Brien had the marriage, which took place at Bethnal Green Register Office in November 1978, annulled because of his wife's refusal to consummate it.

Giving the decree in an undefended suit, Judge Callman wished Mr O'Brien 'better luck next time. It's the old story – a holiday romance is not the same as a steady relationship,' said the judge.

After the hearing, a smiling Mr O'Brien of Goldman Close, St Matthew's Road, Bethnal Green, who works as a salesman when not running the disco in Majorca, said: 'It was in 1977 when we first met.

'There was an international wet T-shirt contest at the club and she was representing Spain and won it.

'We got to know each other and got on like a house on fire. When she finished on holiday and went back to her home in Madrid we continued to keep in touch by letter and I telephoned her and proposed.

'I arranged for her to fly to London and she arrived with a girlfriend. I met them at the airport and put them in a hotel.

'Then after the wedding we were celebrating with champagne when she asked if she could go shopping in the West End to buy some clothes. I gave her £500 to buy a trousseau and put her in a taxi. That's the last I saw of her.'

Photos

'I rang the hotel later that evening and was told she had checked out. Next day I rang her sister in Madrid and was told she'd gone back to a former boyfriend, having realised the wedding was a mistake.

'I've ripped up her photograph and want to forget it all happened.

'I have no plans to marry again. Once bitten, twice shy. I think have learned my lesson. But if anyone wants to marry me I'm open to offers.'

But, it didn't exactly happen like that.

* * * * * *

Back in late 1978, not 1977, after I was kicked off the Rock, Curly and His Nibs were going nuts trying to figure out how to get me back to Alexandra's.

It was me who geed up the salesmen to get them out on the streets hustling for punters and dreaming up new ways to outsmart our competition, the discos and clubs in Plaza Gomila and Cala Major – places like La Sirena, which had been my downfall - just west of Palma proper. And I was the one who made the boat trips and nights at Alex's go with a bang.

I was Louie The Lip. It was what I did. Simple as that.

After they'd tried pleading with the Spanish authorities to overturn my deportation order, His Nibs's lawyers hit on what had the makings of a perfectly legal great plan.

There was a crew of hookers who worked Plaza Gomila and the streets around it and these girls used to like to come and dance at Alex's, especially when the US 6th Fleet was in town. It wasn't difficult for Curly and His Nibs to persuade one of the girls to go to London and marry me, especially when they offered to reward her handsomely - about £3000 quid plus expenses.

The tart Curly and His Nibs found was called 'Marianna', a nice girl as it goes.

Now, the reason 'Marianna' was paid to marry me was because under Spanish law at that time, according to His Nibs's lawyers, a husband was legally obliged to support his wife wherever she was. If I married 'Marianna', I had to look after her and the only way I could do that, my only source of income, was by being in Spain because my job was to run a nightclub in Majorca.

In theory, it was a great idea.

'Marianna' didn't speak a word of English so someone had to make sure she got to the UK. The guy who did this was a suave Filipino named Ricardo. Ricardo managed the boats we used for our beach parties and champagne night disco cruises. In Palma, Ricardo was the owner of Cruceros Palma, the company really owned by Curly and me. He also used to help me arrange work permits for my ticket sellers.

As well as Spanish – and Filipino, I guess - Ricardo spoke excellent, weirdly posh English.

Ricardo brought over 'Marianna' so she could marry me. 'Marianna' insisted on bringing her friend. Another hooker. We checked the two girls into a B&B in King's Cross. My last words to them were 'I'll pick you up at 11 tomorrow morning.' The wedding was at 12 at the registry office.

Ricardo stayed with me at my sister Pat's in Bethnal Green. Ricardo's first morning, Pat made him a full English breakfast. It really was full: twelve sausages, half a pig in bacon rashers, four eggs, a field of mushrooms and another of tomatoes. 'It's an English tradition, Ricky,' she said. 'Now, eat up.'

About 7 in the evening of the day before the wedding, Pat got a phone call. She listened, then said 'Ricardo, it's for you'. She looked confused. Ricardo took the call and Pat and I watched as the colour drained from his face and he kept saying, 'No, no...no, no? NO?' while clicking his fingers for a pen and paper. He scribbled something down and hung up, looking shocked and as white as a sheet as a Filipino with a suntan can look.

'What's wrong, Ricardo?' Pat and I said at the same time.

In his posh voice, which was shaking quite a bit, Ricardo explained that the girls had decided to go shopping in Oxford Street that afternoon and got themselves arrested for shoplifting. They were banged up in Marylebone police station.

Ricardo and I hurtled down to the police station in a taxi. The girls were going to be held overnight and there was absolutely nothing I could do about it. I asked the desk sergeant if the case would be heard the following morning and he said there was no guarantee.

I explained I was getting married at 12 the next day and, if my blushing bride to be wasn't out of the nick by then the wedding couldn't take place. At first he didn't believe my story but I showed him a piece of paper from the registry office which confirmed the time of the wedding. He said he couldn't promise anything but he'd see if he could make sure 'Marianna' and her friend's case was one of the first heard.

The next morning, after a sleepless night – no stag do for me – I was at the nick by 9AM wearing a hopeful carnation in my lapel and sending up prayers to every god I could think of that the desk sergeant had been able to fix things.

Whether he had or not, 'Marianna' and her friend's case was heard at 10 and we were out by 11. The girls were fined £100 each and there was £100 costs to pay. When they were told this, they looked at Ricardo, shrugged and said in Spanish 'we're not paying that'. They knew they had me over a barrel.

We made it to the registry office with ten minutes to spare. The guy did his 'do you take this man?' bit. Ricardo translated what he'd said into Spanish. 'Marianna' repeated the vows in pidgin English. I slipped Pat's wedding ring on her finger and made a mental note to get it back off her sharpish. The last thing I wanted was her scarpering with my sister's pride and joy. Pat would have killed me.

And 'Marianna' and me were man and wife. One thing the Evening Standard got right was the marriage not being consummated. 'Marianna' had cost me an extra £300 in fines and nearly given me a heart attack into the bargain. The last thing I wanted was a night of wedded bliss with her, even if she'd been up for it. I gave 'Marianna' the other half of the three grand she'd been promised and a peck on the cheek and put her and her friend in taxi to Gatwick.

It had been a nightmare but I was legally married and could now present my marriage certificate to the Spanish consulate and I'd be on my way back to the Rock.

But, I wasn't to see the Rock for a couple more years because the only problem with the strategy that his Nibs's lawyers had come up with was that it didn't work. They were legally correct – the Spanish consulate in London didn't dispute that. The problem was that the Spanish dragged their heels. No surprises there.

The first time I bounced up to the consulate building in Sloane Square with my marriage license, the day after the wedding, it felt like I was halfway home to the Rock.

A year later, after I'd trudged back and forth to the consulate Christ knows how many times, I gave up. 'Marianna' had made a tasty £3000 and got away with a shoplifting spree scot-free and I was still stranded in London.

But, after the two years was up and I could have the marriage annulled I did.

* * * * * *

The reason my story ended up in the Evening Standard was because the case for annulment was heard at the divorce courts in High Holborn. Journalists from the big newspapers always hung around outside because this was where the juiciest divorces were dealt with – celebrities, politicians and so on.

Some of the journalists had been in court, listening in on my case and it had obviously appealed to them as a good story. So, when I came out, they besieged me.

Of course, as with the judge, I couldn't tell the real story so I had to carry on making stuff up. Which I did.

I was chuffed to see my picture in the Evening Standard that night but blown away when Pat woke me up the following morning with the news that the story had been picked up by every national newspaper as well.

I was famous. Finally! But not in a way I could have ever dreamed of.

* * * * * *

Now, here's a postscript to the story of my marriage that never was.

A short while after the marriage, I treated Blossy to a trip to New York. He'd never been to America. We had a blast. Peter did a stand up routine at a comedy club that had an open mic night every Monday. You were allowed five minutes onstage to do your thing.

Peter's thing was to get up on the stage, such as it was, and turn his back to the audience before taking off his jacket painfully slowly and laying it over the stool behind him.

The audience, a full house, waited to see what he would do. Slowly, he turned round and looked at them. 'Hello, my name's Peter from London,' he said. The crowd went quiet. I cringed in a corner, nowhere near drunk enough. I knew what he was capable of.

'Once upon a time, a long, long time ago, in the countryside, in England, lived a cow,' he said. 'It was a very happy cow and it had a really full, happy life in a lovely field eating as much grass as it wanted every day.' He paused. 'Now, I expect you're wondering what the name of this really happy cow was?' He turned back to the stool, put his jacket back on, incredibly slowly, before facing the crowd who, amazingly to me, were hypnotised. 'Well,' he said, 'the cow's name was,' very long pause, 'Buttercup'.

Silence. Stunned silence. One person started to clap. Then another. And another. Finally, the place erupted in applause. Peter just stood there deadpan.

When Peter walked off the stage and through the now cheering audience, people were shaking his hand. One guy pulled him aside and said 'man, that was a moment'.

In his own truly original, utterly weird way, Peter still had it. Whatever 'it' was.

* * * * * *

When we got back after our week-long trip to New York, it was back to Pat's for me. I opened the front door, dropped my suitcase and walked into the living room.

Pat was watching TV. 'Have a nice time did you, Lou?' She made it sound like I'd just gone out to get a pint of milk.

'Lovely,' I said.

'I've got a surprise for you,' she said. She stood up, 'I'll just go and get it.'

I sat down in my usual place in front of the TV. She appeared in the door with a huge sack over her shoulder. I looked up at her. She stepped forward and emptied the contents of the sack all over me.

I was ankle-deep in letters and postcards. My mouth hung open. 'They started arriving after you was in the papers and said you was open for offers,' Pat said. I picked up one letter, sniffed it. It smelt of scent and something a bit like curry powder. I thought I was hallucinating from jet-lag. I opened the letter and these photos fell out. I picked one up off the floor. It was a picture of an extremely fat Indian looking woman. I looked at the letter I held in my slightly trembling hand and read it. It was brief and written in very old-fashioned English.

Miss Patel, who'd written the letter, explained she'd only been able to send me an old photo. She'd lost a lot of weight since that picture was taken. Miss Patel, forty years old and a schoolteacher in a small village, lived in Sri Lanka and, God knows how, had read my story. She wanted to come to London, meet me and maybe get married.

There were hundreds of proposals like this from all round the world.

I looked at Pat. She shook her head, started laughing. 'Don't go thinking you're God's gift, Louie,' she said. 'They've read your story and decided you must have a few bob. Who do they think you are? Aristotle bleedin' Onassis? Cup of tea, love?'

AFTERNOON DELIGHT

It was mid-August 1983 when Bernie the Fox, my old mate from back in Bethnal Green called me, said this character he knew was coming over on holiday and would I look after him. The bloke's name was Arthur Donaldson. I'd met him a few times in the boozers with Bernie. Sure, I said. Happy to.

Bernie hadn't really changed. He was still doing the gangster bit round the East End, as he'd done ever since we were kids and coming out to top up his astonishing tan with me at least once a season. Whenever he came over he'd spirit away the bundles of pesetas I had stashed round my apartment, turn them into pounds and bank them for me back in the UK.

This Arthur Donaldson turns up. He was very white. I remember that. Easy-going, chuffed to be on holiday. And he was petrified of water.

I only found this out on his second day, when a couple of my gorgeous Swedish sales girls took him down to Illetes, to the beach down there, to get him some rays.

When I got there, Donald was lying on the beach on his own going a nice shade of lobster. 'Where are the birds?' I said.

'Went for a dip,' he said, pointing in the direction of two lovely curvy brown backs and heads of white-blonde hair.

'Why didn't you go in? The water's lovely.'

'Nah, I'm happy lying in the sun,' he said.

'Come on,' I said. 'You can't come to the Rock and not take a dip in the bleedin' Med.'

He walked down with me but he'd only go in up to his waist. Stood there, shaking with nerves but trying to make it look like the most natural thing in the world. I'd figured it out for myself so I wasn't surprised when, on the way back, out of the side of his mouth he said to me 'can't swim, never learned. Keep schtum.'

And he'd come on holiday to an island, where you're in and out of the sea or the pool all day. Poor sod, I thought.

I was seeing a Danish bird called Lone at the time and she was working as a nurse cum housekeeper for an ancient German couple in Cala Rajada, over on the other side of the island. We'd been spending a lot of time together and her moving away was a bit of a wrench for both of us. And, if you've ever lived on an island you'll know that travelling gets to be a much bigger deal. Forty-five kilometres feels like a drive across Africa. The landscape changes so much in Majorca once you leave Palma, which adds to the feeling that you're going on a continental road trip.

So, when Lone's first day off came round I was gagging to see her but, of course, I'd also promised Bernie I'd show Arthur a great time.

I said to Arthur, this is what I'm doing, do you want to come? See another part of the island. I may have said Lone might have a friend. Probably.

According to Lone, the German's villa was a palace with six bedrooms, an acre of landscaped gardens, pine trees and a pool. So, whatever happened, it would be a great place for Arthur to hang out.

He said, why not? And off we went. I borrowed Curly's car, his pride and joy.

Before coming to the Rock, I don't think Donald had been out of the East End in his life – one of those people who thinks a trip up the West End is a big deal – so he was happy as Larry.

It was a beautiful day. But, that summer they all were. Hot but a nice breeze. You could see for miles, so there were these fantastic views – the mountains looking like folded paper, the sea, empty blue sky, all that. Palm trees. Arthur was loving it. I could tell he thought this is the life. People get that look.

He was fascinated by the people in the villages we went through. When we got away from the tourist spots, it was like the Middle Ages. Women wearing black from head to foot. Windmills everywhere. Horses and carts, even.

After about an hour, we stopped in a small café for coffee. Next door was a souvenir shop with a row of red, blue, yellow and orange pumped-up lilos lined up outside, tied to each other. There was even a blow-up shark. 'Want one?' I said to Arthur. Like he was a kid.

'Why not?' he said. I bought him a bright orange lilo and a towel with a map of Majorca on it. Somehow we squeezed the lilo into the back of Curly's car and headed off towards Cala Rajada and Lone.

* * * * * *

Lone wasn't wrong. The villa was huge. Like an embassy or something. We drove up through lawns of that Spanish grass that never looks real to the front door, standing between two white pillars. Arthur looked at me, eyes wide. 'You're a long way from Valance Road, m'boy,' I said, waggling an imaginary cigar.

Followed by Arthur and the wobbling lilo, I climbed the steps and rang the bell, praying the Krauts weren't around. Lone answered the door, her deep tan set off by a simple white cotton dress over what looked like black lace undies. Lone threw her arms round me and gave me a long, deep kiss and I was very pleased to see her, if you know what I mean. She shook Arthur's hand politely, told us the Germans were out for the day and that she'd made lunch.

I could feel Arthur's eyes going backwards and forwards from Lone to me and, to be honest, it made me nervous more than anything else.

After lunch and a few cold beers I winked at Arthur. 'I'm a bit knackered, mate,' I said. 'Think I'll take a siesta.'

He got my drift right away and said 'no sweat, you carry on, mate. I'll get some sun. Maybe try out the lilo.'

Lone and I waited until he was lying down on a sun-lounger beside the pool, the lilo floating in the shallow end, before we fell on each other and I chased her upstairs.

* * * * * *

There's nothing better than a bit of afternoon delight, especially when you haven't seen each other for a while. We wore each other out and went sparko for a couple of hours.

When I woke up Lone was shaking me. 'Come on, Louie, they'll be back any minute. Time to go.' It took me a while to figure out where I was. You know how deep that kind of sleep is, right? I hopped round the room for a bit till I got my legs in my swimming trunks, pulled on my t-shirt and went out to get Arthur.

The lilo was floating at the deep end of the pool but Arthur was nowhere to be seen. 'Maybe he's gone for a walk,' Lone said.

'Arthur!' I shouted. 'Time to vamos, mate.' No reply. I walked to the pool, bent over to scoop out the lilo and that's when I saw him.

Lying at the bottom of the deep end. I just stood and looked at him down there. 'What is it?' Lone said. She came and looked over my shoulder and that's when she started to scream. I had never heard anyone scream like that. Like they do in the movies. It was horrible.

We looked at each other. 'He couldn't swim,' I said.

'But, the lilo?' She said. 'How...? What are we going to do? The owners...'

I looked down at Arthur, lying at the bottom of the pool face up. 'Should we pull him out?' Lone said.

'No, I said, 'we should call the police'. I ran inside, looking for the phone. The Germans, being organised, had the cops' number next to it. I called and ten minutes later two Guardia Civil turned up. After they'd hauled Arthur out of the pool and called an ambulance, the cops asked me what I thought might have happened. They had very little English and my Spanish wasn't that great so there was no way of explaining Arthur couldn't swim.

Poor sod must have thought it was safe on the lilo and the pool was dead shallow. I guess he fell asleep, rolled off and drowned. Maybe hit his head or something.

Arthur Donaldson, terrified of water, drowned.

As the ambulance was driving away, it met a long shiny red Mercedes which had to back all the way down the drive before heading back up again. A tall guy with a face tanned brown red, who looked like he might have been a tank commander, struggled out of the car, hauling his gut after him.

The German guy marched over to the cops, his small, square, wife trotting at his heels. Lone and I watched as the guy interrogated the cops. His first words to Lone, after he'd stomped over to us, were a choked 'we go away for one day! What on earth happened here? Who is this man?'

I explained as best as I could. Luckily the wife turned out to be sympathetic and understood it was terrible accident. No-one's fault. She hugged Lone, who was crying. The husband started to calm down.

I felt terrible saying it but I said 'sorry, Lone, I need to be getting back to Palma now. Come with me if you want.'

Lone shook her head. The tank commander scowled at me. His wife patted Lone's arm and gave me a sharp look. I felt like saying 'it's not my fault. He was my mate, for Christ's sake.'

Instead, I pecked Lone on the cheek and trudged off to Curly's motor. I was shaking.

* * * * * *

A couple of days later I was having a quiet beer outside the Bally Jay when this bloke I knew who had a bar in El Arenal sidled up to me. 'You're a bit off your patch,' I said.

'I'm a reporter now,' he said. 'Sending stories back to the UK rags. I'm following up this drowning story. That English guy over in Cala Rajada.' He shot me a look from under heavy ginger eyebrows. 'Nasty business that.'

'Yeah' I said. My mind was working fast. I'd told Curly and Bernie the Fox what had happened but that was it. Did this guy know something or was he fishing? I didn't stick around to find out. 'Sorry, mate,' I said, draining my beer, doing my best to stop my hand from shaking too much. 'Can't help you. Don't know anything about it. Good luck.' And I was off.

I ducked into Alex's pronto, slipped into the office and dialled Bernie in London. Luckily, he was in. 'Listen,' I said. 'What's the story? I've just had some herbert who claims to be a reporter sniffing around, trying to find out if I know anything about Arthur's death.'

'You are not going to believe this,' he said. I didn't there and then but, a day or so, it started to sink in.

* * * * * *

You see, Arthur had two older sisters who doted on him. You wouldn't want to cross those two. They didn't believe Arthur drowned in a swimming pool because he was so terrified of water he'd never have gone near one by himself. They'd convinced themselves Arthur was murdered and gone round Bethnal Green telling that to anyone who'd listen. After a day or so of this, they'd whipped up a bit of a storm and forced the British cops to investigate.

They started with Bernie, a known villain, and yanked up his floorboards looking for evidence or clues. I can't believe the cops thought Bernie did it for a second but following up the sisters' story gave them a perfect excuse to rattle his cage. They might not find anything but who knows what else they'd unearth. Luckily for Bernie, they got nada.

When I told Bernie I was sorry he'd got dragged into the whole mad mess, he chuckled. 'It's almost worth it to watch the rozzer's faces when they don't turn anything up,' he said. 'Poor old Arthur, though. He only goes and does something exciting by accident.'

'Bern!' I said, but I knew what he meant. Arthur was just a nice bloke and would have been astonished at being the cause of all this drama.

* * * * * *

After a few weeks everything had died down. The reporter geezer had been given a mouthful by Curly and told never to show his face round the club again.

The thing was, although it didn't look like there'd be any comeback, I still felt terrible. One morning I took myself off to the British consulate to see if there'd been any developments.

'We buried him three days ago,' the geezer said.

I was startled. 'Where? Here?' He nodded. 'Not in London?' He shook his head. 'Why?'

'When I got in touch with the deceased's sisters and asked them if they wanted to have his body flown home to be buried they asked me the cost and, when I told them, said they didn't have the cash. They asked me what would happen and I told them he'd be buried in a pauper's grave. And three days ago that was what happened. Case closed.'

It seemed a bit weird that Arthur's sisters, who thought so much of him, would leave him to be buried that way, no matter how much it cost. I felt gutted that I didn't have the money to ship Arthur back to Bethnal Green. And the thought of him in this Spanish pauper's grave – one of those holes in the wall that looked like a white cement locker – made me feel even worse.

The least I could do, I decided, was to read something from the Bible at Arthur's hole in the wall. I'm Jewish so I know zilch about the Bible but I went along to the English Church. The padre lent me a well-worn Bible and picked out a passage for me to read.

Next morning, I stood alone in front of the box below which they'd written Arthur's name and the day he died in wet cement – 2.8.83. It looked they'd done it with a bent nail. They'd spelt his name 'Artur Danalson'. It was one of those mornings where it's so hot you think you're going to fall over at any minute, when the backs of your knees sweat. I read the bit from the Bible and felt a little bit better. At least I'd done something.

But it took a long time before I stopped dreaming of Arthur poking his head out from behind a palm tree in that garden, his nose bright pink from the sun, giving me the thumbs up and saying 'fooled ya, Louie, didn't I?'

And that orange lilo floating round and round in circles.

RIP Arthur Donaldson.

WET AND WILD

I looked down from the heights of Alexandra's DJ booth at what I had created and saw it was good.

Six soaking wet girls gyrated in front of me in just their panties to Work That Body by Diana Ross, a great disco tune, one of the big hits of the summer before and perfect for the wet t-shirt contests.

Since I'd bought the idea back from Fort Lauderdale three years before, wet t-shirt contests had become a huge draw for Alexandra's. What I hadn't realised was that the contests would attract a whole new audience of young Spanish blokes into the club on top of the Scandies and Germans.

* * * * * *

Only ten years before, under Franco, the Generalissimo, we'd been obliged to make sure no-one even kissed on the dance floor. A geezer called Chris Brown who promoted Alex's down the coast at Santa Ponsa got banged up in a cell once for kissing a girl outside the club. It was easy to forget just how unbelievably strict life was under the old man.

Those were the days when, if the cops found a joint on you, you got six years and a day in El Slammer. You were guilty as charged and it was up to you to prove otherwise. Forget Habeas Corpus in Spain, pal.

What had really kick-started the new permissive Spain was when the Spanish Lieutenant Colonel Antonio Tejero and 200 members of the Guardia Civil stormed the legislature building back in February 1981 and had tried to take the new democratically elected government hostage. They wanted to turn back the clock.

When the attempted coup was foiled because King Juan Carlos appealed to the military to remain loyal and condemn the rebels, it seemed like Spain took that as the signal to really go into overdrive when it came to freedom.

Now hardcore porn was openly available in newsagents and on TV. Majorca was hit by a tidal wave of heroin. Junkies slumped on corners drinking milk, the only thing they could get down.

* * * * * *

A new, anything goes Spain was fine by me if it meant we could put on the wet t-shirt contests.

I grinned, put the mic close to my mouth and sang along: 'Work that body, girls, work that body. Remember, first prize tonight is a bottle of vintage champagne. Alexandra's legendary wet t-shirt contest. The first and still the greatest. And I am Tom Brown, your MC.'

The girls slithered around on the stage we'd made out of a six foot piece of hardwood and placed on top of eight red plastic beer bottle crates. In the middle of the stage, for some reason I couldn't remember, there was a drawing of a skull and crossbones.

The lads gathered round the stage whooped and hollered as the girls danced, their breasts bouncing, panties see-through from the water I'd been squirting on them. One girl's breasts were bright red from sunburn and looked sore but that didn't stop her from throwing herself around with the others. In her mind, that bottle of champagne had her name on it.

I looked up at the ceiling of Alex's, up to where the legendary Jimi Hendrix had rammed his guitar through the roof on 15 July 1968, opening night of the club, back when it was owned by Hendrix's manager, Mike Jeffery.

Hendrix's classic Electric Ladyland album with its famous cover of the naked women was released in October 68. Now I was watching my own electric ladyland, except my ladies were slithering saucy Scandies.

In the couple of years since I'd first introduced the wet t-shirt contests, I'd stopped being surprised at how simple it was to persuade the girls to strip down to their panties which, by now, left practically nothing to the imagination.

I'd worked out a strategy which never failed to work.

* * * * * *

We held the contests at two in the morning. That way, we had a maximum capacity crowd and the girls were tipsy enough to lose whatever inhibitions they'd started out with. Which, in the case of the Scandie girls was, admittedly, not many.

Even though, like I said, I knew we'd end up with five or six girls up for the wet t-shirt contests, there was always tension at the start of the night.

I'd delegate two of my best looking, most charming and persuasive ticket sellers to talk the girls into representing their country. The conversation would usually go something like this:

Oily ticket seller: Hello, darling, where you from?

Giggling Scandie girl: Sveden.

OTS: You're gorgeous. I'm moving to Sweden.

GSG: Sank you.

OTS: Now, what's your name, sweetheart?

GSG: Monica.

OTS: Monica, that's a lovely name. Now, how would you like to represent Sweden in one of the most demanding international challenges in the world?

GSG: Sorry?

OTS: You know about Alexandra's legendary Wet T-Shirt contests?

GSG: No sank you.

OTS: What? You don't know what I'm going to ask you, Monica. Please. Right, I am going to ask you if you'd like to take part in the wet t-shirt contest. Why? Because you're a lovely girl, Monica. And I think you could win this one for the honour of Sweden. Aren't you proud to be Swedish?

GSG: Of course.

OTS: And you're proud of your, you know, natural assets, right?

GSG: My what? *(OTS points at her breasts, spilling out of a tight purple evening dress. She blushes but giggles.)* Of course.

OTS: You should be. You know what, I shouldn't say this but if you took part, I bet you'd win. So, what do you think?

(If Monica was with a gang of other girls or even with her boyfriend, my oily ticket seller would appeal to them to help persuade Monica that taking part in the contest was vital for the honour of her country. Boyfriends were particularly supportive.)

GSG: Do I have to take my t-shirt off?

OTS: Of course not. All that happens is we give you a silk t-shirt which we spray with a little bit of water. Then, you dance. So, really you're just dancing for your country.

(This would confuse Monica because she thought it was all about getting her tits out for the pride of her country. Now, the nice English boy is telling her all she needs to do is dance. And that doesn't sound so bad.)

GSG: *(With a mixture of embarrassment, nervousness, pride and determination.)* OK, what do I have to do?

OTS: *(Punching the air)* Yes! See that curtain over there? Be in front of it at about 1.45 and you'll find out. Fantastic, thank you, Monica!

My oily ticket seller plants a big kiss on Monica's tanned and trembling cheek and disappears into the crowd, leaving her excited but a bit confused as to what she's just got herself into. Come 1.40, the ticket seller mysteriously appears at her side and gently guides her to the curtain. By now, she's had a few free sherberts for Swedish courage, and doesn't need much persuading. We hand out free drink tickets to the contestants precisely for that reason. Every now and again, we'd have a bolter who'd have to be talked back into taking part. My boys were shameless and would use anything they could to talk a reluctant Finn into stripping off.

Once the girls were behind the curtain, we'd hand round the silk t-shirts and they'd undress. By now, all the girls would be looking at each other and Monica from Sweden would be eyeing Petra from Denmark thinking 'I have much better breasts than her. Hers are bigger but mine are the better shape. I should win.' I could feel the competitive spirit getting stronger. And, of course, I'd encourage it by winking at a girl or giving another one the thumbs up.

While I was gleefully egging the girls on – and deciding which one I'd have a crack at later – my boys would be setting up the stage. They'd have also picked out fifteen guys to be judges, making sure there was a good representation of blokes from each girl's country to get everything good and heated, and given them pens and paper so they could vote. Eddie from Luton, the DJ, would be whipping things up even more so that when the girls did come out they were met with a massive blast of applause, whistling and hooting which I could tell psyched them up even more.

So, I open the curtain. The girls dance out, hands over their heads, breasts shifting suggestively in their silk t-shirts. The roar of approval nearly takes the roof off the club. I follow out, waving my hand-held water spray over my head, grinning like a maniac.

First off, I introduce each girl and she dances onstage by herself. I usually pick the one who looks most nervous to start so she doesn't have a chance to chicken out. Once she's up there, I spray her with water which I've made sure is icy-cold so she gasps and the old chapel hat pegs stick out even more. She goes bright red and I grin like the devil.

One by one, the girls take their place on stage and submit to the icy spray. When they've all been introduced and they're standing at the side of the stage, raring to go again by now, I spray them all once more, really drenching them this time.

Now, with Eddie whipping things up even more, my two most persuasive lads single out the girl most likely to take her t-shirt all the way off – they're always right. They lift her wet t-shirt up over her head while she's protesting but not really. Now, she's up on stage dancing about, breasts bouncing. The guys in the crowd are going crazy – ridiculous really because they've been surrounded by topless girls all day long on the beach.

My boys move to the next girl who looks most likely to take her t-shirt off. By now, all the other girls are thinking that the topless ones have a better chance of winning. In a flash, they've all stripped off and are dancing on the creaking stage.

The girls are really into it by now, sticking out their chests and wobbling around as they dance. Monica from Sweden who, a couple of hours ago, wouldn't have been caught dead doing what she is now, is throwing her hair around and has her hands in the air. I make a note to try it on with her later. Eddie fades the record down and asks for someone to collect the paper and pens from the fifteen judges. I'm handed the pieces of paper and I look through them. Four of the guys have voted for Monica from Sweden but six of them have gone for Petra from Denmark, probably because of the size of her breasts. But, there can only be one winner.

I, ask for silence and announce tonight's winner of Alexandra's legendary wet t-shirt contest: 'Monica from Sweden'. A roar of applause. Monica's thrilled and squealing with delight. Petra looks pissed off. I step down onto the stage. Invite Monica back up. Strip off my 'Miss Wet T-Shirt 1982' t-shirt, give it to her and she puts it on. I give her a smacking kiss on each cheek, hand her the first prize of a bottle of champagne and start to schmooze her for real.

And, standing in the shadows smoking his cheap cigar, Curly smiles to himself.

HELLO SAILOR!

'You know we just about blew you out of the water last night?'

I almost fell off my bar stool. 'You what?'

'Yep,' said the big black guy sitting next to me. He chuckled, a deep low gurgle. 'You don't know how close you came, man.'

* * * * * *

Curly hadn't been wrong about the rise and rise of Magaluf. More and more clubs opened and, as they did, the number of punters making the trip into Palma shrank. Magaluf also had beaches full of oiled up topless birds, unlike Palma, which didn't have a natural beach. The horror stories the tour reps spread about drug dealers and muggings in Plaza Gomila and Terreno didn't help. And we had to out-hustle the other clubs in Gomila for the punters that did come.

The regular yachtie day workers we'd had who worked on the luxury yachts that moored in the Bay of Palma also disappeared when a new marina was built down the coast at a place called Puerto Portals.

Which is why the American 6th Fleet became our lifeline.

* * * * * *

The US navy had been coming to Majorca and mooring in the bay of Palma since after WWII ended and the start of the Cold War with Russia.

Because the Generalissimo Franco had encouraged tourism to Majorca from very early on – it was the Love Island for thousands of Spanish couples, the place where babies were conceived - the island could handle the US navy and offer them plenty. It soon became a favourite port of call throughout the navy.

So much so that the Rock received around 50,000 sailors a year on average and one year an incredible 150,000 discovered the delights of Majorca.

The Yanks may have loved the Rock but they sometimes didn't quite get it. One of my favourite places to hand out flyers for Alexandra's was opposite the cathedral, on a street called the Born that ran down to the sea. The spot was also big with the gypsy shoeshine boys who, when they knew the navy was in town, came out in force looking for shoes and dinero.

I once watched in amazement as an American sailor let a shoeshine boy polish his suede shoes. I guess the guy must have been too polite to say no. One way to earn the goodwill of the natives and make them think you're nuts at the same time, I suppose.

* * * * * *

Over the years since 1975, when Alexandra's opened,

we'd built up a great relationship with the Yank sailors, especially the black guys. The difference between the whites and blacks was that the white boys usually got so pissed they were out for the count very early on. The blacks didn't do that because they liked to dance and we always made sure we played their music, which wasn't a hardship because everyone loved it. Over the years the word had spread throughout the US navy that Alex's was the place to head for in Palma.

The black guys weren't any trouble because they stayed sober but there were sometimes fights between them and the white sailors and, if that happened, I had to run up to Plaza Gomila and find a couple of Shore Patrol, big buggers with long white sticks and short fuses. Just the sight of them coming through the door of Alex's was enough to stop trouble in its tracks.

Even though the movements of the US navy were meant to be top secret, the hookers who came to dance at Alex's and loved the black sailors always knew they were coming a couple of days in advance so we had time to plan our campaign with military precision to make sure they headed our way.

* * * * * *

Ours was a two-pronged operation, as it were.

The day the fleet arrived, my team would be tracking down every halfway decent bird with a pulse they could find. Their pitch went something like this: 'Scuse me. Do you speak English? You do? Fantastic. Listen, it's the 10th anniversary of Alexandra's. You know Alexandra's right? You don't? Just arrived, have you? Right, because it's the anniversary of the club, we're giving away free passes tonight and a legendary Alexandra's cocktail. You'll come, won't you? Course you will. See you tonight, girls!'

What we didn't tell the girls was that when they turned up at Alex's they'd be surrounded by a couple of hundred Yank sailors circling them like starving sharks. Most of the sailors had shore leave that ended at midnight, which made them doubly desperate to cram in as much action as possible the minute they got through the club doors. We also didn't tell them it was the 10th anniversary of Alex's every week.

While my PRs were hustling potential bait, I'd be making sure I was the first one up the metal gangplank and piped aboard when the navy docked in Palma. That way I'd get the jump on everyone trying to part the Yank sailors from their precious spending loot.

To give myself the front to do this I channelled the spirit of Sergeant Ernie Bilko, my hero from the classic TV show. Dressed in a homemade uniform of sailor's cap, short-sleeved crisp white shirt with gold epaulettes I'd found in a flea market and sown on myself, pressed white strides, ID round my neck in a clear plastic holder and an important-looking bulging briefcase, I'd force my way to the head of the queue waiting to get onboard.

In the queue would be Tumi Bestard, the Acting US Consular Agent and, just behind him, the Mayor of Palma with his heavy Mayor's gold chain round his neck, followed by tour guides, a shoe salesman and a Majorica pearl salesman. Tumi and the Mayor would be looking at me trying to figure out who I was. The salesmen, who knew a chancer when they saw one, would be scowling.

Most times it was Tumi, the Mayor then me in the line. Tumi was proud of the fact that he was always the first on board to greet the fleet. One time, I beat him to it by just steaming in front of him. He didn't like that.

As soon as I could, I shot up the gangplank with my hand outstretched and a big grin slapped on my face. Shaking hands with the captain and senior officers at a rapid rate of knots, I'd invite them to the official welcoming party which was going to be held at Alexandra's that night. I had to do this pronto before the real officials got a sniff of what I was up to.

'Don't forget,' I'd say. 'There'll be VIP tickets for you and the United States Office staff and free drinks.' Next I'd raise my voice and, sounding as important as I could, I'd ask the captain to please delegate two men to accompany me to the mess deck so I could invite some of the lower-ranking men to the official welcoming party. By now, the captain was even more confused and embarrassed at keeping the actual official officials waiting and he'd bark out orders for two men to escort me down below decks. And off we'd trot.

* * * * * *

One time, as I was walking away from the captain, I conjured up a scene from an imaginary episode of Bilko that had me in stitches. Picture this.

I'm dressed in my homemade uniform. One of my fake scrambled egg epaulets is coming loose. I'm moving fast so that I can get below decks without being rumbled. But, without warning, I stop.

Turning, I walk back to the captain. I wipe a fake tear from behind my shades, bow my head and say 'such brave men'. I start to place a hand on the captain's shoulder but leave it hanging in mid-air before attempting a crisp salute that somehow goes wrong. I turn on my heels, look at the two open-mouthed waiting jarheads and bark 'come on, come on, move it, move it! What is this, a staring contest?' before marching off downstairs.

Once below decks, I pop my head into the ship's galley. A fat tattooed chef in a filthy vest and a crumpled chef's hat is stirring something bubbling and terrifying with a ladle. A scowling Chinese guy peels potatoes. A transistor radio wedged behind a pipe plays tinny pop.

'Don't make anything special for me,' I say to the startled chef. 'I'll,' gulp, 'have what the fellows are having.' I salute him. He raises his own hand, forgetting it's the hand holding the ladle, and splatters the Chinese guy with boiling hot, bright red liquid. The Chinese guy screams.

Just before I walk away, I say again 'such brave boys'.

* * * * * *

Once I was safely away from the top brass, I'd set up a table and start dishing out invites to Alex's from my bulging briefcase, talking up the wet t-shirt contest and doing my spiel. I'd also be putting up posters promoting the wet t-shirt contest. The news went round the men like wildfire.

Then, mission accomplished, I'd stroll off the ship congratulating myself. One time, in the company of one of my salesmen called Pete Dixon, who for some reason had come with me – and who I'd introduced to the captain as 'Vladimir, the official photographer' – I half-inched a side of bacon from a conveyor belt in the kitchen and stashed in my holdall. So, let's work this out, I'm Jewish and I'm pinching bacon.

The next thing was to make sure that, as soon as the sailors put a foot on dry land, they were steered in the direction of Alexandra's by four of my best-looking PR girls handing out more tickets and reminding the guys about the wet t-shirt contest that night. 'Don't forget, guys' they'd say, 'it's the tenth anniversary of Alex's tonight so it's going to be a very special night'.

By ten, when we opened, I could guarantee there would be at least a couple of hundred guys clamouring to get in. When they did, I'd be in full-on Tom Brown mode – complete with rainbow coloured afro wig – talking about how tonight was 'ladeez night' and there were hundreds of 'ladeez' on their way down to the club right that very minute, while playing 'Ladies Night' by Kool and the Gang.

This was always a bit of a hairy moment because if the girls didn't show, there were only the local hookers available. Not that *they* would have minded, I'm sure.

But the tourist girls always arrived and we never had riots.

Our routine worked perfectly until the competition just got too much for us.

The first blow was struck when a Yank who was pally with some of the captains who came to Majorca opened a bar in Magaluf called Daiquiri Palace. He may have been an ex-sailor. Above Daiquiri Palace was a penthouse apartment the guy made available to the captains and senior officers - for whatever shenanigans they got up to - and, in return, they did everything they could to steer their men to Magaluf short of ordering them to go.

And when the delights of Magaluf also included beaches with bronzed topless birds as far as the eye could see, it wasn't difficult to persuade blokes who'd been cooped up with each other, no booze, plenty of farting and only copies of Playboy and Hustler for entertainment where the action was.

For a while I managed to avoid a total mass desertion from Alex's and complete disaster by sticking up official looking posters that said 'Palmanova and Magaluf strictly off limits' whenever I was able to get onboard ship. Palmanova was another popular resort with great beaches not far from Magaluf.

Now, when the sailors in their Hawaiian shirts hit Palma's Paseo Maritimo and my PRs fell on them they would ask them where they were headed that night. If a sailor said Palmanova or Magaluf, they would be told it was 'off limits. Didn't you hear?'

But, soon, the brass got wise to that one. The aircraft carrier USS John F Kennedy started stopping in Majorca, along with six warships and its own supply ship in tow and that changed everything all over again.

When the Kennedy started calling at Majorca, the USO in Palma began organising free buses to take the men who had shore leave straight to Palmanova or Magaluf, potentially bypassing us altogether.

I got desperate and my competitive spirit got the better of me.

It was this fatal combination which nearly got me and a disco boat party of 150 very merry party people blown out of the water.

* * * * * *

We were heading back from a champagne night party cruise round Palma Bay when we spotted the grey bulk of the USS John F Kennedy moored out in the bay. As we got closer it loomed above us like the cliffs of a metal country shining in the moonlight. I thought of the six thousand sailors onboard. Even if only a couple of hundred of them came down to Alex's, it would be an amazing result.

Which is why I decided to divert my disco boat in the direction of the Kennedy and drum up a bit more interest in Alex's. I instructed the captain to head towards the floating battleship grey island and really started blasting the music.

Once we got closer to the Kennedy I cut the music, grabbed the mic and, as loud as I could, bellowed 'USS John F Kennedy, this is the Alexandra. We demand that you put down your weapons. I repeat, put down your weapons and prepare for boarding. This is Alexandra, prepare for boarding.' The sound of my voice echoed across the Bay of Palma.

I thought this was hilarious, as did my boatload of party people who'd been guzzling cheap Spanish champagne, sangria and God knows what for the past hour or so. They started jumping about so much that the boat really did start to rock, which pissed my captain off even more. A few of the girls were inspired to take off their tops and shake their suntanned breasts in the direction of the Kennedy.

As we got even closer, I repeated 'USS Kennedy, this is the Alexandra. Prepare for boarding. Prepare for boarding. Put down your weapons.'

By now, a row of heads had appeared over the side of the Kennedy. Seachlights from the ship began raking the boat. My party people started waving and got even more excited. A couple of girls and one bloke bent over and mooned the Kennedy. I, of course, wound them up as much as I could. I found my copy of 'In The Navy' by the Village People and played that a couple of times.

I finished by inviting the crew of the Kennedy down to Alex's for the world famous wet t-shirt contest and we putt-putted away and back to shore.

I was well pleased with myself and I didn't think any more of what we'd done until the following night and I wound up having a drink next to the black guy.

* * * * * *

'Why were you going to blow us out of the water?' I said to the black guy, my voice trembling as I thought of the Kennedy's big guns and the damage they could do. 'You could see we weren't exactly a threat.'

'Nah,' he said. 'I think you just pissed off our captain.'

* * * * * *

Later, I found myself having a drink at the British American Club in the Son Armadans area of Terreno with Tumi Bestard and I discovered he was a real character. He was the son of a director of the bank of Spain and the kind of posh Majorcan I hardly ever rubbed shoulders with, a proper gent. Tumi was one of those guys who'd fallen in love with everything the States stood for – like I had, in a way.

He'd first become obsessed with the navy and all things American as a boy of around eight or nine years old. His family had a place on the edge of a small bay called Portarosa just to the right of Gomila, heading away from the cathedral. This would have been back in the 1940s, when Portarosa was just a settlement of a few houses used as summer places by some of Palma's grander families and the city hadn't reached out to stretch around the bay, joining up the smaller villages.

Tumi would row out to the US navy boats in the bay and ask the sailors to throw down anything they could spare – chewing gum, coins, baseball cards. One time, a sailor with a wicked sense of humour threw him down a pack of condoms. When he got them home he started blowing them up, thinking they were funny-looking balloons, much to the horror of his very proper Majorcan mum.

Tumi had been the Consular Agent since 1961, and the only non-Yank in the whole state department. He loved his job and took it very seriously. Not only was it a big responsibility – it was Tumi the navy turned to if they needed to get their guys sprung from Palma nick – he also got to meet the US top brass, including Presidents, and a fair few legendary stars.

'And, do you know?' Tumi said when we met, 'I was always the first on board to greet the fleet when it arrived in Palma.'

'Not always,' I said. And I told him the story of my Bilko routine.

POOR LAMBS

There's not much you can do to bring in the punters when they're simply not there. Plaza Gomila was no longer the place to be. By summer 1985, Alex's was on the ropes. It was a struggle to put on my curly rainbow wig and my Union Jack clogs every night, go out there and be Louie The Lip, Clown Prince of Clubland to an audience which had shrunk because we could no longer run the boat trips. The authorities had decided the only people who could legally run these were recognized travel companies with kosher insurance.

So, one night I was a little surprised and nervous when Curly strolled across the nearly empty dance floor, followed by His Nibs and, a little way behind them, Paco the bouncer. It was probably the second time I'd seen His Nibs at Alex's since we'd opened back in 1975. Still, he didn't look like he'd come to pronounce the death sentence on the club – there was no skull in one hand, scythe in the air. He was relaxed, beaming and rubbing his hands. I could feel the excitement and confidence coming off him in waves.

'His Nibs is taking us for a ride,' Curly shouted in my ear, his nasal voice going through my head like a dentist's drill as he made himself heard over 'Into The Groove' by Madonna. 'Come on.'

'Now?' I shouted. I couldn't help but think of what the Mafia said to people they were about to wack.

'Now. Come on. You'll be back in time for the toga party later. Pete can play some records.' Pete Dixon was a PR who DJ'd any chance he got. Because he was hungry, he did it for free, which Curly appreciated.

I stepped down from the DJ booth and followed Curly and His Nibs across the dark, cavernous club. Into The Groove and Three Little Birds by Bob Marley blasted out. Pete loved his reggae.

I trailed after Curly and His Nibs as they chatted away in Spanish to each other. We stopped at a powder-blue convertible Bentley. It was a measure of His Nibs's confidence that he could leave a brand new convertible Bentley unlocked in Plaza Gomila. Almost drooling, Curly climbed in the passenger seat and I took the backseat, sinking into the shiny, new cream leather. His Nibs pulled away smoothly, we headed down to the Paseo Maritimo, turned right – me sliding the length of the seat - and headed out of town. A Bentley, millions of pounds worth of pristine white yachts creaking in the harbour under a heavy Mediterranean moon, my own nightclub, I should have been thrilled but all I could think about was whether Alex's was going to get the axe or not.

We cruised along the coast, Curly and His Nibs making small talk. I smoked, looked out at the sea, bit my nails, worried. Once, a bug so big it looked like it should have had people steering it smashed into my glasses, stunning me. I wasn't enjoying myself.

My misery deepened when we got in sight of Magaluf. The sky was lit with a million different shades of neon. The delighted whoops of party people and the blare of car horns cut through the steady thump of music from the open doors of a thousand bars. It was magnificent! Everything Plaza Gomila had been but a lot bigger and much more in your face.

His Nibs steered the Bentley through the crowds of tanned kids striding the sticky streets, wearing next to nothing and looking for adventure, Curly scowling at anyone who got too close to the beast, until we turned the corner into a slightly quieter street. His Nibs eased the Bentley to a stop opposite a field next to a hotel called the Samos, the only one on the street. There were sheep in the field, sleeping and deaf to the sounds of Magaluf in full effect.

His Nibs climbed out of the car. Curly and I followed him over to the field. His Nibs said something to Curly, who nodded and said 'fantastico, muy bueno'. A mosquito bit me on my forehead. I lit a cigarette, pushed my rainbow wig back and scratched.

'So we're going to become sheep farmers, are we?' I said to Curly. 'Business isn't that bad, is it? I don't know anything about sheep.'

'Be serious for once in your life, Louie,' Curly said. 'No we are not going to be bleedin' sheep farmers. He's making us an offer.'

I puffed out my cheeks and, in my best Marlon Brando voice, said 'one we can't refuse?'

'Tell you later,' Curly said. He went back to nodding at everything His Nibs said, his Afro bobbing. A sheep woke up. I looked at it. It looked back at me. Both of us with no idea what was going on. But, whatever His Nibs and Curly were talking about, it didn't sound too bad. His Nibs slapped Curly on the back, shook my hand, grinned and motioned us back towards the Bentley. Once again, we crawled back through the well-oiled kids until we were heading back down towards Palma and the comparative graveyard that was Plaza Gomila.

His Nibs dropped us off outside Alex's and as soon as he'd pulled away, I said 'what was that all about?'

'He's only going to build the biggest disco not just in Majorca but in Spain.'

'And...?'

'He wants us to manage it.'

I looked at Curly's mask-like face, felt like falling to my knees. 'Fantastic. I hope you told him yes!'

'Not exactly.'

'What?'

'He wants his answer tomorrow.'

'So, how will it work? Will we be partners in the new gaff?'

'No, he'd pay us to manage it but we'd get a percentage of the profits. And we'll stay partners in Alex's, for as long as that lasts. I guess he'll get new people in to manage it.'

'Wow,' I said. 'That's amazing. All our troubles are over.' I held out my hand, 'put it there, Curly. I knew something would come along.' I looked up at the sky 'thanks, Angel,' I said.

Curly looked down at the cigar he'd just stubbed out on the street. 'I told him we weren't interested.'

'You what?' I squealed. The night started to spin around me. 'You are joking?' Then I remembered, of course, that Curly didn't joke. My shoulders slumped. 'Why?'

Still looking down at the ground, Curly said. 'Because I know His Nibs. The first year will be great. The second year he'll probably want to do the place up, totally reform it in a different style. We won't have a say in it but it'll come out of our profit.'

'But, still...'

Curly looked at me. 'I don't want to do it, Louie. Got that?' I looked at him. I knew him well enough to see that his mind was made up and wasn't going to be changed. But, I couldn't do anything without him. We were partners.

But, I knew we were missing out on another opportunity of a lifetime.

As I trudged down the glass stairs of Alex's, now filled with cloudy water and a few dying fish, I heard the opening beats of Frankie's 'Relax'.

Yeah, right, I thought, as I changed into my toga, in reality a customized hotel sheet.

* * * * * *

It's the opening night of BCM in Magaluf, the club that Curly and me could have been part of. All day long I hear commercials on the radio saying 'BCM, BCM, grand opening tonight'. Every hour or so a plane crosses the sky trailing a banner that says 'BCM opening tonight, Magaluf'.

That night, we know Alex's will be dead. Everyone's heading down to Magaluf to see this amazing club, His Nibs's glorious achievement. I decide to join them, with Nick, one of our best PRs and a good mate. We leave Curly back at Alex's. He doesn't want to come. We whizz off down to Magaluf on our mopeds around 11. To celebrate the opening, His Nibs has organised a launch party with champagne from ten to midnight. The show, with lasers, special guest DJs and a sound system that had to be brought over from Madrid, starts then.

I know the people on the door. They wave Nick and me through. The club is amazing, designed to look like a Moroccan palace, with water fountains. I can well believe it's the biggest nightclub in Europe. It wouldn't surprise me if it was the largest in the world. His Nibs has said it's designed to hold 6,000 people and, knowing the Spanish and regulations, I'm sure they'll be squeezing in a fair few more.

Nick and me make our way through the His Nibs's guests sipping champagne. He is at their centre, looking like the Godfather in an impeccable cream linen suit, hair slicked back, radiating power. I shake his hand, resisting the temptation to kiss the ring on his finger. Fair play to him, I think. He's pulled it off.

I stand with Nick, sipping champagne. The huge dance floor is empty and waiting. The music fades out. One of His Nibs's mouthpieces makes a speech in Spanish and English which ends with him saying that BCM is now officially open and the night's entertainment will start. Nick and me look at each other. It has to be done. I drain my glass of champagne. He does the same. I stride out into the middle of the vast dance floor and, to a thumping beat, I go wild.

We are the first people to officially dance on the floor of BCM.

It feels like the beginning of something Big, Colossal and Magnificent and that's exactly what BCM and Magaluf becomes.

But not for me, sadly.

BOMBED AT LA BARAKA

I could tell at the interview who would make it selling tickets or not.

On the surface, life on the Rock looked like it was sun, sea, sand and shagging – and it was, of course – but it was also tough and lived without a safety net. So, when I picked people to work for me, I had to feel they had what it took to survive and also that they really were prepared to be part of a team.

The thing I couldn't predict was who would become a victim of the Rock's temptations or not. It was so easy to become a drunk, a drug addict or to simply lose it. Like Peter Bloss had.

I always thanked my lucky stars that it just wasn't in me to become an alcoholic or druggie. It sounds corny, but I was addicted to making people laugh.

But, in some ways, the temptation to reinvent yourself as someone different from who you really were was the biggest danger. It was simply so easy. The Majorcans had no idea if what you said was true and no real way of checking. Most of the time, as long as you didn't do something really serious, they didn't actually care.

I lost count of the number of pretend toffs, pop stars, film stars and hitmen I met over the years. And there were also the charismatic lunatics with amazing secrets or incredible inventions they simply couldn't tell you about unless, of course, you bought them a drink or invested in their demented schemes.

For instance, there was a guy who used to come into Alex's who claimed to be the son of one of the infamous British spies. It was either Burgess or Maclean, I can't remember which. This guy said that that whichever spy it was used to smuggle microfilm and all that under his blankets in his pram. So, on the one hand, why would you go to the trouble to make up something like that but, on the other, if you feel you've got nothing to lose, why not?

My salesmen who really took to the life – who didn't become hopeless alcoholics or junkies or become convinced they were Batman or Jesus - often went on to do great things back in the real world. They always told me that, apart from becoming tough enough to stand on their own two feet, they learned how to read people, overcome their objections and give the punter what they think they want. That's all selling is to me.

And if they thanked me for teaching that to them, I always said, 'No mate, you had it in you. I just gave you a way to bring it out.'

Over the years, I'd lost contact with many of the salesmen and women who'd worked for me which was fair enough, there must have been hundreds of them. But, plenty kept in touch and liked nothing better than a trip back to the Rock.

The island had got into their blood and they loved to come back whenever they could, reminisce and relive their wild years with me. And I was always up for it.

* * * * * *

'And this,' Johnny Kwango held up a huge orange lobster's tail, 'is the loot. The world is our lobster, lads.' Micky Jenkins, one of the Crawley Crew, laughed so hard at that he inhaled the forkful of paella rice he'd been about to eat, coughed, and a grain of yellow rice shot out of his nose, which made the rest of us laugh even harder.

A gang of my ex-salesmen and me were at La Baraka, an incredible bar in Palmanova owned by a Frenchman named Claude and one of my favourite places on the Rock. Inspired by what was rumoured to go on there, we'd got into character as a mob of London villains planning a caper. Now we were sitting round a table using bits of paella as props – me, Johnny Kwango, Micky Jenkins, Clive Williams, Steve Mills and Tom Jackson and Brian Ruttledge, two guys from Coventry. These were all guys who'd been great ticket sellers and used what they'd learnt to make it big in sales in the real world.

We'd been taking turns topping each other. 'Right, lads,' I said, 'this calamare ring's the security van. This crab claw is the getaway car. Clive, you'll be the driver and Millsy,' I held up an empty muscle shell, 'you'll be the...' And it was too much, Micky fell off his chair laughing in a high-pitched shriek.

'Muscle,' Brian finished for him.

By now we were on a fourth jug of Claude's innocent-looking sangria and it was beginning to find its mark. The other guys were on holiday but I was due at Alex's that night and knew I had to try and quit while I was ahead but it wasn't proving that easy. I was having too much fun to stop.

* * * * * *

Claude always seemed to me to be a pretty generous sort. In the late 1960s and early 70s, he'd often put the genius Manchester United and Ireland footballer George Best up in an apartment he owned near La Baraka, and carried George's monstrous bar tabs without a murmur. Of course, Claude wasn't daft and Bestie was a huge attraction. But, even that was a mixed blessing, what with geezers turning up wanting to have a go at George to prove something or other that they'd usually forgotten because they were so plastered.

Perhaps Claude just looked after Bestie because he thought the world of him. Underneath the tough guy persona, Claude was a good guy. One of the chaps.

Claude first fired up the La Baraka barbeque back in 1971 and it had been an immediate success. At that time, Palmanova was pretty undeveloped but, like Magaluf, it had a fantastic beach. The rich and famous would lazily drop anchor just offshore, row or swim in and have long lazy lunches that sometimes lasted for days, running up tabs that ran into hundreds of bottles of beer and countless jugs of sangria.

Claude claimed to get through around 400 lambs every summer for his famous lamb cous-cous or barbeque.

Which is a pretty big flock of sheep to disappear every year.

They all came to Claude's. Throughout the 1970s, Freddy Laker, the pioneer of low cost flying and the man who had single-handedly done the most to make Majorca an affordable holiday destination, would anchor his yacht 'Lady Jacqueline' – and later 'Lady Jacqueline 2' – and head for Claude's with his latest lady in tow. Women were Freddy's weakness.

Like I said, Claude wasn't daft and he loved women himself, which was why there were always plenty of gorgeous birds at La Baraka or sunbathing topless nearby. One time, Claude told me he did a deal with a friend of his who owned a model agency in Birmingham to send over six of her prettiest girls for a free holiday in exchange for enhancing the already considerable appeal of La Baraka or, in other words, acting as a honeytrap.

The deal was that the girls would share Claude's large apartment with him rent-free and have all the food and drink they wanted at La Baraka. The only condition was that, apart from joints, they weren't to bring drugs into his apartment. Don't forget, these were the days when coke was beginning to be a permanent blizzard on the island.

Claude's plan worked perfectly for most of the summer. The girls were a hit with the roues and gigolos of La Baraka and word of their beauty soon spread like wildfire. There was even a high-powered judge, who claimed to be a guardian of morality on the Rock and had it in for Claude, who'd come down and ogle the gorgeous, oiled up girls from behind his newspaper.

But, the girls had to go when they started to forget where they were and wander round Claude's apartment naked. It was just too much for Claude, he told me, shaking his head.

Apart from Freddy and George, the list of rich and famous people who came to La Baraka was amazing and, whoever they were, Claude treated them exactly the same as he would anyone else. Even the villains.

For some reason, La Baraka was always popular with villians. Some English writer described the South of France as 'a sunny place for shady people' and this definitely applies to Majorca. But, as Claude always said in his defense, 'if you only accepted doctors and lawyers, you'd be empty'.

So, La Baraka became a watering hole for mafia from all over Europe and beyond. The Corsican, Sicilian, German, British, Russian and Yank mafia all loved to hang out at Claude's place and, because they were on their holidays, they were no trouble at all. Like most villains I've met, apart from the obvious psycho, they were hilarious and generous. Two great qualities in a bloke, whoever they are.

These were different people from the lowlifes and petty criminals who had knocked about Plaza Gomila. Now, it was all about drugs and serious, organised crime.

It was rumoured that a couple of legendary heists were planned at La Baraka – which is what inspired our Paella Caper that very long hot afternoon in summer 1988.

One of these was the 1978 kidnapping of a French business tycoon by the name of Baron Édouard-Jean Empain. The kidnappers, led by a guy called George Bertoncini, demanded a ransom of 17 million Swiss francs and cut off Empain's little finger to show his family they were serious.

The kidnapping itself was planned like a military operation and, as it was around the time of political kidnappings by the Baader Meinhof gang and the Red Brigade, Empain's kidnappers made it look like they were a French extreme left-wing political faction called the NAPAP.

But, although the operation was extremely well-organised, it didn't appear to be carried out by serious villains but by a cast of petty crooks, including a pimp called 'Joe The Marseilles' and his wife.

The connection to La Baraka came about when the police discovered airline tickets to Majorca as they were going through the gang's stuff after securing the release of the Baron. This was clear evidence that the gang, who claimed not to know each other, had spent a week on the Rock planning the kidnap.

It wasn't suggested that Claude knew anything about the Baron Empain kidnapping. But that wasn't the case with another famous heist planned at La Baraka. The cops definitely thought he was involved.

Some time in the late 1970s or early 1980s, a crew of crooks came up with the fantastic idea of robbing a van loaded with used currency on its way to Majorca airport. The money was French francs, German marks, British pounds and so on that was being sent back from the bureau de changes on the island after people had exchanged their money for pesetas to the country it came from. The gang's haul was rumoured to have been worth around 780 million pesetas. A lot of cash.

One morning not so long after this, Claude threw open the curtains of his apartment, stepped out onto the balcony and found himself looking down the barrels of 40 rifles trained on him by Spanish police lying on their bellies on the white sand of Palmanova beach.

According to Claude, a jealous Arab who was convinced Claude was knocking off his wife persuaded the police he had a hand in the heist. Claude hotly denied this, the same way he always told the police he was innocent of the crimes they accused him of. Claude always said 'if I was involved in these heists and stealing millions, would I be sweating away making steak and chips. Do you want to see my varicose veins?'

But, for whatever reason, the police still kept coming. They'd raid La Baraka, smashing bottles of wine and booze because they claimed to believe that was where Claude stashed his loot.

So, was Claude really a criminal mastermind or one of these guys who took the opportunity to reinvent himself? He liked to give the impression he was The Godfather – El Padrino – but this could just as easily have been him having fun playing a part. He was also a great businessman and knew that an air of mystery is an excellent asset, whoever you are. Whatever the case, he was certainly a fantastically colourful character so I don't care either way.

This is what some of what Claude told me about his life.

* * * * * *

Claude said that 'baraka' was an Arabic word that meant spirit and he had plenty of that.

He was born in Tunisia, North Africa, in the early 1930s, to French parents. He'd been a middleweight champion boxer in Tunisia and, looking at the way he carried himself, you could believe it.

Claude was certainly in Paris in the late 1950s and early 60s, knocking around with the glamorous characters who were the legends of Parisian nightlife.

One of Claude's closest pals was a guy called Porfirio Rubirosa, a Dominican diplomat, jet-setter and international playboy. Rubirosa had two claims to fame, which were closely related to each other.

First of all, Rubirosa was a legendary womaniser and counted two of the richest women in the world among his five wives. He was married to the American heiress Doris Duke for a year in the late 40s. When they divorced, Rubirosa received an alimony, a fishing fleet off the coast of Africa, several sports cars, a B-25 bomber converted into a passenger plane and a 17th century Paris mansion house.

Rubirosa's marriage to American heiress Barbara Hutton lasted a couple of months longer than a year and in their settlement he received a coffee plantation in the Dominican republic, another converted bomber, polo ponies, jewellery and a cash payoff reported at $2.5 million.

Apart from his wives, Rubirosa was, as they say, romantically linked to an astonishing list of the world's most beautiful women, including Marilyn Monroe, Ava Gardner, Rita Hayworth and Eva Peron.

This may have been one of the reasons why. The gay American writer Truman Capote described Rubirosa's old chap as being 'an 11-inch café au lait sinker as thick as a man's wrist'. Apparently, the jet-set nickname for a pepper grinder was a 'Rubirosa'.

After World War II, Rubirosa became a keen racing car driver and polo player. He was to die in a car crash after a drinking session at Jimmy's, the famous Parisian nightclub, at which Claude was also present. Rubirosa was plastered and Claude begged him not to drive home. Rubirosa insisted, as his house was only a short distance away from Jimmy's.

Rubirosa drove his car into a chestnut tree doing about 12 miles an hour and died. Whenever Claude talked about Rubirosa, he shook his head sadly.

After Paris, Claude drifted down to the South of France where he owned a bar in St Tropez, when it really was St Tropez, as he put it. Bardot became a great friend and he may or may not have had a tumble with her.

Like so many of us, Claude discovered the delights of Majorca pretty much by accident and was one of the first to really see its potential. Unlike the overstuffed South of France, Majorca was quiet, tranquil and pretty much uninterested in the rich and famous people who came to the island. It was also cheap and, despite the Spanish cops and life under Franco, offered an enterprising foreigner like Claude a huge amount of freedom.

And, I guess, he fell in love with the place.

* * * * * *

But, let's get back to that long hot summer afternoon in 1988. After we'd washed down our paella and a couple of shared plates of Claude's legendary lamb cous-cous with more jugs of sangria, he suggested we take our drinks outside onto his barbeque terrace and enjoy the view – ladies sunning themselves, brilliant white boats moored in the glittering Med and a view clear across the huge bay of Palma to the mountains beyond.

By now, though, the combination of ferocious heat and the light bouncing off the white sand had started to get to us. The first to go was Clive Williams from London. He keeled over off his chair muttering 'me not well,' and lay on the floor gasping, eyes closed. Millsy stood up, staggered over to where four topless Swedish girls were quietly bronzing and threw up dramatically beside them but fortunately not all over them. Tom and Brian, two guys from Coventry, went for a walk along the beach and just didn't come back.

Soon only Johnny Kwango, Micky Jenkins and I were left. We settled the bill and somehow managed to pour ourselves into a taxi and back to Palma, where I even managed to do my Tom Brown show at Alexandra's.

* * * * * *

If you're wondering who Johnny Kwango was, he'd worked as a salesman for me back in the 1970s – one of the first guys Curly and me had hired - and we'd stayed in touch. He wasn't the real Johnny Kwango, who was a black middleweight wrestler famous in Britain for moves like his airplane spin and leaping head butt.

Our Johnny used to love to give himself different names from time to time to impress the punters and new salesmen. 'The name's Lomax,' he said, 'Johnny Lomax'. Or it would be 'Johny Estufado, it's a pleasure to meet me.' Estufado is Spanish stew but Johnny Stew doesn't exactly have the same ring to it.

It was Johnny Kwango which stuck. 'Johnny Kwango from Kingston, Jamaica.'

But he was Johnny Burns from Borehamwood, a few miles north of London. And the real Johnny Kwango was African.

For what it's worth.

JACKPOT!

You couldn't miss the sign I'd put out on the balcony of my trendy penthouse flat in a red-brick block at Playfair Mansions, Queen's Club Gardens, Fulham. I'd painted it myself and it read FOR RENT. No estate agents for me.

It was December 1989 and I was flat broke.

* * * * * *

That summer on the Rock had been the worst ever. We'd only opened Alex's for ten weeks and there were plenty of good reasons why business was so bad.

Magaluf was now firmly established as the 'Brits on the piss, the nightmare returns' holiday destination for anyone below the age of 30. But even Magaluf was suffering as long-haul flights got cheaper and tourists headed to places like Florida instead.

The area around Plaza Gomila had been going down for years. The stories reps used to spread about how dodgy the place was were now true. Dealers, junkies, hookers and transvestites prowled among the punters who did still come down to the Plaza.

Tito's closed its doors in 1984 and with it went the last traces of any glamour in the square.

If it hadn't been for the big spending Finns and the US navy, we wouldn't have had any punters at all.

So, apart from Curly, Pepe and me, we were down to just two barmen and my best PRs, Nick Lang from Brighton and Jasonip Glynn from Burnley, who'd both been with us from the 1970s.

The days of the boat and beach parties were long gone so Nick and Jason had to make do with the punters they could drag in off the scruffy streets around Gomila.

Of course, money was short so we did everything we could to make it, as well as tightening our belts. Curly started recycling the discount tickets we gave out on the street to avoid having to print more.

I taped a night of my antics at the club and called it The Tom Brown Show, made some copies and designed a cover. Nick and Jason sold these on the street for 1000 pesetas each and we split the proceeds 50/50. On average, the lads sold around 20 of these a day and one amazing day Jason shifted 40.

Apart from my wages from the club, this was the only money I made all summer.

Perhaps the saddest blow of all was having to get rid of the tropical fish that had swum in the glass floor of Alex's for all those years. Remember the fish? They'd been our pride and joy when we opened.

Curly loved those fish.

He replaced them with baby terrapins. Can you imagine? And, as they grew, the terrapins ate each other. To Curly's horror.

* * * * * *

So why did we stay? For me, it was all about loving those hours when I was Tom Brown, life and soul of the party. And, as long as the club was open, I was going to give it everything I had, even if I didn't make any money.

By now, Curly had made his life out in Majorca too. Outside of Alex's, he had other business interests. His son went to a posh English school called Kings College, high on a hill in a smart suburb called Bonanova just outside Palma up from Marivent, the King's summer palace.

My reasons were irrational and sentimental, Curly's were entirely practical. Sounds about right.

* * * * * *

One of the great things about my penthouse apartment in Fulham was the view. I used to love to stand out on the balcony with a cup of Nescafe and a fag on a clear morning and look out across the city.

It was bitterly cold today, without a cloud in the sky but I was determined to make the most of every minute I spent in what had been my pride and joy. I used to love to give my address to people - 'Playfair Mansions, Queen's Club Gardens, Fulham, actually' – and watch the occasional eyebrow raise.

I watched a pair of couples playing tennis in the square below, listened to the way they laughed and shouted encouragement to each other in their posh voices and wondered when I'd have to go. Sebastian Coe, the Olympic gold medallist, and the brother of Nick, a mate in Majorca, was running laps of the square. Every time I saw him I thought 'he'd have made a good paper boy.'

I thought about the £40,000 left on my mortgage, like I did every other minute of the day and winced. I had no money coming in and zero idea how I was going to carry on paying the bank.

Like all gamblers, I lived on optimism but I also knew that when your luck's out, there's nothing you can do about it. You just have to wait for it to come back. But, was my number really up this time?

I shivered, went back into the thick centrally heated air and closed the French doors behind me. Maybe Bern could cheer me up.

Me and Bernie the Fox were meeting for our post-Christmas, pre-New Year's Eve ritual pub crawl round Bethnal Green and, if nothing else, that would make my troubles go away for as long as I was knocking back the Christmas spirit.

It was Bern who'd sparked the idea of renting my place out. He'd offered to put me up on his sofa until I got back on my feet. I appreciated the offer but was praying it didn't come to that.

* * * * * *

I woke up out a terrible nightmare I'd been having that I was reduced to sleeping on Bernie's sofa. I opened one gummed up eye. I actually was on Bernie's sofa.

I sat up, coughed, swung my feet onto the floor. Bernie's front room was painfully hot. My head was thumping, my mouth tasted like a parrot had crapped in it. I had a kingsize hangover. I got up, nearly fell over, went to the window, wrestled it open and inhaled a lungful of painfully cold London air. By the angle of the sun in the gunmetal grey sky it was early afternoon. I stumbled to the kitchen, drank water from the tap, made myself a cup of tea with milk that was just on the turn, lit a cigarette and sat shaking in Bern's front room until I felt strong enough to get dressed and attempt the journey back to Fulham. There was no sign of Bern. Maybe he'd got lucky.

I left Bern a note saying I'd see him New Year's Eve, shut the door behind me, tramped down the piss-smelling stairs and out into the empty dusk. I'd never felt more sorry for myself than I did then.

In my mid-40s and kipping on Bern's sofa.

* * * * * *

At least when I woke up later that afternoon I was on my own sofa. I looked at my watch. Time for the football results. I used the remote to switch on the TV. '...And that was the football results.' Missed them. 'Now for the pools numbers...'

Out of habit I jotted the numbers down. I'd had a standing order coupon with Littlewoods Pools all year but had never come close. Not surprising, the way my luck was running. I fell asleep again.

Around 3 AM I woke up with a thumping heart and no idea where I was. For a minute I thought I was back on Bernie's sofa but when I recognised my own front room, I calmed down. I couldn't sleep so I went looking for my pools coupon. When I began to check it against the numbers I'd scribbled down earlier, I really started to shake and my battered heart pounded even harder.

I always did the 'any eight numbers out of fourteen' permutation or, as it was called, 'perm'. I had eight numbers and they had to fall in a winning line for me to win. The perm gave me 240 chances to win. I could have won big but there was no way to check because I'd lost the perm book which gave all the possible combinations. I'd have to wait until the Littlewoods office in Liverpool opened in, I looked at my watch again, five hours.

For the rest of that night I lay awake, my mind circling from delicious fantasies about what I'd do with my winnings to the voice of reason which told me to look at the way my luck had been going recently and not get my hopes up too high.

* * * * * *

I was on the blower and talking to a deadpan Scouser at nine sharp that morning. She took my details and said that if I was a winner I'd get the call on Tuesday, the next working day after New Year's. I bit back my frustration, wished the Liver Bird Happy New Year and accepted that I couldn't do anything to move the process along.

That night, in the boozer back in Bethnal Green I sang Auld Lang Syne with the rest but my mind was on Tuesday morning and the call from Littlewoods. I hadn't told anyone I was possibly a pools winner in case I jinxed my luck so my sisters, Bern and the rest of the gang all thought I was preoccupied and down because of the problems with my flat. I lost count of the amount of times I had my cheek tweaked and someone said 'cheer up, Lou, it might never happen'. Tuesday morning, I forced myself not to get on the blower bang on nine and waited for the call as calmly as I could.

When the call came, I shot to the phone, slid on a rug and nearly went gliding through the open French window over the balcony. I let it ring a couple of times, took a deep breath, and said '0171 7296328'.

'Hello, is that Mr O'Brien?' The bloke sounded just like John Lennon. 'Congratulations,' he said. 'You've won first prize on the pools.' The blood rushed to my head. I thought I was going to pass out.

'Great,' I squeaked. 'Wha...?'

The man chuckled. 'We'll be sending someone down to you tomorrow, to confirm your claim so please have your coupon and some identification ready.'

'How much?' I said. 'How much? Sorry, I just...'

'I understand, Mr O'Brien but, I'm sorry, I can't tell you how much. We won't know the full amount until mid-day tomorrow.'

'How much? How much?' I repeated. I couldn't stop myself.

This time, he laughed. 'I can tell you this. We never send a representative to a winner's home unless they've won at least £100,000.' The blood surged up into my head again. 'Mr O'Brien,' the man said. 'Are you still there.'

'Yes.'

'Good. A Mr Maxwell will be with you at ten tomorrow.'

'Thank you.'

'And congratulations again.'

'Thank you.' I hung up, put the phone down slowly, walked out onto the balcony, took the For Rent sign, ripped it into little pieces, scattered them onto the street below, walked back into my front room and started to dance round the room screaming 'I won, I won, I won, I wooooonnnnn' until I collapsed on the floor.

* * * * * *

'Can I use your phone?' I handed Mr Maxwell the handset. He left the room with it, my coupon and passport in his other hand. I lit another cigarette, waved away some of the blue fug that had filled the room. When Mr Maxwell came back in, he was smiling. He sat down, took a sip of his tea, bent over his notepad to double check – I felt like grabbing it away from him but took a deep breath – before looking up at me. 'Mr O'Brien, Louie, my office has just told me the first prize payout for this week. There were six winners and the winning dividend is...' he paused, looked down again, grinned,'£235,000'.

I leapt up, whooped, grabbed Mr Maxwell in a bear hug, kissed him on both cheeks before letting him go. He straightened his Littlewoods tie, adjusted his blue blazer and said 'shall we go to your bank, Louie, arrange the transfer of the money?'

We took a taxi to my bank in the East End. It was a beautiful day or it looked that way to me. It could have been snowing purple snow for all I cared.

Mr Maxwell explained to my bank manager that I'd won the pools. The guy, who only weeks before, had been giving me a hard time about my mortgage arrears, was all smiles and handshakes. He even magicked up a bottle of champagne from somewhere. After they'd done the business and transferred the money to my account, the bank manager asked me if there was anything I wanted. 'First, I want to pay off my mortgage.' He nodded. 'And then I'd like £10,000 in cash, please.'

The bank manager nodded. 'Very good,' he said. 'Perhaps we could make an appointment to discuss some extremely attractive investment opportunities when it's convenient?'

'Sure.' I knew I wasn't going to do that. As soon as my money arrived, I scarpered from the bank with what was left of the bottle of bubbly and Mr Maxwell in tow. I peeled off a £50 note, thanked him for all his help and flagged him down a cab. I got in the next one that came along and headed back to my home in Fulham's exclusive Queens Club Gardens.

Back in the flat, I called my sisters, gave them the news and told them to expect some cash very soon. The next call was to Bern. 'You doing anything tonight, Bern?' I said.

'No plans. Bit skint after New Year's, as it goes,' he said.

'I've got a surprise for you,' I said. 'Can you come over tonight?'

He grunted. 'Can't you tell me over the phone?'

'No I can't. Come on, it'll be worth it.'

'All right.'

* * * * * *

'I'm going to get some crocodile shoes,' Bern said. 'That's what I'm going to do.' He looked at the cheque I'd given him for the third time, shook his head. 'What can I say, Louie? Thanks, mate.'

'My pleasure,' I said. I grinned, loving seeing his glee. 'Shall we go up West? Somewhere nice? My treat.'

'Abso-bleedin'-lutely,' Bern said. 'Looks like your luck's well and truly turned.'

'Looks that way,' I said.

Later that night, as we sat in a deep, red leather banquette in some Mayfair joint, Bern said 'so what are you going to do now, Lou? Not going back to Majorca, are you?'

I hadn't given the future a moment's thought but I said 'I am. Course.'

'Why? You can do whatever you want.'

'And that's what I want to do. It's not about the money. I've put years of my life into Alex's. And I'm not walking away.'

He looked at me, started to say something, shrugged and went back to eyeing up the posh crumpet.

* * * * * *

Next morning, remarkably fresh considering the amount of champagne I'd put away, I cabbed it to Harrods and bought a deluxe Roulette wheel. Roulette was my game, and, of course, I had a system. Also, it was the numbers I always used while playing roulette that had won the pools for me. I figured I could practice on my own wheel before taking on the casinos.

Like all gamblers, now that I'd won big I thought I knew all the answers. And you could forget about investing wisely.

It took a long losing streak and a good chunk of my money before I realised that wasn't the case.

But, when I got back to the Rock I knew that, whatever happened, I always had my flat to fall back on. Once again, I became Tom Brown, Showman. Richer but none the wiser.

And, you know what? I never told Curly about my win.

FLOGGING ALEX'S

For most of the summer of 1992 we might as well have not been open. It was soul-destroying but a few things made me carry on.

I loved Alex's and, despite the writing on the wall in dirty big letters, I hoped against hope that things would turn around. I hated giving up on anything and Alex's had been my baby for nearly 20 years. Winning the pools and being able to buy my apartment in Fulham outright had given me a financial cushion which meant I could stick things out.

Curly had no such romantic feelings and wanted to get shot of Alex's. He asked His Nibs if we could sell the place and His Nibs agreed, as long as we didn't advertise but only put the word out locally. Majorcans are like that, they really don't want anyone knowing how badly they're doing – or how well.

You might bump into a Majorcan guy in the street – tanned, looking great, huge gold Rolex on his wrist, beautiful young chica on his arm, carrying a sack of money to deposit at the bank – and, when you ask him how he's doing, he'll say 'business is terrible, my back's killing me, my daughter's run off with a gypsy,' whatever. I think they hate the idea you might want something off them. But, they'll be generosity itself if they don't feel hustled.

Once His Nibs had agreed with Curly, I had no choice but to go along with it and, really, we couldn't afford to be sentimental. Curly was right.

We hired a professional crew to make a video of some Spanish geezer walking round the club selling its features: 'the cracked, scuffed, dirty glass staircase filled with half-dead terrapins floating in cloudy water was imported at great expense from London in 1975'.

I ran an ad in the Sunday Times and we sat back and waited for the enquiries to come flooding in. We were looking for offers in the region of £200,000 to £300,000 There were plenty of time-wasters but we got a call from this Liberian guy who sounded dead keen.

Mr Wakpele flew over from Switzerland to look at the club. He was a charming, coffee-coloured dude in a smart suit who explained that he 'had many interests in Europe but had always wanted my own club so I could have some fun.' I guess he saw himself as some kind of African Hugh Hefner character. We told Wakpele that if he bought the club, me and my PRs would stay on. That wasn't going to happen. Wakpele barely looked at the cooked set of books Curly put in front of him before waving them away and assuring us everything was fine. All of us had a meet at His Nibs's office in Palma and it looked like the deal was done. We shook hands all round and Wakpele said he'd go back to Switzerland and make a transfer of 50% of the money as a deposit. That was good enough for me but Curly was suspicious, as he always was.

'There's something about him that don't smell right,' Curly said as he dialled the number of a Swiss banker contact he happened to have, a Herr Smitt, 'it's all too easy. I don't like it'. He got Smitt on the line, explained he wanted to know what there was to know about a Mr Wakpele, a Liberian gentleman. Smitt asked Curly to wait for his call back, which would be in a few minutes. It didn't even take that long before the phone rang.

Curly listened, nodded, smiled his tight smile, thanked Smitt and put the phone down. 'Smitt says Mr Wakpele's suspected of embezzlement in Switzerland and we should definitely not do any business with him. Told ya, Lou.'

'Let's wait to see if he transfers the loot for the deposit, at least. We've got nothing to lose.'

Curly shrugged. 'If you want,' he said. He looked at his watch. 'Soon be time to open, though Christ knows what for.'

Even though I knew he was right, I couldn't help but be stung by Curly's 'it's only business' attitude to watching our dream go down the khazi. This combination of Curly's hard-headedness and my concentration on the bright side had been what had made us so successful. Now it divided us.

I pulled my rainbow Afro wig down tight on my head, slipped into my Union Jack clogs and clumped across the empty dance floor to get set for another night.

We never heard from Mr Wakpele again. Nor did we find out what was the real reason behind his offer for the club. Something didn't smell right but we had no idea what.

After this, we tried everything we could to shift Alex's but there were no takers. Mr Wakpele had been the only serious contender for the club, and he was a joke.

The writing was on the wall in letters so large even I had to see them though I did everything in my power not to.

Later that year my dream finally went up in a puff of smoke and Alexandra's closed its doors for the last time.

EPILOGUE: SUMMER 2011

20 Elvises. 10 Fred Flintstones. A gang dressed as prisoners in black and white striped outfits including little hats. A bride to be in a wedding dress with an L-plate on her back, followed by a shrieking gaggle of her mates, all wearing pink sparkly cowboy hats, some of them sunburned bright red. One of the girls has already had a bit too much and sits down on a kerb, her head in her hands. A bunch of lads all wearing t-shirts that say 'Billy's Stag Do, Magaluf 2011'.

I look down at my brand new t-shirt, given to me by my mate Paul of hangoutonholiday.com, a great website where people going on holiday can meet up with people going to the same place at the same time and make friends before they travel. I wish we'd had hangoutonholiday.com back in the 1970s.

A solitary pirate weaves by. He looks like Jack Sparrow if he'd had his head slammed in a door a few times. I don't know if he's on his way to Pirates, the show, or is part of a pirate stag gang who he lost somewhere down the line.

And, in among the hen parties, stag do lads and other sunburned punters wearing their team colours there's always the Looky-Looky Men, the African guys who come up from places like Senegal to work the streets selling funny hats, huge sunglasses, badges that light up, handheld loudspeakers and anything they can move. A very black Looky-Looky Man wearing sunglasses with blue eyes built into the lenses comes up to me and starts to make his pitch. 'No thanks, mate,' I say. 'I work here.' This is not strictly true but in my heart I've never stopped being a ticket seller and part of the whole merry hustle.

Only I don't go back to Plaza Gomila much these days. To be honest, it feels too much like a ghost town for me and I'm on nodding terms with plenty of the ghosts.

Sometimes I'll meet a pal in the Bally Jay café down in Plaza Meditterànea, which doesn't look that much different from when we used to hang out and plan our strategy for world domination through ticket selling there. The lovely Maria left years ago and I often wonder where she is.

Alexandra's is still there. It's wholly owned by His Nibs now and there's no reason for him to sell it. As you can imagine, walking past the locked gate at the top of the steps that lead down to Alex's is weird for me. I've got so many amazing memories but plenty of not so great ones.

Nearly all of the bars and clubs I knew have gone. The Majorcan kids drink outside now. They have botellón parties, named after the Spanish for a big bottle of beer, and say they can't afford to get into clubs. In the mornings, the pavements are sticky with spilt drink and worse.

What clubs are left are pretty much Latin American, gay or heavy metal.

But Jaimé who made the most fantastic boccadillos still has his place on Calle Robert Graves, which we called the hole in the wall or the boc shop. If I am in Gomila, I'll buy a huge, delicious tuna boc and be unable to eat anything else for the next few hours.

So, now, I like to head down to Magaluf and soak up the energy. The buzz really puts a spring in my step all over again.

It feels to me like Magaluf will never go the way of Gomila, just continue to change. His Nibs had definitely seen the future when he opened BCM back in 1986. When easyJet revolutionised budget air travel all over again in 1995 they gave Magaluf another huge shot in the arm. Today, so many people who live on the Rock or come and go regularly have a lot to thank easyJet for. They've made it possible for many of us to live on the island and do business all over Europe without paying a fortune for travel. I love 'em!

Right now, I'm plotted up on Punta Balena, or, as I call it, Hamburger Hill, Magaluf, outside a bar run by a couple who worked for me at Millenium, downstairs at BCM, back in 1997 – when I came back to the island for one last roll of the dice and managed the place.

They're all over Magaluf, the other island resorts, mainland Spain, Gran Canaria, Florida, Mexico and in all kinds of kosher businesses, the people who worked for me when they were starting out. I've had plenty of ex-PRs tell me they've applied what I taught them about reading potential punters in all kinds of businesses.

This may be an art but there's no mystery to it. It's only what I learned on the streets of the East End, Stockholm, New Orleans, Copenhagen, Miami Beach, Venice Beach LA and, of course, El Arenal where it all began for me.

Always approach from the front. Make eye contact right away. Give the punter a big smile. Stop them in their tracks any way you can, within reason. Offer something free. Talk fast.

Hamburger Hill is the big hill in the middle of Magaluf where all the action goes on. If you know Magaluf, it's right by the bunji jump. I'm sipping a Cuba Libre, smoking a Ducados and mentally playing one of my favourite games: deciding who I'd have taken out on of the PRs and ticket sellers working the sticky, scorched streets of Magaluf.

'Oi, Louie The Lip!' Laura Cameron, the daughter of my friend Debbie, strides past me on the other side of the road, leading a huge crowd of giggling, singing, well-oiled punters down the hill for the final stop on the Magaluf Pub Crawl she runs - BCM. She gives me a wave and, over her tanned shoulder, calls out '179 tonight, Lou. That's a record for May!'

I go back to my game, looking up and down the street for PRs. I watch a girl try to blag four big young lads. She hasn't got it, I tell myself. Why? Because she didn't meet them face on. She delivered her line as they were halfway past her. Too late. That's not how it works. Sure enough, they walk on and she starts looking for someone else.

Another gang of lads, all wearing stag do t-shirts is heading in my direction. I don't see the girl coming but, out of nowhere, I smell suntan lotion and perfume. A tray of jelly shots and Jäger Bombs – Jägermeister and Red Bull - followed by a lovely long pair of suntanned legs appears out the door of the bar where I'm sitting. The owner of the legs and the tray looks down at me and winks. She stands directly in front of the lads and, in a loud, confident, Scottish accent, says 'free shots, fellahs?'

The guys whoop and reach for the drinks. The girl pulls the tray away and, walking backwards, leads them into the bar. 'Have to drink them inside, lads,' she says, smiling. The guys follow her into the bar without protesting, like tipsy sheep.

That's how it's done. She blagged the first one, offered them something free and cheekily gave them no choice but to come inside. I'd have given her a job all day long.

And, I ask myself the same question I always do every time I come back to Majorca. Would I do it all over again?

What do you think?

WHERE ARE THEY NOW?

These are some of the real-life characters who feature in Hasta La Flip-Flops! In my 25 years in Majorca, I must have hired and fired hundreds if not thousands of salesmen so please forgive me if I've left you out.

Peter Ratcliffe AKA DeLovely

Peter became successful with his company Legends In Time, selling Formula One memorabilia to the masses. Peter's million-pound boat is moored in Palma harbour and we're still great buddies.

Peter Bloss

Blossy finally got his act together and became a born again Christian. He married Rose and raised two daughters. Today, Peter lives near me so we can reminisce whenever we feel like it. He's still one of the funniest guys I know.

Curly

Curly retired from the Rock and now lives in Sweden. He's still married to Yvonne. Without Curly's business brains and drive, I couldn't have done half of what I did in Majorca. All the best, mate.

John Burns AKA Kwango

Johnny lives in Manchester. He's married to Jackie and has a son called Lee. Johnny works as a joiner and is currently doing his bit to help make the 2012 Olympics happen on time. The real Johnny Kwango, the wrestler, died in 1994.

The Crawley Crew
Micky Jenkins married Sally, had two sons and runs his own construction company in West Sussex. Lee Dorrington and Jinksy moved down under. Steve Cubbitt runs an estate agents.

Nick Lang
Married with two kids, Nick has his own restaurant, La Marinara in Kemptown, Brighton.

Brian Ruttledge and Tom Jackson
Alive and well and living in Coventry.

Clive Williams, Steve Mills and Gary Graham
Curly originally turned down Clive and Steve when they wanted to become ticket sellers but I saw the potential. They soon become two of my best and earned the nickname Los Pollos from His Nibs. Today, Clive is the director of a major homeware company in Manchester and Steve runs a football academy for the underprivileged in Los Cabos, Mexico.

Gary Graham was another South London ticket seller now running his own businesses.

Chris Brown and Solvie
Dividing their time between homes in Sweden and the Caribbean.

Jim and Steve, the Clancy Brothers

Both very successful businessmen with their own companies.

Derek 'Jughead' Avis

Has his own company in Florida.

The Brighton Boys (and girls)

Gary Rice, Russell, Dutch Barbara, Jim and AnnaLee, Mike Pinker – and these are just the names I can remember – all made it.

The Jocks

Gerry Richie runs clubs and pubs in Edinburgh. Terry Cameron lives in Majorca. Brian and others all run their own companies.

Jack McCulloch

Lives in Bornholm, Denmark.

Peter Dixon

Ex-DJ, has his fingers in lots of different pies.

Hugh Grant

Yes, that Hugh Grant! Hugh never mentions this in interviews but he won Mr Majorca at Alexandra's back in the mid-80s and I like to think this gave him the confidence to become the superstar he is today. Seriously, Hugh was a lovely guy – probably still is – and I was very flattered that he took my advice all those years ago.

And everyone who knows me...

Many of us still meet up at reunions, weddings and birthdays. One of the things ex-salesmen and women often say is that they've used what they learned from me to succeed in their careers and have fantastic adventures.

My answer is always 'all I did was show you how to survive on your own. You chose to come to Majorca to live the dream and selling tickets was the way you did it.'